UNSOLVED MURDERS
AND MYSTERIES

EDITED BY JOHN CANNING

WARNER BOOKS

A *Warner* Book

First published 1987 by Michael O'Mara Books Limited
Published in 1988 by Futura Publications
Reprinted 1989, 1990 (twice), 1991
Revised edition published by Warner Books 1992
Reprinted 1993, 1994 (twice), 1995, 1996, 1997, 1998, 2000

A CIP catalogue record for this book
is available from the British Library.

ISBN 0 7515 0896 9

Printed in England by Clays Ltd, St Ives plc

Warner Books
A Division of
Little, Brown and Company (UK)
Brettenham House
Lancaster Place
London WC2E 7EN

CONTENTS

ENIGMAS OF AIR AND SEA

EDITOR'S NOTE

'Truth will come to light; murder cannot be hid long.' Thus said Launcelot Gobbo in *The Merchant of Venice*. But though murder can seldom be hidden the murderer can be – and frequently is – as exampled by some of the accounts that follow.

The crime of murder has always exercised a horrid fascination over the minds of men. 'Thou shalt not kill' has seemed to many to be the starkest of Mosaic injunctions. But an extra chill is added when the crime is unsolved. Could the murderer strike again? Might he be sitting next to one in the bus or underground? Indeed, might one even have met him within the past few days?

Edgar Lustgarten has written of the spell amounting almost to obsession which the Wallace case exerted over the celebrated dramatic critic James Agate, who believed the weight of evidence for and against Wallace's guilt to be exactly evenly balanced. At the end of one of their many discussions on the matter Lustgarten asked Agate to adopt the theory that Wallace was innocent. What sort of person would have committed the crime?

'A genius,' replied Agate flatly. 'A brutal, bloody fiend – and a genius.'

'I wonder whether he reads the stuff written on the crime,' Lustgarten said, 'and sometimes talks about the case among his friends.'

'That,' said Agate sombrely, 'is the most shocking thought of all.'

Research on this case has turned up new findings, discussed in a following chapter, so that the evidence is not perhaps quite as baffling as it once was, but Agate's reaction strikes a reciprocating chord.

The mystery surrounding Robert Maxwell's death is one where the balance of possibilities again is so finely drawn as to defy any definite solution. The persuasive hypothesis of suicide is contradicted by the gigantic optimism and resolution of the man; the very plausible theory of death from natural causes is counterbalanced by the opinions of three Israeli doctors and two respected French pathologists which point to murder. The case truly fulfils

7

Winston Churchill's dictum used in another connection of 'a riddle wrapped in a mystery inside an enigma', and is set to run and run.

However, murder or possible murder is but one facet in the kaleidoscope of the unsolved. There are areas of speculation hardly less intriguing. Is it really possible that a modern prime minister could have been a spy for a foreign power? Might the prisoner in Spandau not have been Rudolf Hess, and did his death have sinister overtones? Could Caryl Chessman, in San Quentin's Death Row awaiting execution for more than a decade and afforded every legal facility to establish his case, have been innocent after all? On the face of it such questions may seem far-fetched, even absurd, and yet there is solid, well-researched evidence which supports these suppositions.

What is not in doubt is that the subjects discussed in this book will be focal points of controversy and passionate argument for years to come. Indeed, some of them have already survived undimmed the battering of time.

Our modest hope is that the ensuing essays will provide a modicum of light rather than heat for the debates.

My thanks are due to the contributing authors for a happy collaboration, to Georgie Evans for editorial assistance, to Sarah Coombe for illustration research, and to my paperback editor Alice Wood for guidance and help with this new edition.

JOHN CANNING

WHO WAS THE MURDERER?

DR JOHN BODKIN ADAMS

'Scotland Yard's murder squad is to investigate the suspected mass poisoning of wealthy women in Eastbourne during the past twenty years. Because the vast extent of the murder suspicions is not yet known they will start by examining the wills of more than 400 m⟨ ⟩ and women who died in the town, and their investigations may uncover the most sensational episode in British criminal history.'

This strange little paragraph appeared in the *Daily Mail* on 22 August 1956 – strange because it is obviously accusing some person, or persons, of mass murder, while it at the same time admits that the inquiry has not yet even begun.

The 'mass murderer' was an unprepossessing fat man named Dr John Bodkin Adams, and the *Mail* paragraph marked the beginning of his trial – not his trial in a court of law, but his trial by the British press. What followed is, in itself, one of 'the most sensational episodes in British criminal history . . .'.

'It is expected,' added the *Mail* as an afterthought, 'that the names of twenty-five people will be picked out as possible victims of a maniac.'

Bodkin Adams certainly looked as if he had been specially cast for the role of maniacal mass murderer, with a figure like that of Sidney Greenstreet, the urbane villain of *The Maltese Falcon*, and plump, pendulous cheeks that made him look like a rather sinister baby.

The event that had brought Bodkin Adams to the attention of the press – and the police – was the apparent suicide of one of his patients, Mrs 'Bobbie' Hullett. Bobbie Hullett had been

9

shattered by the death of her second husband Jack, a rich, retired businessman, who was suffering from a cancer of the bowel. This was the second husband that she had lost in five years, and the death of the first had also brought her close to suicide.

In July 1956 Bodkin Adams spent an evening with her, and she gave him a cheque for £1,000 – money that she said her husband had intended to give the doctor for a new car. Two days after this, she retired to bed suffering from dizziness and headache. Bodkin Adams called to see her. The next afternoon she went into a coma, and died in hospital a few days later. It looked to the doctors very much like suicide. Bodkin Adams wrote a letter to the coroner, mentioning that he had been prescribing small doses of sodium barbiturate as a sleeping tablet, and added the odd phrase: 'She could not possibly have secreted any of this.' He added that he had examined her room for empty bottles or cartons, and found nothing to suggest she had any poison.

When the coroner, Dr A. C. Sommerville, read this letter his suspicions were immediately aroused, and he called for a second post-mortem. When that proved inconclusive, he asked for a third post-mortem to be performed by the famous 'crime doctor', Francis Camps. Camps took some of Mrs Hullett's organs back to London with him. The coroner made an unusual decision to hold the inquest in private and without informing the press. That in itself suggested that he suspected there was 'dirty work afoot'. When the inquest was adjourned awaiting further information, a journalist on the local newspaper, the *Brighton Argus*, was informed about the secret investigation. He hurried to the police station for more details but the Chief Constable shook his head saying, 'I cannot go into it further.' As he was leaving the police station, a police officer remarked casually, 'You on this Hullett job? Well it's about time somebody caught up with that bloody doctor.'

What had 'that bloody doctor' done to incur suspicion? He had, to begin with, been phenomenally successful. Adams was an Ulster Protestant, who had arrived in Eastbourne in 1923 in answer to an advertisement for 'a Christian young doctor-assistant'. He started his rounds on a motorbike. Two years later he was driving a two-seater car. And within three years of joining the practice, he was being driven by a chauffeur. Eastbourne was full of rich, retired businessmen, and Bodkin Adams was always a popular guest at their social gatherings.

There were also many lonely but wealthy old ladies in Eastbourne and Dr Adams seemed to have a natural gift for bringing them comfort. In 1935 one of these old ladies, Mrs Matilda Whitton, left him £3,000, a very substantial sum for those days, and equivalent to about £30,000 in the devalued currency of today. He was also the executor of her will, which caused many raised eyebrows. The will was challenged in court by the family, but it was upheld. That was the beginning of the whispering campaign against Bodkin Adams. Then, over the years, the doctor received many more bequests: £1,000 from a spinster, Irene Herbert, £4,000 in shares from Mrs Emily Mortimer, £1,000 from Mrs Amy Ware, a Rolls-Royce from Mrs Edith Morrell, £200 from Mrs Annabella Kilgour, £100 from Mrs Mary Prince, £100 from Mrs Theodora Hullett – the previous wife of Jack Hullett, £800 from Mrs Julia Bradnum, £500 from Mrs Annie Dowding, £5,200 from Mrs Clara Miller, £750 from Miss Florence Cavill, £100 from Sidney Prince, £250 from George Blunt, and £1,000 from James Downs. These bequests amounted to a total of nearly £22,000, most of it from elderly widows and spinsters, some of whom had left Dr Adams a substantial part of their fortune. (Clare Miller, for example, left Adams £5,200 out of a total estate worth £7,000.) Not to mention the Rolls-Royce, silver cutlery and other such items . . .

It can be seen that Bodkin Adams was both a very charming and a very lucky man. It would not be surprising if overworked police officers felt a certain envy as they saw his name figure again and again in reports of legacies in the *Brighton Argus*. Yet a dozen or so legacies do not constitute proof that the man who received them is guilty of murder. In late August 1956 most of the British press chose to ignore this simple piece of logic. The Bodkin Adams case was discussed as if there could be no doubt that he would shortly be charged with mass poisoning. One of the few sane voices was that of Percy Hoskins, the *Daily Express* crime reporter. He wrote an article in which he pointed out that, so far, it was a case of smoke without fire. It was not true that 400 wealthy widows had been murdered; it was not true that the murderer had been at work for 20 years; it was not true that more that £1 million was involved. But this was not the kind of story that the great British public wanted to read. It was not even the kind of story that Hoskins's boss, Lord Beaverbrook, wanted to read; he told Hoskins that he had better be right, or his head would be on the chopping-block.

Bodkin Adams seemed to have a gift for putting his own head on the chopping-block. Just before the continuation of the inquest of Bobbie Hullett he wrote the coroner another letter, admitting that two months before her death he had been on a trip to Dublin with Mrs Hullett and two other ladies. Mrs Hullett had forgotten her sleeping tablets so he had given her eight barbiturate tablets. Looking back on it now, he realized that she was in possession of more barbiturates than might be good for her – enough to kill herself, for example. The coroner felt that this was highly suspicious. At the inquest, he went out of his way to ask a police superintendent, 'Has the Chief Constable of Eastbourne invoked the aid of Scotland Yard to investigate certain deaths in this neighbourhood?' The superintendent replied that he had done so. The question was totally irrelevant but the coroner seemed to be telling the press to expect further spectacular developments. However, the verdict of the inquest was that Bobbie Hullett had committed suicide.

Two days later, Hoskins travelled up to London on the same train as Bodkin Adams and was startled that the doctor seemed unaware of the seriousness of the situation. He warned him that his whole future, perhaps his life itself, was in danger. Yet Bodkin Adams seemed wholly unconcerned. He was either innocent or supremely confident.

Whether he liked it or not, Bodkin Adams had become a celebrity. Newspaper men from all over the world flooded into Eastbourne. One French newspaper ran a headline: IS THE BLUEBEARD OF EASTBOURNE ABOUT TO BE UNMASKED? The British press had to be slightly more cautious, but the implication was as plain as a banner headline.

Superintendent Herbert Hannam, who was in charge of the Scotland Yard investigation, had a difficult task ahead of him: studying the records of over 100 deaths. But on 2 November 1956 he was ready to present his case against Bodkin Adams. There were 13 charges, nine of them fairly minor accusations about 'feloniously' giving drugs to patients who were not supposed to receive them. These were mainly to prepare the ground for the major accusations: that Bodkin Adams had concealed the fact that he had a pecuniary interest in the deaths of Amy Ware, Edith Morrell, James Downs and Jack Hullett, and had 'procured their burial' or cremation. In other words, that Bodkin Adams was anxious to conceal that he was a beneficiary in the wills of these patients until he had their bodies safely buried or burned.

Bodkin Adams may have been unaware that his life was in danger but his solicitor had no illusions about it. He asked the doctor if he had any detailed records about the various cases, particularly the Morrell case. Adams shook his head vaguely. Probably not. All he could remember was that he did receive a parcel of nurses' records after her illness, but he could no longer remember what had happened to it. His solicitor made him search the house. At 3 a.m. they unearthed the missing parcel containing eight small notebooks. It was these that would provide the most dramatic moment of the trial.

On 18 December 1956 Superintendent Hannam arrested Bodkin Adams, and charged him with the murder of Mrs Morrell. The solicitor's instinct about her case had been correct. The next morning, Bodkin Adams faced a long list of charges, the last of which was that in November 1950 he did 'feloniously, wilfully and of malice aforethought . . . kill and murder Edith Alice Morrell'. Adams was then taken to Brixton prison.

Why was Adams in the dock when there was no real proof against him? Superintendent Hannam's inquiries had led him to believe that he was dealing with a cunning swindler and an infinitely subtle killer. He came to believe that Adams had altered wills on several occasions and the bodies of his patients were cremated instead of being buried. He believed that in the last few days of one woman's life, Adams had forged cheques to the value of £18,000. He uncovered one suspicious deal in which

Adams had influenced two women to leave their house and live in a flat. He then sold the house, and kept the money for three years until he was forced to reimburse it after a writ was served on him. Whether or not Adams was a murderer, he was certainly a greedy and rather dishonest man. On one occasion, he had been struck by a gold-headed cane and chased out of the house by an indignant husband after saying, 'Leave your estate to me and I'll look after your wife' – the man's wife was lying seriously ill in bed at the time.

Then there was the case of Mrs Annabella Kilgour, not mentioned in the indictments. In 1950, Adams called on Mrs Kilgour, and her nurse reported that she was restless. 'I'll give her an injection to give her a good night's sleep', said Adams; and, to the nurse's astonishment, gave the old lady an injection with a dose that seemed far too high. Mrs Kilgour fell into a coma immediately and died the next morning. When Adams called that morning the nurse told him, 'Mrs Kilgour is dead. You realize, doctor, that you've killed her?' She recalled later, 'I have never seen a man look so frightened in my life.' Mrs Kilgour left Adams £2,000.

It would appear, therefore, that Hannam had every reason to suspect Bodkin Adams of being a mercenary and greedy man who had no hesitation in administering overdoses to his patients.

The trial opened at the Old Bailey on 18 March 1957. The case against Bodkin Adams was presented by the Attorney General, Sir Reginald Manningham-Buller, and it sounded damning. Mrs Morrell was 81 years old when she died. She was suffering from hardening of the arteries of the brain and from the effects of a stroke, which had left her paralyzed in the left side. She was rarely in any pain – such a condition is seldom attended with pain. Yet Bodkin Adams prescribed huge doses of pain-killing drugs – morphia, heroin, barbiturates and sedormid. Why should he do that unless it was his aim to make his patient a drug addict, who would be grateful to him for keeping her supplied?

Adams had called on Mrs Morrell's solicitor, and told him that Mrs Morrell had promised to leave him a Rolls-Royce and a case of silver cutlery. He also said Mrs Morrell had recollected that she had forgotten to do this, so she wanted her solicitor to prepare a codicil. If it did not meet with her approval it could be destroyed later. The solicitor called on Mrs Morrell and she executed the codicil. It was then that Adams made a tremendous increase in the quantity of drugs he was prescribing her, and she spent much of the time in a coma. It would seem that Adams killed her by giving her these massive overdoses. On the last evening of her life he had prescribed an injection in a 5cc syringe, instead of the usual 2cc syringe. Three hours later he had repeated the dose. One hour after that Mrs Morrell died.

But for those who, like the reporter Percy Hoskins, felt that Adams, was 'a dead duck', there was a great surprise to come.

Four of the chief prosecution witnesses were undoubtedly the nurses who had attended Mrs Morrell at the end of her life, and who had provided the prosecution with the evidence about massive overdoses. On the second morning of the trial, the prosecution questioned Nurse Stronach, a stocky woman with a firm jaw. She testified that the patient had been 'rambling and semi-conscious'. She admitted that the patient had told her she was suffering pain, 'but I considered it neurotic'.

Then the defence, Mr Geoffrey Lawrence, took over. He asked her what injections she had given the old lady and whether it had been a quarter grain of morphia? The nurse agreed. Had not Dr Adams then arrived and given Mrs Morrell a further injection, without telling her what it was? The nurse agreed. Lawrence asked her if it was not the practice that all injections were noted down in a book. She agreed.

The defence now exploded its bombshell. Mr Lawrence produced an exercise book. He asked, 'Is that the night report for June 1950? Is that your handwriting?' The nurse had to agree that it was. Lawrence then read aloud a long passage, which demonstrated that Nurse Stronach had, indeed, recorded exactly what she had given the patient – milk and brandy, a sedormid tablet, more milk and brandy. She had also recorded that the patient had called her a nasty, common woman. Then Lawrence read out another entry – a description of the old lady's lunch consisting of partridge, celery and pudding, followed by brandy and soda. Hardly the lunch of a semi-conscious woman. . .

Lawrence pressed home the attack. Nurse Stronach had declared earlier that Mrs Morrell had been dopey and half asleep when Dr Adams had given her an injection; this was because she had already given Mrs Morrell an injection. But the record showed that Nurse Stronach had not given her an injection . . . Nurse Stronach had to agree that her memory had been at fault.

This was, in fact, the turning point of the trial. The defence had established that the nurses were not as reliable as the prosecution believed. The same point was reinforced when the other three nurses were cross-examined. Nurse Randall was asked about the normal dose of paraldehyde, the drug that was supposed to have killed the old lady. She answered, 'Two cc would be a normal dose.' Lawrence pointed out that the British Pharmacopoeia gave the full dose as 8cc, and the embarrassed nurse admitted that she had not known that.

The crucial point, of course, was that last injection of 5cc, which Dr Adams was alleged to have prepared, and which had been given by Nurse Randall. The record showed that no such injection had been given. The trial was to continue for 13 days more; but in effect, it was now over. It was almost a formality for the judge to find Bodkin Adams not guilty. When Percy Hoskins returned to his office, Lord Beaverbrook rang him and told him, 'Percy, two men have been acquitted today – Adams and Hoskins.' After that, Adams and Hoskins left for a secret hideaway, perhaps where Hoskins could write up the story of Dr John Bodkin Adams at his leisure.

But were two men acquitted? Was Hoskins right to believe that Bodkin Adams was innocent? He was possibly right to believe Adams was no sinister Bluebeard who carefully planned the murders of his patients. Yet we must remember that Adams was tried only for one murder. Would the verdict have been the same if the jury had known as much about him as Superintendent Hannam knew? He was found innocent because it was proved that the nurses had been mistaken on so many minor points. But were they lying when they alleged that Bodkin Adams had turned Mrs Morrell into a drug addict?

We know that Bodkin Adams was almost childishly greedy and avaricious. We know he was capable of putting pressure on his patients to make them leave him money in their wills. We know he was capable of giving at least one old lady an overdose that killed her – whether deliberately or out of carelessness. Is it not conceivable that he did the same to others when it suited his purposes? It is difficult to believe that Bodkin Adams was the wronged innocent that Percy Hoskins makes him out to be. In fact, it is hard not to feel that if the jury had found him guilty, no great injustice would have been committed.

JANICE WESTON

A lay-by on the northbound carriageway of the A1 is one of the most unlikely spots for a murder. Not only is the A1 one of the busiest roads in Britain but the lay-by in question is extremely narrow and completely exposed to view. But one has to remember that the murder took place at night, and that it was raining hard.

Nevertheless, the man who struck down Janice Weston, a wealthy solicitor, on the night of Saturday, 10 September 1983, must count himself remarkably lucky that he was not seen committing the deed in the headlights of a vehicle flashing past.

The body was discovered the following morning by a cyclist who had stopped to answer a call of nature. The body had been thrown into the ditch alongside the lay-by. It was badly battered – particularly the back of the head – but the murderer had made no attempt to cover it before hurriedly driving off in the victim's car.

Within 48 hours the police knew that the dead woman was 36-year-old Janice Weston, a brilliant company-law specialist and a partner in the Lincoln Inn's firm of Charles Russell & Company.

Janice Weston came from a comfortable background. After doing well at her convent school she had gone on to read law at Manchester University. When she qualified as a solicitor she was offered a post with the well-known London firm of Herbert Oppenheimer, Nathan & Vandyk. She was a career girl and dedicated to her work.

It was during her time at Oppenheimer's that she met the two men who were to play an important part in her life. The first was Tony Weston, a property developer, one year older than herself. He was married with two children. The other was Heinz Isner, 40 years older than she, and chairman of the Mettoy Company which made children's Corgi cars. He was a wealthy merchant banker and a Jew who had fled to Britain from Nazi Germany. Janice was Mettoy's legal adviser.

In 1975 Isner's wife died. Soon he began to invite the firm's petite and well-turned out legal adviser to dinner at his Chelsea flat and to take her out to the theatre and ballet. The relationship developed until one day Isner revealed to his step-granddaughter that he had proposed marriage to Janice but that she had turned him down. Nevertheless, the couple continued to see each other until Heinz Isner died in July 1977. Janice was a major beneficiary in his will and she received paintings, furniture, shares and money totalling some £140,000.

Her career continued to prosper, and five years later at the age of 35 she married Tony Weston, who was by now divorced. The couple together bought an old country mansion, Clopton Manor in Northamptonshire, which they began to modernize and convert into flats, using one of the flats themselves. They both continued their separate careers – Janice, by now, a partner at Charles Russell. She also began researching for a book on computer law. Meanwhile, Tony Weston was negotiating the purchase of a château in France. As a successful professional young couple they had a lifestyle many would envy.

Janice had made her will 39 days after her wedding. Of her £300,000 estate, nearly £100,000 was to go to her sister and £10,000 to her widowed mother. The income from the rest of the estate was left for life to her husband, with the capital after her death being shared between his two children and her nephews and nieces.

During the weekend of 10–11 September 1983, Tony Weston was away in France on a business trip concerning the château. Janice, being the perfectionist and hard-worker that she was, took the opportunity of going to her office to work. At about 5 p.m. that Saturday afternoon one of the other partners called into Russell's and found her there. He thought she had been expecting someone, but she was still alone when he left a short time later. It appears she returned home to the couple's flat in Holland Park where she had a light snack. The police subsequently found that nothing had been cleared away afterwards – uncharacteristic of the fastidious Janice. It seems she left the flat in a hurry for she did not take her handbag with her. She did, however, take her purse which was eventually discovered, with £37 in it, tucked under the driving seat of her silver Alfa Romeo.

19

It was a filthy night and one wonders why she had gone out. Was she driving somebody somewhere? Had she received a telephone call summoning her to a meeting place? Or was she going to Clopton Manor – only 15 miles from the lay-by on the A1? It hardly seems likely as their flat was unfinished and sparsely furnished; there were not even sheets on the beds, only sleeping-bags.

After the discovery of Janice's body at 9 a.m. on the Sunday morning, the police, under the supervision of Detective Chief Superintendent Leonard Bradley, were soon at the scene together with Dr Ian Hill, a Home Office pathologist. After examining the body his verdict was that she had been killed with the car jack found by the police in the nearby field. She had probably died between 9 p.m. on the Saturday night and 2 a.m. on Sunday morning.

On Monday morning colleagues at Charles Russell became concerned when Janice did not appear for her appointments. They had telephoned her home and then, knowing that her husband was away, they telephoned her sister. News of the body of an unidentified woman found beside a lay-by on the A1 had already been reported in the press that morning. Her sister became worried and her husband contacted the police. Later that morning they identified Janice's body.

Tony Weston returned from France that Monday and told a reporter that he called 'on any member of the public with knowledge or reasonable suspicion of the person who committed this crime to come forward to the police'. Within a further 24 hours a keen-eyed policeman found Janice's Alfa Romeo. It was parked in Camden Square, London NW1, not three miles from her flat. The interior was smeared with blood but there were no fingerprints.

The police investigation intensified but, if anything, the mystery deepened. The owner of a car-spares shop in Royston, Hertfordshire, telephoned the police to say that at about 11 a.m. on the Sunday a man between 25 and 35 years of age had bought a couple of spare car plates from him. Their number was that of Janice's car. Two other witnesses corroborated his story. Neither the man nor the number plates have been seen since.

20

It also transpired that on the Saturday morning, Janice had collected a spare tyre that had been repaired. Before leaving for France Tony Weston had had a puncture while visiting Clopton Manor. A workman on the site had changed it for him and one of his staff in London had taken it to be repaired. A mechanic had put the spare tyre, with Tony Weston's name and telephone number still chalked on the inside, into the boot of the Alfa for Janice. The old spare remained on her rear nearside wheel. When the car was discovered, the newly repaired tyre was back on the Alfa and the spare was missing. Later police inquiries revealed that Janice might have stopped at the lay-by because a tyre needed changing. Six witnesses said they had seen a man changing her tyre.

In December 1983 Tony Weston was held for 55 hours by the police. His solicitor appealed to a High Court judge that he should either be charged or released. Later Tony Weston said, 'I walked into a London police station for a progress meeting. Nine hours later TV News showed me leaving St Neot's Police Station, 60 miles away, handcuffed and with a blanket over my head. To most people that blanket means only one thing. No smoke without fire . . . Guilty.'

He does, indeed, seem to have been a leading suspect for a while, although he could prove his movements in Paris that weekend, and a hotel clerk remembered him collecting his room key on the Saturday evening. He was later completely eliminated from police inquiries.

Police investigations continued. Isner's step-granddaughter was questioned about his will and the relationship between Janice Weston and her step-grandfather. She was asked where she had been on the night of the murder – her alibi was checked and her fingerprints taken. Janice's legacy had been slightly reduced after Isner's stepdaughter appealed to a High Court over his will. But clearly no member of the Isner family was involved in the murder.

At the inquest in April 1984 the jury returned a verdict of unlawful killing. What really happened that night in September 1983 may never be known, but there are several possibilities. Janice may have given a lift to a hitch-hiker who then killed her.

But why then did her car not turn up further north on the A1 rather than in London? Or a passing motorist may have stopped to change her tyre – and killed her. It is baffling.

Detective Chief Superintendent Bradley says, 'We're still pursuing active lines of inquiry and interviewing people, such as persons detained in other parts of the country who might have had an opportunity to commit the crime. We are still hopeful of bringing our efforts to a successful conclusion.'

THE LINDBERGH BABY KIDNAPPING

On 21 May 1927 Charles Lindbergh became the most famous young man in the world. For 33 hours, the whole of Europe and America had held its breath as his tiny plane, *Spirit of St Louis*, made the first solo flight across the Atlantic. As one biographer remarked, he had single-handedly christened and launched the air age.

Less than five years later, however, Lindbergh had become one of the most deeply pitied men in the world. On the evening of 1 March 1932, his 19-month-old son, Charles junior, was kidnapped from his cot. It was the beginning of a ten-week ordeal that left Lindbergh an embittered man whose only desire was to escape from America.

The Lindberghs were all suffering from colds on that rainy and windy day in March, which is why they had decided to delay their departure to the home of Lindbergh's in-laws at Englewood, New Jersey, by 24 hours. At 7.30 that Tuesday evening, Anne Lindbergh and the nurse Betty Gow put the baby to bed in his cot, and closed and bolted all the shutters, except one which was warped and refused to close. Fifty minutes later, Charles Lindbergh arrived back from New York – only half an hour's drive away from their new home in Hopewell, South Jersey. Supper was waiting, and they ate in front of a blazing fire. At about 9.10 Lindbergh looked up sharply. 'What was that?' He had heard a sound, he said, like an orange crate smashing. But there was no further noise, and he forgot about it.

Just after 10 o'clock, Betty Gow knocked on the door of the Lindberghs' bedroom and asked, 'Mrs Lindbergh, do you have the baby?'

'Why, no.'

They went down to the library to see if Lindbergh had taken the child – he was fond of practical jokes. Then all three rushed back to the baby's bedroom. They could see the imprint of young Charles's head on the pillow, and it would obviously have been impossible for him to have climbed out on his own. Lindbergh said, 'Anne, they've stolen our baby.'

Then he saw the envelope on the radiator under the window. He told them not to touch it. When the police opened it an hour later, it was found to contain a ransom demand for $50,000.

There were few clues. Under the window, the police found some smudged footprints; nearby there was a ladder in three sections and a chisel. The ladder – a crude home-made one – was broken where the top section joined the middle one; this was almost certainly the noise Lindbergh had heard earlier. There were no fingerprints; the kidnapper must have worn gloves.

The kidnapping caused a nationwide sensation. But at this stage the Lindberghs were not too worried. Anne wrote to her mother-in-law: '. . . the detectives are very optimistic though they think it will take time and patience. In fact, they think the kidnappers have gotten themselves into a terrible jam – so much pressure, such a close net over the country . . .' And the pressure was indeed tremendous; crooks all over the east coast had reason to curse the kidnappers as the police turned on the heat. Sympathetic letters arrived literally in sackloads – 200,000 of them in a few days. Carloads of police, F.B.I. agents and secret servicemen arrived in Hopewell; so did many reporters and photographers. The Lindberghs were given no privacy. The great American public continued to love 'Lindy', but Lindy's love affair with the American way of life was at an end.

The note offered few clues. It had various spelling mistakes; 'anyding' for anything, and 'gut' for good; a handwriting expert said it had been written by a German with low educational qualifications. It was signed with two interlocking circles, one red and one blue.

But the kidnapper was obviously scared off by the hullabaloo; he made no attempt to contact the Lindberghs. From his prison cell, Al Capone, America's most famous gangster, offered to recover the baby if he was allowed out; the authorities declined. Mrs Lindbergh broadcast an appeal, and newspapers printed a diet sheet of the baby's meals. This drew a letter from the kidnapper – signed with the two coloured circles – explaining: 'We can note [sic] make any appointments just now', and promising to adhere to the diet. It had the typical German spelling errors: as before 'gut' for good, and 'aus' for 'out'.

A week after the kidnapping, a well-wisher named Dr John F. Condon sent a letter to his local newspaper in the Bronx, offering $1,000 of his own money for the return of the child. The result was a letter addressed to Condon signed with the two circles. It began: 'Dear Sir, If you are willing to act as go-between in the Lindbergh cace pleace [sic] follow stricly instruction.' It asked him to collect the money from Lindbergh and then place an advertisement in the *New York American* reading: Mony is Redy. Then further 'instruction' would be forthcoming.

When Condon succeeded in speaking to Lindbergh, the famous flyer sounded exhausted and indifferent – until Condon mentioned the signature of interlocking circles. Then his voice became excited, and he offered to see Condon immediately. The advertisement duly appeared in the *New York American*: 'Money is ready, Jafsie.' That same evening, a man's deep voice spoke to Condon on the telephone – Condon could also hear another man in the room speaking in Italian – and told him that the gang would shortly be in touch. The next day he was handed a letter that instructed him where to find yet another message.

The second message told Condon to meet the writer at a cemetery at 233rd Street. At the cemetery gates, a young man wearing a handkerchief over his face asked Condon if he had brought the money – the demand had now been increased to $70,000. Condon explained that the notice had been too short. Suddenly the man took fright. 'Have you brought the police?' Condon replied, 'No! You can trust me.' But the man ran away. Condon chased after him, and caught up with him in a nearby park. Here the young man, who identified himself as 'John', asked a peculiar thing, 'Would I burn if the baby is dead?' Appalled, Condon asked, 'Is the baby dead?' But 'John' assured him it was alive. It was on a boat, about six hours away (he pronounced it 'boad'). Finally, 'John' offered a token of his good faith – he would send Condon the baby's sleeping suit. And, in fact, it arrived by post; the Lindberghs identified it as that of their son.

On 2 April a second rendezvous at a cemetery was made.

25

This time, Lindbergh himself accompanied Condon; he was carrying $70,000 in a cardboard box. Unknown to Lindbergh, the Treasury had listed the number of every bill. Condon spoke to the kidnapper, and managed to persuade him to accept only $50,000. As he returned to Lindbergh's car, the kidnapper shouted after him, 'Hey, doctor'. Lindbergh heard the voice clearly. A moment later Condon handed over the money, and 'John' promised to send details of the whereabouts of the missing baby by the next morning's post.

The letter, when it arrived, claimed that the child was on a boat called the *Nelly*, near Elizabeth Island. Condon accompanied Lindbergh on the flight to look for the boat at the specified location. It was not there. Bitterly, they realized they had been tricked.

Five weeks later, on 12 May 1932, the last hope vanished when a Negro teamster, walking in the woods near the Lindbergh home, found a shallow, leaf-covered grave. It contained the decomposing body of a child. The shirt in which the body was dressed had been made by Betty Gow from a flannel petticoat. Charles Lindbergh Junior – 'Buster' – had been dead since the night on which he was taken from his cot; he had died of a blow on the head.

The trail seemed to be cold, yet the hunt for the kidnapper and killer was intensified. A member of the Lindbergh household was for a time widely suspected by the public, but the Lindberghs were convinced she was innocent. Another person suspected of complicity – Violet Sharpe, a maid at the home of Lindbergh's in-laws – committed suicide with poison.

Meanwhile, a wood technologist named Arthur Koehler was continuing his own investigations and examining the ladder used by the kidnapper. He had written to Lindbergh offering to try to trace its wood, using the laboratory of the Forest Service. It took him 18 months, and dozens of visits to lumber yards but eventually he found the place where the wood had been bought: The National Lumber and Millwork Company in the Bronx. It confirmed what the police had already come to accept: that the kidnapper of the Lindbergh baby lived somewhere in the Bronx – the reason he had seen Condon's original advertisement so quickly . . .

In May 1934, President Roosevelt abandoned the gold standard. This was unfortunate for the kidnappers, for $35,000 of the ransom money had been in gold certificates. These were now called in as they had ceased to be legal tender.

A break finally came on 15 September 1934. A dark-blue Dodge sedan drove into a garage in upper Manhattan; the man who drove asked for fuel with a German accent, and paid with a $10 gold certificate. The gas attendant hesitated but the man said, 'They're all right – any bank will take them.' So the attendant gave him his change. But not before he made a note of the number of the car. Other gold certificates had been exchanged in New York and they had proved to be part of the Lindbergh ransom money, but no one had ever noticed the person who had changed them. The certificate was taken to the local bank.

Four days later, a bank teller realized that this was another gold certificate from the Lindbergh ransom money. On the back of the note was a car registration number: 4U-13-41-N.Y. He tracked the gold certificate back to the service station in Manhattan. The police now checked with the New York State Motor License vehicle bureau as to who owned a car of that number. The answer soon came back: Richard Hauptmann, 1279 East 222nd Street, the Bronx.

Police surrounded the small frame house all that night, and when a man finally stepped out of the front door, they still waited, watching him climb into the blue Dodge sedan and drive off. A few minutes later, they forced him over to the kerb – perhaps working on the theory that a man with a steering wheel in both hands would not be able to pull out a gun and start shooting. But Hauptmann was unarmed. In his wallet, they found a $20 bill that was also from the Lindbergh ransom. Back at Hauptmann's home, in the garage a further $14,600 in ransom bills was found, carefully concealed. On a strip of wood in a dark closet they found Condon's telephone number. When asked to write down a passage containing words used by the kidnapper, Hauptmann misspelled them exactly as they appeared in the notes.

When asked how he came to be in possession of the money,

27

Hauptmann said it had been left in his care by a friend, Isidor Fisch, who had since died.

Hauptmann was a carpenter by trade, and he was 35 years old. He also had a criminal record in Germany – burglary and highway robbery – and had been sentenced to five years' imprisonment. He had been released on parole but had been arrested for more burglaries. He escaped and fled the country. He had entered the United States illegally, married a waitress, and set up in business as a carpenter. He was extremely successful, earning $50 a week. He had not worked for the past two years, and his account books, which he kept meticulously, showed that his fortunes had improved considerably since 1932.

Hauptmann's own story was that he and Fisch had gone into business in 1932, and that Fisch owed him $7,500. In 1933 Fisch had gone to Germany, but had died in Leipzig in 1934. Later that year, heavy rain had seeped into a closet in which he had left a shoe box that Fisch had consigned to his care, and only then had Hauptmann discovered it was full of money, which he dried out. But he failed to tell his wife, or Fisch's family, about his find. He had started using occasional bills from the shoe box because, after all, Fisch owed him money.

But perhaps the most damning piece of evidence at Hauptmann's trial, which opened in Flemington, New Jersey, on 2 January 1935, was the ladder. In Hauptmann's attic, claimed the prosecution, the police had discovered that a floorboard was missing. Sawdust showed that it had been sawn off. And the left-hand board of the kidnap ladder – known as 'Rail 16' – was of the same type of wood as the missing board. When placed in position in the attic floor four nail holes in Rail 16 matched exactly the four nail holes in the joist below. That seemed to prove emphatically that Hauptmann had made the ladder. Hauptmann replied scornfully that he was a skilful carpenter and that the ladder had been made by an incompetent amateur, not a man who took pride in his work. But the jury discounted his protest.

On 13 February 1935 the jury found Hauptmann guilty of murder. By October, the Court of Appeals had denied Hauptmann's appeal. The prison governor Harold Hoffmann interviewed Hauptmann in his cell in December, and emerged a puzzled man. Hauptmann again pointed out that he would never have made such a ladder, and begged to be given a truth drug or lie detector test. Hoffmann felt that his pleas rang true and began an investigation into the case. A few days after Hauptmann's arrest, Mrs Hauptmann had left home, unable to stand the continual commotion. A short time afterwards, the police had 'found' the missing board. Could they have removed it themselves? They could certainly have planted Condon's phone number in the dark closet. Condon had at first been uncertain that Hauptmann was 'John'. It was only later that he changed his mind. The prosecution had insisted that Hauptmann was alone in planning and carrying out the kidnapping, but what about the Italian voice Condon had heard on the telephone?

Governor Hoffman's intervention was interpreted by most of the American press as an attempt to get publicity, and others felt he was politically motivated – he was attempting to sack the Attorney General, David Wilentz, who had prosecuted Hauptmann. For Lindbergh this was the last straw. Totally convinced that Hauptmann was the man who had killed his son – and that American justice could be influenced by politicians – he sailed for England. He would remain in Europe for nearly five years, and was to become an admirer and frequent guest of the Nazis. During World War II he would try hard to prevent America entering the war on the side of the Allies.

Hauptmann was finally electrocuted, on 3 April 1936. For many years, there were no doubts that justice had been done. Everyone felt that the villain had finally got his 'come-uppance'. Only Hauptmann's wife Anna continued to plead that her husband was innocent.

But as the years went by, an increasing number of people began to agree with her – or at least, to agree that Hauptmann had not been proved guilty. Anthony Scaduto's book *Scapegoat* is an extremely powerful presentation of the evidence in favour of Hauptmann. But another book, *In Search of the Lindbergh Baby*, by Theon Wright, a reporter at the trial, raises a startling possibility: that 'Buster' Lindbergh was not murdered at all. A Connecticut businessman named Harold Olson had been told as a child that

29

he belonged to a family of gangsters, who had placed him with Roy and Sarah Olson when he was a baby. His real father, he was told, may have been Al Capone. But when he was an adult, his mother's cousins had told him that he might be the son of Charles Lindbergh. Furthermore, a woman who had been his nurse as a baby told him authoritatively that he was the Lindbergh child. Olson was certainly the right age for the Lindbergh baby, and photographs of him as a child show similar eyes to 'Buster' Lindbergh's, and the same scar on the chin. Olson spent years trying to track down his origins, and finally came to believe that the Lindbergh kidnapping was a plot organized by Capone lieutenants to get their boss out of jail – it may be recalled that Capone offered to locate the Lindbergh baby in exchange for his freedom.

But what about the child's body? A photograph in Wright's book shows that it was little more than a skeleton. The shirt in which it was wrapped was rotten, so little faith can be placed in Betty Gow's identification of it as the one she made. In *The Trial of Richart Hauptmann* there is one rather odd piece of evidence, given by William J. Allen, the truck driver who found the body; he said that the land on the other side of the road belonged to 'a Catholic home – a kind of hospital for children that ain't got no home'. Could the skeleton – which even Lindbergh was doubtful about identifying – have come from there?

This may seem a far-fetched theory. Yet one thing is certain: Bruno Richard Hauptmann should never have been found guilty on the evidence offered by the prosecution.

WILLIAM HERBERT WALLACE

The Wallace murder case might have been devised by Agatha Christie. In spite of recent evidence that seems to point towards a solution, it retains that tantalizing quality of a classic unsolved mystery.

William Herbert Wallace gave the appearance of being a completely ordinary little man. The critic James Agate once said of him: 'That man was born middle-aged.' But this undistinguished appearance concealed a certain sadness and unfulfilment. Wallace was born in Keswick, in England's Lake District, in 1878, the child of lower-middle-class parents. But he had an intellectual turn of mind, and when he discovered the *Meditations* of the Roman emperor Marcus Aurelius, decided that he was by nature a stoic – that is, one who doesn't expect much out of life, but who thinks it can be improved by hard work and discipline.

Like H. G. Wells's Kipps or Mr Polly – of whom he constantly reminds us – he became a draper's assistant, and found the life just as boring as they had. His quest for adventure took him to India – but still as a draper's assistant – then to Shanghai; he found both places a great disappointment, and caught a bad dose of dysentery which further undermined his already delicate constitution. So with his Marcus Aurelius in his pocket, he returned to England.

He became a Liberal election agent in Yorkshire, and while on a holiday in Harrogate met a mild-looking, dark-haired young lady named Julia Thorp. She was undoubtedly more intelligent than Wallace; she was well read, spoke French, played the piano and made excellent sketches. They talked about Marcus Aurelius and other intellectual matters and, in a rather leisurely manner, decided they liked one another enough to get married. They married in 1913 and lived in Harrogate. In the following year the outbreak of World War I cost Wallace his job – political agents were not needed during a war. Fortunately, it also caused many job vacancies and he soon found employment as an insurance agent in Liverpool, working for the Prudential.

The couple moved into a rather dreary little terrace house in a cul-de-sac called Wolverton Crescent, in the Anfield district, and for the next 17 years lived a life of peaceful and rather penurious dullness.

Wallace pottered about in a chemical laboratory in his home, and even gave occasional lectures at the technical college. He also joined a chess club that met regularly in the City Café in North John Street. Julia read library books and sang at the piano. They had no children and, apparently, no real friends. And although life on less than £4 a week was hardly idyllic, they seemed happy enough.

The evening of 19 January 1931 was chilly and damp, but by 7 o'clock a few members had already arrived at the chess club in the City Café. Shortly after 7.15, the telephone rang. Samuel Beattie, captain of the club, answered it. A man's voice asked for Wallace. Beattie said that Wallace would be in later to play a match and suggested he ring back. 'No, I'm too busy – I have my girl's 21st birthday on.' The man said his name was Qualtrough, and asked if Beattie could give him a message. Beattie wrote it down – it asked Wallace to go to Qualtrough's home at 25 Menlove Gardens East the following evening at 7.30. It was, said Qualtrough, a matter of business.

Wallace slipped quietly into the club some time before 8 o'clock. Beattie gave him the message and Wallace made a note of the address in his diary.

The following evening, Wallace arrived home shortly after six, had 'high tea' – a substantial meal – and left the house at a quarter to seven. He instructed his wife to bolt the back door after him – that was their usual practice. Julia Wallace, who was suffering from a heavy cold, nevertheless went with him to the back gate and watched him leave. Wallace walked to a tramcar, asked the conductor if it went to Menlove Gardens East, and climbed aboard. The conductor advised him to change trams at Penny Lane, and told Wallace where to get off. The conductor of the second tram advised him to get off at Menlove Gardens West.

Wallace now spent a frustrating half-hour or so trying to find Menlove Gardens East. Apparently it did not exist; although there was a Menlove Gardens North and Menlove Gardens West. Wallace decided to call at 25 Menlove Gardens West, just in case Beattie had taken down the address wrongly; but the householder there said he had never heard of a Mr Qualtrough. Wallace tried calling at the house of his superintendent at the Prudential, a Mr Joseph Crew, who lived in nearby Green Lane, but found no one at home. He asked a policeman the way, and remarked on the time, 'It's not 8 o'clock yet.' The policeman said, 'It's a quarter to.' He called in a general shop, then in a newsagent's, where he borrowed a city directory, which seemed to prove beyond all doubt that Menlove Gardens East did not exist. He even asked the proprietress to look in her account book to make sure that there was no such place as Menlove Gardens East. People were to remark later that Wallace seemed determined to make people remember him. Finally, even the pertinacious Wallace gave up, and returned home.

He arrived back at 8.45 p.m., and inserted his key into the front door. To his surprise, it seemed to be locked on the inside. He tried the back door; that was also locked. Receiving no reply to his knock, he called on his next-door neighbours the Johnstons, looking deeply concerned, and asked them if they had heard anything unusual – only a thin partition wall separated them from the Wallaces. They said no. John Johnston suggested that perhaps Wallace should try the back door again. And this time, to Wallace's apparent surprise, it opened. He entered the house, and the Johnstons waited outside politely. A few moments later, Wallace rushed out, looking shocked. 'Come and see – she's been killed.' They followed him through to the sitting room, which was at the back of the house. Julia Wallace was lying on the floor, face downward, and the gash in the back of her head made it clear that she had been the victim of an attack. The floor was spattered with blood.

Wallace seemed curiously calm as he lit a gas-mantle, walking around the body to do so, then suggested that they should look in the kitchen to see if anything had been taken. There was a lid on the kitchen floor, which Wallace said had been wrenched from a cabinet. He took down the cash-box from a shelf, looked inside and told the Johnstons that he thought

33

about £4 had been taken. Then, at Johnston's suggestion, Wallace went upstairs to see if anything was missing, and came down almost immediately saying, 'There's £5 in a jar they haven't taken.'

At this point, Johnston left to fetch the police. Wallace had a momentary breakdown, putting his hands to his head and sobbing, but quickly recovered himself. Mrs Johnston and Wallace then returned to the sitting room, where Wallace commented, 'They've finished her – look at the brains.' And indeed, Julia Wallace's brains were oozing on to the floor. Then Wallace exclaimed with surprise, 'Why, whatever was she doing with her mackintosh and my mackintosh?' There was a mackintosh under her body, which Wallace identified as his own.

Shortly afterwards, a policeman arrived. Wallace told him about his fruitless search for Qualtrough, then accompanied him upstairs. Constable Williams felt that Wallace seemed 'extraordinarily cool and calm'. The bedroom appeared to have been disturbed, with pillows lying near the fireplace.

Another policeman arrived, then, just before 10 o'clock, Professor J.E.W. MacFall, the professor of forensic medicine at Liverpool University. MacFall concluded that Mrs Wallace died of a violent blow or blows to the back left-hand side of the skull – and deduced that she had been sitting in an armchair, leaning forward as if talking to somebody, when the blow had been struck. She had fallen to the floor, and the attacker had rained about 11 more blows on her. He also reached the interesting conclusion that Mrs Wallace had died about four hours earlier – that is, at 6 o'clock . . .

This, it later proved, was impossible, for the 14-year-old milk boy, Alan Close, was to testify that he had delivered a can of milk at 6.25 p.m., and that Mrs Wallace advised him to hurry home because he had a cough.

But MacFall had planted suspicion on Wallace in the minds of the police. Two weeks later, on 2 February 1931, Wallace was charged with his wife's murder. He became very pale and replied, 'What can I say to this charge, of which I am absolutely innocent?'

34

His trial began on 22 April, before Mr Justice Wright. The prosecution case was that Wallace had concocted an elaborate plan to murder his wife, and had phoned the café to make the appointment with Qualtrough on the evening before the murder. The endless and elaborate inquiries about Menlove Gardens East were intended to provide him with a perfect alibi; but Mrs Wallace was already lying dead in her sitting-room when William Herbert Wallace left the house. In the closing speech for the Crown, Mr E. G. Hemmerde made much of the 'inherent improbabilities' in Wallace's story: that surely an insurance agent would not spend his evening on such a wild goose chase – that he would have hurried back home the moment he knew that a Menlove Gardens East did not exist. He also made much of Wallace's apparent calmness immediately after the discovery of the body, and mentioned in passing the possibility that Wallace had stripped naked and then put on his mackintosh, and battered his wife to death, before leaving the house to look for Qualtrough.

The judge's summing up was favourable to Wallace, and there was some surprise when, after only an hour, the jury returned a verdict of guilty. Wallace was shattered; he had been confident of acquittal. But he appealed against the verdict, and indeed the following month, the Court of Criminal Appeal quashed it, and Wallace was freed.

He was taken back at his old job. But most of his colleagues had doubts about his innocence. He was given a job in the office. He moved house, to Meadowside Road in Bromsborough, a Liverpool suburb. And on 26 February 1933 – less than two years after his ordeal – he died in hospital of cancer of the liver. Ever since that date, writers on crime have disputed his guilt or innocence.

The main problem, of course, is that of motive. Wallace was a lifelong keeper of diaries, and his diaries make it clear that his married life was peaceful and serene. There was no suggestion of another woman, or that he was tired of his wife. His diaries after his trial continue to protest his innocence, with entries like: 'Julia, Julia my dear, why were you taken from me?' The crime writer Nigel Morland, who examined the case at length in

Background to Murder and who was convinced of Wallace's guilt, has to fall back on generalizations like: 'The human heart is always a vast mystery . . .'

Yseult Bridges, who also wrote about the case, became convinced of Wallace's guilt when she read a series of 'ghosted' articles about his life which appeared in *John Bull* in 1932. There Wallace remarks that he had matched his brains against some of the greatest chess players in the world. Yseult Bridges comments that 'he was never more than a third-rate player in an obscure little club', and concludes that Wallace was a pathological liar. But another writer, Jonathan Goodman, looked more closely into the matter, and concludes (in *The Killing of Julia Wallace*) that Wallace was telling the truth after all; in the 1920s he had played in 'simultaneous exhibition matches' against world-famous players like Capablanca – and been thoroughly beaten.

Kenneth Gunnell, a parliamentary candidate from Redruth, Cornwall, independently discovered that Wallace was telling the truth about his chess opponents, and so began to study the case in detail. He made one odd discovery. Amy Wallace, the wife of Wallace's elder brother Joseph, was a tough and dominant lady, and Gunnell found out that in Malaya – where she had lived in the 1920s – Amy had been a member of a flagellation sect, and indulged in beating black boys. He noted that after his acquittal, Wallace sometimes acted like a man with something on his mind – not murder, perhaps, but some guilty secret. Could it be that Amy Wallace was Herbert Wallace's mistress, and that she murdered Julia? Mr Gunnell even speculated that the murder weapon was the metal handle of a riding whip. Unfortunately, Mr Gunnell's stimulating theory remained unpublished. Yet when I read the typescript of his book, I found myself ultimately unconvinced. Although my view of Wallace was rather negative – he seemed to me a cold-hearted egoist who had married Julia for her money (which he used to pay his debts), then treated her purely as a piece of domestic furniture – it seemed clear that he was simply not the type to engage in affairs with highly dominant women. Amy Wallace probably terrified him.

36

In 1960, I collaborated with Patricia Pitman on *An Encyclopedia of Murder*. Mrs Pitman was convinced of Wallace's guilt; I, in spite of misgivings about his character, of his innocence. He simply had no reason to kill Julia. Two or three years later, she surprised me by telling me that she was now convinced of Wallace's innocence. It seemed that she had been talking to one of Britain's leading crime experts, J. H. H. Gaute, a director of the publishers Harrap, and he had told her the real identity of the murderer. I hastened to contact Joe Gaute, with whom I had had much friendly correspondence about murder. It was from him that I first heard the name of the man he was certain was the killer of Julia Wallace: Gordon Parry. Wallace himself, it seemed, had believed that Parry murdered his wife, and after his retirement he had made a public statement to the effect that he had had an alarm button installed inside his front door as a safety precaution.

After the murder, Wallace had been asked by the police what callers might have been admitted to the house by his wife; he named 15 people (including his sister-in-law Amy). Asked if he suspected any of them Wallace hesitated, then admitted that he was suspicious of a young man named Gordon Parry. This man had called at his house on business, and was trusted by Julia. But he had a criminal record. And he knew where Wallace kept his collection money. At the time of the murder, Parry was heavily in debt. Questioned by the police, he alleged that he had been with 'friends' on the evening of the murder, and his friends corroborated this. However, two years later, Parry admitted that this had been 'a mistake'.

Joe Gaute had been curious about Parry's present whereabouts, and had casually looked him up in the London Telephone Directory. It was a long shot, but it paid off. Parry was listed at an address in south London. The author Jonathan Goodman, who was writing his book on the Wallace case, and another crime expert, Richard Whittington-Egan, went to call on him. Parry, a powerfully built, little man with sleeked-back grey hair and a military moustache, received them with the 'bogus bonhomie of a car salesman', and talked to them on his doorstep. They decided that 'his manner masks . . . considerable firmness, even ruthlessness. He would be a nasty man to cross.' Parry hinted that he could reveal much about Wallace, and described him as 'a very strange man' and 'sexually odd'. He seemed to know what had become of everybody involved in the case, as if he had been carefully following its aftermath over the years. And when he finally dismissed Goodman and Whittington-Egan, they both had the feeling that he was thinking that he had fooled better people than they were. In his book *The Killing of Julia Wallace*, Goodman refers to Parry as 'Mr X', and it is fairly clear that he regarded him as the chief suspect.

In 1980, a news editor in Liverpool's Radio City, Roger Wilkes, became interested in the Wallace case, and started researching it for a programme. He contacted Jonathan Goodman, who at first was understandably cagey about revealing Parry's identity, in case he found himself involved in a libel suit. But through Wallace's solicitor, Hector Munro, Wilkes tracked down Parry's identity. At the time of the murder, Parry was 22, the son of well-to-do parents. He had worked for the Prudential for a while, but had failed to pay in various premiums he had received; his parents had paid the money. Parry had been charged at various times with theft, embezzlement and indecent assault – at his trial for the latter a medical expert called him 'a sexual pervert'.

Wilkes persisted; but when he finally tracked down Parry to North Wales he discovered that he had died a few weeks before, in April 1980. Nevertheless, he continued with his investigation. Who were the 'friends' who had given Parry his alibi for the night of the murder? It emerged that there was only one – a Miss Lily Lloyd, to whom Parry was engaged. And from Jonathan Goodman he learned that when Parry had jilted her two years later, Miss Lloyd had gone to Wallace's solicitor and offered to swear an affidavit saying that the alibi she had given for Parry for the night of the crime was false. Wilkes then managed to track down Miss Lloyd. She had played a piano in a cinema in the 1930s and if the police had taken the trouble to check her alibi they would have discovered that she could not have been with Parry at the time of the murder as she was working in the cinema.

Finally, Wilkes uncovered the clinching piece of evidence. At the time of the murder, a young garage mechanic named John Parkes had been working near Parry's home. He knew Parry as a 'wide boy' – he had been to school with him. On the night of the murder, Parry had called at the garage in an agitated state, and washed down his car with a high-pressure hose. Parkes saw a glove in the car, and pulled it out to prevent it getting wet. It was soaked with wet blood . . .

Wilkes had finally tracked down the murderer of Julia Wallace – but half a century too late.

ADELAIDE BARTLETT

The Adelaide Barlett poisoning case does not qualify as one of the great murder mysteries; yet most students of Victorian crime will agree that it is one of the most peculiar cases of all time.

Theodore Edwin Bartlett was a hard-working and highly ambitious grocer; by the time he was 29, he and his business partner owned a chain of small shops in south London. Although he was a good-looking man, fond of the open air, he had never married – life was too busy for romance. Then, one day in the early 1870s, he went to call on his brother Charles, who lived in Kingston, and was introduced to a dazzlingly attractive 18-year-old girl named Adelaide Blanche de la Tremoile. She had dark curly hair, large and appealing eyes, and a sensual mouth. Edwin found her fascinating. But it seems likely that, at this stage, marriage did not enter his head.

Adelaide was definitely a lady, and therefore far above him socially. Then he learned that there was an odd secret in her background. Adelaide's mother had borne her out of wedlock. Her father was a wealthy Englishman who preferred to keep his identity secret – it has been suggested that he was a member of Queen Victoria's entourage when she visited France in 1855, and was therefore probably titled. Now Adelaide lived with a guardian in a house in Richmond – she was staying in Kingston as a guest of Charles's 16-year-old daughter. So it seemed that, although she was a lady, her chances of being accepted into English society were minimal. Edwin saw his opportunity, and pursued it with single-minded vigour.

He called on her when she returned to Richmond, and seems to have persuaded her guardian – or her father – that a virtuous and successful grocer would make a desirable husband. He explained to Adelaide solemnly that his intentions were more than pure; there was no element of carnal desire in his feeling for her, and when they were married, their relationship would be wholly platonic. By way of proving his good faith, Edwin Bartlett packed off his newly wedded bride to a ladies' finishing school in Stoke Newington. She came to stay with her husband during the school holidays but – according to Adelaide – their relationship was like that of father and daughter. And when she had finished at the Stoke Newington school, Edwin sent her off to a convent in Brussels. She stayed there until 1877 – two years after their marriage – when she returned home to a newly furnished flat above Edwin's largest shop in Herne Hill. For just one month, life was pleasant and peaceful, and Adelaide no doubt enjoyed being a young married woman in charge of her first home. Then Edwin's mother died, and the dutiful son invited his father to come and live with them.

It was a mistake. The old man was a bad-tempered old sponger and he had never liked Adelaide. He made himself so unpleasant that Adelaide ran away from home – possibly to the house in Kingston where Edwin had first met her. This seems to have led to further trouble. Edwin's younger brother, Frederick, also lived in the house, and the old man suspected a love affair. One writer on the case states that Adelaide became Frederick's mistress, but there is no evidence whatsoever for this assertion. All we know is that the old man accused Adelaide of having an affair with Frederick, and that Edwin was so incensed he made his father sign an apology drawn up by a solicitor. Then an uneasy peace reigned in the household.

Four years later, in 1881, two things broke the monotony of their lives: Edwin had a nervous breakdown (brought on, according to his father, by laying a floor), and Adelaide had a stillborn baby. The latter incident was Edwin's fault; the nurse he engaged to look after his wife had sensed that this might be a difficult birth, and begged Edwin to call in a doctor. But the Victorian Edwin was rather shocked at the idea of another man 'interfering with her', and refused. By the time a doctor was finally called in, the baby was dead.

Soon after this, perhaps to distract her, they moved to the village of Merton, near Wimbledon. Edwin's motive may also have been to get rid of his father. He selected a house that had no spare bedroom, so the old man was forced to find a home elsewhere.

Early in 1885 – the Bartletts had now been married ten years

– the couple decided to try another place of worship one Sunday morning. They attended the Wesleyan Chapel in Merton. The preacher that day was a young man named George Dyson; he had a black moustache, a receding hairline, and was of slight build. Dyson made a pastoral call on the Barletts soon after that. And when he told Edwin Bartlett that he was about to go to Trinity College Dublin, to take his degree, Bartlett was deeply impressed. He had an almost pathetic admiration for anyone with education – he himself was an avid but disorganized reader. He cross-examined Dyson about his studies and pressed the young man to come and visit them again as soon as he returned from Dublin. Slightly overwhelmed – for he was modest and not very clever – Dyson agreed. And a warm, if peculiar, friendship began between these three rather lonely people.

Dyson found Edwin Bartlett 'exceedingly odd'. He seemed to have eccentric ideas on all kinds of subjects. For example, he was a devotee of a work called *Esoteric Anthropology* by Thomas Low Nichols, whose long sub-title declared it to be a 'confidential' treatise on the passionate attractions and perversions of the most intimate relations between men and women. It was not, as the judge later assumed, disguised pornography, but an early 'women's lib' discourse on the unfairness of using women as sexual objects. It recommended birth control and suggested that sexual intercourse should only be practised for the purpose of begetting children. Another of Edwin's rather peculiar beliefs was that men should have two wives, one for 'use' and one for intellectual companionship. He was also, like many Victorians, interested in hypnotism, and in the doctrines of Anton Mesmer, according to which human beings possess a 'vital magnetic fluid' that can be passed from one to another.

Soon, Edwin Bartlett was professing the warmest affection for the Reverend Dyson. In fact, he proposed that Dyson should continue Adelaide's education, teaching her geography, history, Latin and mathematics. Dyson, who was making a mere £100 a year, agreed. He would arrive in the morning, while Edwin was out at business, and often stay all day. During most of this time, he was alone with Adelaide. Whether she became his mistress

42

depends on one's final view of her guilt or innocence; but certainly she often sat at his feet, with her head on his knee, and he often kissed her – alone and in her husband's presence. And, oddly enough, Edwin seemed delighted with the whole arrangement. His wife was lonely – she had only one close female friend, a Mrs Alice Matthews – and now he had found her a male friend and teacher who could be trusted implicitly. Edwin had unlimited faith in clergymen. If he found Dyson still in the house when he came in for supper, he warmly pressed him to stay for the evening.

When the Bartletts went to Dover for a month, Edwin tried to persuade Dyson to accompany them too, and offered him a first-class season ticket so that he could rush down from London whenever he was free. Dyson refused, but Edwin still found time to travel to Putney and whisk him off to Dover as an overnight guest. He also asked Dyson to be an executor of his will, in which, naturally, he left everything to Adelaide.

In the September of 1885 the Bartletts moved into a new lodging in Victoria – it was to be their last. Edwin told their landlady, Mrs Doggett, that they would be having a regular visitor, a clergyman, as a dinner guest. George Dyson continued to call as regularly as ever, travelling from Putney, where he was now in charge of his own church, on a season ticket given him by Edwin Bartlett. They even kept a special jacket and slippers for him to change into. Dyson was finding this close friendship with a young married woman disturbing, and he confessed openly to Edwin that he was growing attracted to Adelaide and that it was upsetting his work. He felt he ought to stop seeing them. Edwin dismissed the idea, assuring Dyson that Adelaide had become a better and nobler woman since she had known him. He seemed to be trying to throw them into one another's arms. Mrs Doggett noticed one day, after Dyson had left, that the window curtains were not merely drawn, but pinned together. It is hard to imagine why they should do this unless they were having an affair.

Suddenly Edwin became ill. One day he felt so exhausted at work that he hurried home. The next morning, he and Adelaide and Dyson went to a dog show – dogs were one of Edwin's main interests – but he felt so ill that they had to return home. Adelaide went out to fetch a doctor. She found a young man called Alfred Leach, whom she had never met before, but who immediately accompanied her to her home. Edwin was suffering from sickness, diarrhoea and bleeding of the bowels; he had also had toothache. When Dr Leach looked into his mouth, he observed a blue line round the gums – a symptom of mercury poisoning. When he asked Edwin if he had taken mercury, Edwin denied it, but admitted that he had swallowed a pill he had found in a drawer – he had no idea what it was for. Leach arrived at another explanation. Edwin's teeth were in an appalling condition, and his breath smelt foul. Apparently the dentist who made his false teeth had failed to draw the stumps; for some reason, he had sawn off the teeth at the gums. When these had rotted, the dentist merely made more false teeth, and the condition of his mouth made it impossible for Edwin to clean his remaining teeth. Leach's theory was that Edwin had, at some time, got a dose of mercury into his system, and that the sulphides produced by his rotting teeth had combined with it to form mercuric sulphide – hence the blue line.

A dentist who was called in verified that Edwin was suffering from mercury posioning, and extracted 15 roots and stumps. So throughout December the patient remained in bed. On Christmas Day 1885, he received an unpleasant shock when he went to the lavatory and passed a round worm. He was naturally something of a hypochondriac, and this gave him 'the horrors'. He swore that he could feel worms wriggling in his throat and became deeply depressed.

On the last day of December – and the last day of Edwin's life – he went to the dentist for yet another tooth extraction. Young Dr Leach, who had become a devotee of Adelaide, went with them. On the way Adelaide remarked that they had just been saying that they sometimes wished they were unmarried, so they could have the pleasure of getting married again. Later, when Edwin got home, his appetite had improved, and he ate a large meal of oysters, jugged hare and cake, with a helping of chutney. He told Mrs Doggett that he would have a haddock for his breakfast. It seemed he was at last on the road to recovery.

Just before 4 a.m. on New Year's Day, Adelaide knocked on the Doggett's bedroom door. 'Go and fetch Dr Leach. I think Mr Bartlett is dead.' She explained that she had fallen asleep, holding Edwin's foot – which apparently soothed him – as she sat beside his bed. She had awakened and felt that he was cold. She had tried to revive him with brandy but without success. Dr Leach observed a glass of brandy on the shelf, with a smell of chloroform.

The moment old Mr Bartlett heard of his son's death, he concluded he had been murdered. He sniffed his son's lips, then turned to Dr Leach and said, 'We must have a post mortem.'

The post mortem revealed a baffling and astonishing fact: that Edwin Bartlett had died of chloroform poisoning. This was so astonishing because chloroform is an unpleasant-tasting substance that would be almost impossible to swallow; moreover, it causes vomiting. If chloroform was poured down someone's throat when he was unconscious it would get into the lungs – which seemed to point to the completely mystifying conclusion that Edwin Bartlett had drunk the chloroform voluntarily. Yet his cheerfulness before he went to sleep, and the fact that he had even ordered his breakfast, made it unlikely that he intended suicide.

Where had the chloroform come from? This was soon revealed. The Reverend Dyson had bought it, at Adelaide's request. He had even gone to three separate chemists to get a fairly large quantity, claiming that he wanted to use it as cleaning fluid. Adelaide had told him she wanted it to make her husband sleep. And now, when he heard that chloroform had been found in Edwin's stomach, Dyson was panic stricken. He saw it as the end of his career. He rushed along to see Adelaide, and when Mrs Matthews came unexpectedly into the room, she heard Dyson saying, 'You did tell me Edwin was going to die soon.' When Adelaide denied it, he bowed his head on the piano and groaned, 'Oh, my God!' Later that day, he saw Adelaide alone, and she asked him to say nothing about the chloroform. Dyson refused and said he was going to make a clean breast of it.

And so he did. The result was that Adelaide Bartlett found herself on trial for murder. When, in the spring of 1886, it became known that he was to be tried for poisoning her husband, and that the Reverend George Dyson would probably stand in the dock beside her, public excitement was intense. It had all the signs of being a thoroughly scandalous murder case, complete with revelations of secret adultery and a plot by the lovers to kill the husband. When it was known that the great advocate Edward Clarke would defend Adelaide, people nodded significantly. Clarke was not one of those barristers who depended on verbal fireworks and bullying to win his cases; he was known for a certain quiet sincerity. Yet for all that, he had a formidable reputation. It was obvious that no suburban grocer's wife could afford his services, which could only mean that her mysterious father had intervened.

In the event, Adelaide finally stood alone in the dock; Dyson had managed to clear his own name by shamelessly doing his best to hand her over to the hangman. Edward Clarke had an apparently impossible task – to convince a Victorian jury that this pretty Frenchwoman, quite probably an adulteress, was innocent of her husband's murder. He had only one thing on his side: the total mystery of how even the most cunning murderess could have got the chloroform into Edwin Bartlett's stomach.

Clarke's defence was brilliant. His line of argument was that Edwin was a highly eccentric man who had almost thrown his wife into the arms of the clergyman, and who had told them that he expected them to marry when he was dead. He had insisted that his marriage to Adelaide should be purely platonic, and they had only had sexual intercourse once, as a result of which a baby had been born. But in the last days of his illness, Edwin had suddenly shown a desire for sexual intercourse. Adelaide felt this was wrong, since she now regarded herself as affianced to Dyson. So she asked Dyson to get her chloroform, so she might wave it in his face if he made sexual demands. However, she had been unable to go through with it. She had never been able to keep a secret from Edwin, and on that last evening of his life, had confessed her intention and showed him the bottle of chloroform. Edwin had been rather upset about it, and had placed the bottle on the mantelpiece. Somehow, while Adelaide dozed by her husband, holding his foot to comfort him, some of that chloroform had got into Edwin's stomach. (She admitted she had disposed of the rest by throwing it from the window of a train.) The main point of the defence was that Edwin was eccentric to the point of insanity, and that such an unpredictable man might easily have swallowed chloroform – perhaps simply to upset his wife and gain attention.

Amazingly enough, the jury believed this unlikely story of a wife too virtuous to permit her own husband sexual intercourse, even when it was revealed that Edwin had rubber contraceptives in his pocket and undoubtedly used them in making love to Adelaide. But the central point of the defence, of course, was that baffling mystery of the chloroform; if Adelaide poisoned her husband, how did she get it into his stomach? To that question the prosecution had no answer. After that, there could only be one verdict. 'Although we think there is the gravest suspicion attaching to the prisoner, we do not think there is sufficient evidence to show how or by whom the chloroform was administered.' So the verdict had to be not guilty.

The question of Adelaide's guilt or innocence has been argued by criminologists ever since. Some, like Nigel Morland, have no doubt that she was innocent, and that Edwin took the chloroform himself in a spirit of resentment or mischief. The majority is inclined to believe that Adelaide was poisoning Edwin from the beginning with some mercury compound, and only decided on the dangerous expedient of ether when he looked like recovering. Yseult Bridges believes that Adelaide somehow used hypnosis to induce Edwin to swallow the chloroform. None, as far as I know, has hit upon what seems to be the simplest and most obvious solution.

Let us try to reconstruct a hypothetical scenario. When Edwin Bartlett meets the beautiful Adelaide, he is too shy to hope that she will become his mistress as well as his wife, and so he assures her that their relationship will be a purely platonic one. But after two years of marriage, he is less humble and self-effacing, and insists on his marital rights. Adelaide becomes pregnant but, due to her husband's peculiar ideas about doctors, she loses the baby.

Edwin's curious attitude – his feeling that a doctor who

47

examined his wife would be 'interfering with her' – indicates a powerful physical jealousy. It is surely the attitude of a man who has the utmost difficulty in persuading his wife to let him make love to her, so the idea of another man examining her intimately arouses intense jealousy. Adelaide, for her part, finds sex with her husband rather unpleasant, perhaps because his rotten teeth cause permanent halitosis, and she does her best to persuade him to abide by their 'platonic' contract by petting him, fussing over him, showing him a great deal of affection – in fact, everything but allowing him into her bed. (At the trial, it was emphasized that they seemed to be an extremely happily married couple.) She makes use of the standard excuse, that she is afraid of becoming pregnant again, but Edwin counters that by buying contraceptives.

For Edwin, life becomes a permanent siege on his wife's virtue, with very infrequent successes. In his efforts to soften her, he deliberately introduces the Reverend George Dyson into their household and encourages a flirtation. In effect, he is asking the clergyman – whom he trusts implicitly – to 'warm her up'. While she is feeling kindly and grateful to her husband, she can hardly refuse him the occasional embrace.

Edwin falls ill. We do not know whether – as Yseult Bridges believes – she has been administering small doses of lead acetate or some mercuric poison. But it gives her a flash of hope; she sees the end of her martyrdom in sight. Then he begins to recover, and to indicate that his sexual appetites are returning to normal. Perhaps she finds the contraceptives in his pocket.

It is at this point that she asks Dyson to buy the chloroform. Presumably the idea of killing Edwin is at the back of her mind – it is hard to believe that she intends to soak a handkerchief in the drug and try and press it over his nose whenever he becomes amorous. But she also knows Edwin well enough to know that, as a hypochondriacal invalid, he quite enjoys taking 'medicines'. He is in a state of neurotic depression about his 'worms'. Dr Leach has given him all kinds of medicines for them, without effect; Edwin is convinced he is still swarming with worms. All Adelaide needs to do is to produce the chloroform and tell Edwin that Dr Leach has recommended this to get rid of worms.

Perhaps only the lightest of hints is needed. Perhaps she offers him a little chloroform mixed with brandy, but he finds it unpleasant. Then, as she sits beside him, he decides that he will win her approval by taking his medicine, and he cautiously reaches out for the bottle . . .

Sir James Paget, a well-known doctor, made the famous comment, 'Now the case is over, she should tell us in the interests of science how she did it.' The answer is surely that she did not do it; Edwin did. Whether it was at Adelaide's suggestion we shall never know.

LIZZIE BORDEN

The crime of Lizzie Borden has entered the realm of folklore; there is even a ballet about it called 'The Fall River Legend'. But was it Lizzie's crime? And if so, what was her motive in committing it? This is the problem that has intrigued students of crime for almost a century.

Fall River is a small mill town in Massachusetts, and in 1892, one of its most respected residents was Andrew Jackson Borden, a man who made a fortune in property and banking. He lived at 92 Second Street with his second wife Abby and his two daughters, Lizzie and Emma. Oddly enough, the house in which this wealthy family lived was thoroughly uncomfortable; the lavatory was in the basement and the only running water in a sink room off the kitchen. But Andrew Borden was of Puritan stock, and regarded these discomforts as minor inconveniences.

The day dawned hot and bright on 4 August 1892; by 7 in the morning the temperature was already in the eighties. Andrew and Abby Borden and John Vinnicum Morse, Andrew's brother-in-law by his first marriage, ate a breakfast of mutton and mutton soup. This may sound surprising in such hot weather but Mrs Borden had cooked a large joint of mutton on the previous Sunday, and now they were eating mutton for every meal – Andrew Borden was a notoriously tight man. Fall River had been struck by a heat wave that week and the repeated appearance of the mutton may explain why the family was suffering from stomach pains and vomiting; Mrs Borden even suspected that someone was poisoning them. The Irish maid Bridget Sullivan, who had been ordered to clean all the windows, had to break off to be sick in the garden.

Lizzie rose rather late. Her sister Emma – nine years her senior – was away staying with friends. Lizzie was feeling tired and depressed. She was plain, overweight and 32 years old, and no man ever looked at her twice. She adored her father – although she disliked his rudeness and meanness – and detested her stepmother, who was even more overweight and unattractive than Lizzie herself. To add to her problems, it was the wrong time of the month, so she felt physically miserable. Listlessly, she began to do some ironing. Her stepmother was upstairs, cleaning the guest room. Poor Bridget was still cleaning the windows and struggling with nausea.

At 10.45 a.m. Andrew Borden came back from his office and was surprised to find the screen door latched and the front door locked. Bridget let him in and discovered that the patent lock had been released, and that both bolts had been drawn. She exclaimed out loud, and at that moment heard Lizzie laugh. Then Lizzie came forward and asked her father how he felt now – he had been as ill as the rest of them. He was still feeling weak. Lizzie told him that her stepmother had gone out to visit someone who was sick -- a note had been delivered to the house. Andrew Borden then went into the sitting-room, which was a little cooler than the rest of the house, and lay down on the horsehair sofa. Bridget decided to sneak upstairs and have a rest; as she lay on her bed, she heard the town hall clock chime 11.

Ten minutes later, Lizzie shouted upstairs, 'Come down quick. Father's dead. Somebody came in and killed him.'

Andrew Borden was lying on the sofa, his face a mass of blood. His skull had been cleft open, and an eye hung out on its socket. Bridget was hastily dispatched for the doctor, who lived across the road. He arrived together with several neighbours. When Dr Bowen had cleaned the blood from Andrew Borden's face, and ascertained that he had been killed by blows from a hatchet, he asked Bridget to find a sheet to cover the body. Bridget said she was afraid to go upstairs alone – after all, the burglar might still be in the house, perhaps hiding under a bed. A neighbour named Mrs Churchill accompanied her upstairs. And when she returned, she asked Lizzie what had become of Mrs Borden. Lizzie's reply was, 'I don't know but she is killed too, for I thought I heard her come in.' Again Bridget and Mrs Churchill went upstairs. They found Abby Borden lying, face downward, in the guest room. Her skull had been even more savagely battered than that of Andrew Borden.

For about 24 hours the inhabitants of Fall River were in a state of nervous tension; there was a maniac at large who crept into houses and killed with a chopper. News of the murders flew by means of Mr Edison's telegraph all over America. Then suspicion settled on a member of the family: Uncle John Vinnicum Morse, Andrew Borden's brother-in-law, who had stayed in the house the previous night. Morse was running one of Borden's farms and was in effect his business manager. Rumour had it that his arrest was expected hourly. When he walked out of the Borden home, a menacing crowd, estimated at 2,000, followed him along the street. But a policeman, Special Officer Harrington, had already fixed on Lizzie as his chief suspect. It was not a matter of evidence: merely that her demeanour seemed too calm for one who had just suffered a bereavement.

Bridget, by comparison, was in a state of terrified hysteria. And it was Harrington who made another important discovery: on the day before the murders, a woman answering Lizzie's description had tried to buy prussic acid in a local pharmacy — she said she needed it to kill moths in a fur coat. The pharmacist declined to sell her the poison, but it later emerged that the woman had tried two other pharmacists, with the same result. Later that day, it also emerged, Lizzie had visited a friend named Miss Russell, and had mentioned her suspicion that their food had been poisoned. She had also talked about a mysterious burglary that had occurred in the previous June; over $100 had been taken from Mr Borden's desk. Lizzie thought the thief had probably entered through the cellar door. (Oddly enough, Andrew Borden had told the police to drop their investigation because the 'real' culprit would probably never be found.) And finally, before leaving Miss Russell, Lizzie had made a curious prediction: 'I'm afraid somebody will do something . . .'

Now suspicion began to focus on Lizzie. Another uncle, Hiram Harrington, a blacksmith, told the press that there had been constant disputes in the house about money — the girls were jealous of the money that Mr Borden made over to his wife, and insisted on being treated identically. Lizzie often quarrelled with her father and would refuse to speak to him for days. His refusal to allow her to spend money on entertaining her church friends angered her, and she was resentful of his meanness.

Harrington added significantly that the motive for the crime was unquestionably money and pointed out that Andrew Borden would probably leave half a million . . .

One week after the murders, as everyone now expected, Lizzie was arrested. The following morning she was arraigned and a date was set for the preliminary hearing. The town split into two factions: those who were convinced of her guilt, and those who were sure she was a persecuted innocent. After all, there was no real evidence against Lizzie. The murder weapon had not been found – although the police had located in the cellar the head of a hatchet covered in ashes, with a short piece of broken handle attached. If Lizzie had killed her parents – her stepmother with 17 blows and her father with nine – surely she would have been covered with blood? Yet no bloodstained dress had been found. It is true that Lizzie had burned one of her dresses the Sunday after the murder, saying that it seemed to have some blood spots on it, but that itself was unsuspicious. If she had been wearing this dress to kill her family, it would have been soaked in blood. Besides, she would have had two bloodstained dresses, for Mrs Borden had been killed at least an hour before her husband. In short, there was no real evidence against Lizzie, who had been, as she claimed, out in the barn when the murders had taken place.

The anti-Lizzie faction pointed out that only Lizzie could have killed the Bordens. Nothing was less likely than that some homicidal maniac had sneaked into the house around 9.30 a.m. and killed Mrs Borden, then waited, concealed, for an hour or so until he could creep down and kill Andrew Borden as he lay asleep. And why had she been trying to buy poison on the day before the murders, if not to kill her stepmother?

The trial opened on 5 June 1892. The prosecution pointed out that Lizzie had tried to buy poison, and suggested that she had tried to lure Bridget out of the house by mentioning a sale of cheap cotton goods. She claimed that Mrs Borden had left the house after she received a note saying that someone was sick; but no such note had been found. She claimed that she had been in the barn at the time, but there were no footprints in the dust.

When Uncle John Morse was called to the stand, he proved to

Lizzie Borden with her sister and friends in court

have a cast-iron alibi – he had been to visit a nephew and niece in the town, and had not arrived back until 20 minutes after the bodies were discovered. There was not the remotest possibility that Uncle John was the murderer.

When finally asked if she had anything to say to the jury in her own defence, Lizzie replied, 'I am innocent. I leave it for my counsel to speak for me.' The jury believed her; after retiring for an hour, the foreman announced the verdict of not guilty. There were wild cheers and Lizzie found herself something of a popular heroine.

There were those who expected her to move to some other place; but she did nothing so obvious. She and her sister stayed in Fall River – they only moved to a larger house. They could afford to: Andrew Borden had left them $175,000 each. Five years later, Lizzie once more appeared on the front pages of the newspapers. Two paintings that had been stolen from a big store had been traced back to her, and a warrant had been issued for her arrest. But nothing more was heard of this matter as it was settled out of court. In later life, she became an ardent theatregoer, and caused some scandal by throwing a lavish party for an actress, Nance O'Neil. This seems to have caused a separation between Lizzie and her sister Emma. When Lizzie died in 1927, at the age of 67, she left an estate of $265,000, much of it to the animal rescue league.

When the American crime expert and bibliophile Edmund

Pearson came to edit *The Trial of Lizzie Borden* in 1937 he left no doubt that he regarded Lizzie as guilty; he said the same thing in two essays on the case. He was convinced that the murders had been planned several days before. But if that was so, why had Lizzie tried to buy poison on the day before she killed her parents with a hatchet?

In 1961, a crime writer named Edward Radin challenged Pearson's verdict. In *Lizzie Borden, The Untold Story,* Radin admitted that he had always considered Lizzie guilty – on the strength of Pearson's books – until he came upon one small anomaly. Pearson had always emphasized that Lizzie had given the police a silk dress to examine, claiming it was the dress she had been wearing on the morning of the murders. Who, asked Pearson, would wear a silk dress to do the housework? Radin discovered that the dress was made of a material known as bengaline silk – a cotton or wool fabric with a few threads of silk interwoven. Disturbed by this and some other minor errors, Radin went to Fall River to look at the minutes of the trial. They revealed that Pearson had been highly selective. 'To put it bluntly, Pearson presented such a biased version of the case that it might be considered a literary hoax.' Pearson had deliberately omitted evidence that revealed that, far from being heartlessly calm, Lizzie had been in tears just after the bodies had been discovered, while another witness said she was so pale she thought she was going to faint. Radin found evidence that suggested Lizzie had indeed been up in the barn, as she claimed. And he listed many other points on which he felt that Pearson had shown deliberate bias. He shows beyond all doubt that Pearson was inclined to omit evidence that pointed to Lizzie's innocence.

All this, says Radin, leaves only three possible suspects: Uncle John Morse, Emma Borden and Bridget Sullivan. He soon eliminates the first two. That, inevitably, leaves Bridget. He points out that there is a basic discrepancy between Bridget's evidence and Lizzie's. Lizzie said Bridget began washing the windows at 9 o'clock. Bridget said it was 9.30 a.m. That half hour would have sufficed for Bridget to kill Abby Borden. But why should Bridget have killed Mrs Borden? Perhaps because she was angry at having been ordered to wash the windows when she was feeling sick. Radin speculates that she may have asked Mrs Borden if she could leave the windows until later, and Mrs Borden refused. So she went to get an axe, sneaked up behind her employer, and battered her to death with 17 blows. Why then should she kill Andrew Borden? Perhaps because he had overheard Mrs Borden's refusal, and therefore knew Bridget had a motive.

Three years after Radin's book appeared, a selection of Pearson's crime essays was published under the title *Masterpieces of Murder*, and its editor, Gerald Gross, takes the opportunity to defend Pearson. He points out that if Pearson omitted evidence of Lizzie's innocence, Radin omits evidence of her guilt – he plays down Lizzie's hatred of her stepmother. Yet Gross admits that Radin has made some telling points. He ends up believing that Bridget was Lizzie's accomplice in the murder. There is a legend – repeated by some writers on that case – that Bridget went back to Ireland with a large bank balance. Gross believes Lizzie paid Bridget to help her with the murders. His final comment is that, until someone finds a signed confession, we shall never be sure who killed the Bordens.

In fact, such a signed confession had been published, in a book called *Mutiny and Murder* by Edgar Snow (1959). Snow tells how he received a letter from an elderly gentleman named Thomas Owens, who claimed that he had Lizzie's confession. He harked back to the story that a warrant had been issued for Lizzie's arrest for the theft of two pictures; the store in question was called Tilden-Thurber, and it was in Providence, Rhode Island. After Lizzie visited the shop, the assistant found that two expensive portraits on porcelain were missing. Some time later, another lady took one of the portraits into the shop asking if a crack could be repaired; asked where she obtained it, she said from Lizzie Borden. According to Owens, the manager of the store had then offered Lizzie a deal: confess to the murders, or be prosecuted. Lizzie refused, and the story appeared in a Providence newspaper. This led Lizzie to change her mind, and she typed the confession which read: 'Unfair means force my signature here admitting the act on August 4, 1892, as mine

56

alone, Lisbeth A. Borden.' Owens, who was a photographer, had been asked to make a photograph of the confession, and had made an extra one for himself. He tried to sell it to Snow for $100; Snow persuaded him to take $50.

But Radin decided to look into this piece of evidence. He soon established that the signature was a forgery, lifted straight from Lizzie's will. So the 'confession' story was a hoax, although the story about the theft of the paintings is true enough, and, indeed, indicates a peculiar and dishonest side to Lizzie's character.

In 1967, there appeared yet another book on the Borden murder but this time by someone who had known Lizzie when they had lived on the same block in Fall River. *A Private Disgrace, Lizzie Borden by Daylight* finally supplies some of the missing pieces that enable us to understand the Borden murder case. Its author, Victoria Lincoln, knew one family secret: that Lizzie often suffered from fits of dizziness. She argues carefully, from medical evidence, that Lizzie suffered from psychomotor epilepsy of the brain, which afflicted her about four times a year, usually during menstrual periods.

The book is not an attempt to prove that Lizzie committed the murders in some kind of trance. Miss Lincoln is convinced that Lizzie did intend to murder her stepmother – but by poison. Furthermore, Victoria Lincoln was able to unearth the motive. The Borden sisters and their stepmother had been involved in a quarrel about a house that Andrew Borden intended to give to his wife. A similar quarrel five years before, again about a house, had led to immense bitterness, and Lizzie had then ceased to call Abby 'mother', and called her 'Mrs Borden'. On the morning of the murder, the transfer was due to be signed. That was why Andrew Borden came back home, bringing the transfer deed with him. The deed vanished, but a half-burned roll of paper was found in the stove by a policeman. Lizzie knew about the transfer – that may have been why she had forced her way into her father's desk in June, taking money to pretend it was a burglary. Having failed to buy poison, she took the hatchet from the cellar and killed Abby Borden. Miss Lincoln believes she then killed her father to spare him the

57

horror of realizing she was a killer, as he inevitably would have guessed. Yet, knowing of Lizzie's increasing resentment about her father's meanness and rudeness, it seems more likely that killing him was the only logical way of obtaining some kind of freedom for herself and her sister – and, no doubt, a diet of something less uninspiring than boiled mutton.

In *Blood in the Parlour*, Dorothy Dunbar provides an amusing footnote to the case. Before Lizzie's arrest, children in the streets of Fall River were chanting:

Mr Borden he is dead
Lizzie hit him on the head!

Obviously this was the original crude form of the far more celebrated quatrain:

Lizzie Borden took an axe
And gave her mother forty whacks.
And when she saw what she had done,
She gave her father forty-one.

TONY MANCINI

Brighton has the unusual distinction of having been associated with two trunk murders. And, as if to stretch the coincidence to its limit, both occurred at the same time and the bodies were discovered within 200 yards of one another. One murder was easily solved, although the full story did not emerge for another four decades; the other remains unsolved to this day.

Mancini was a small-time crook, but an exceptionally unpleasant one. His real name was Cecil Lois England, and while still a teenager he deserted from the RAF. Almost immediately, he became a member of London's underworld, working for a gangster named 'Harry Boy' Sabini as a strong-arm man. He admitted later that he began to get 'kicks' out of violence: 'It was like a drug addiction.' He was once ordered to mark a man for life as a punishment for 'informing'; he walked into the pub where the man was leaning on the bar, pulled an axe from under his coat, and chopped off his left hand; leaving the axe embedded in the bar, he walked out of the pub. Everyone knew he was responsible, but his associates had arranged for him to have a cast-iron alibi, and witnesses were afraid to talk. On another occasion, he turned the handle of a meat grinder while a gangster had his hand forced into it – this was a punishment for dipping his hand into the till.

On his 'collecting rounds', Mancini met a pretty, slim ex-showgirl, a blue-eyed blonde named Violet Saunders, who preferred to be known as Violette Kaye. She was 42 years old, 17 years Mancini's senior. Her work as a dancer became more difficult to obtain so she had turned to prostitution. Mancini became her pimp. In September 1933, just after Mancini had emerged from a six-month spell in jail for theft, they decided to move down to Brighton, 'the place where it was all happening in those days'. Many of Violette's wealthier clients still called to see her, travelling from London in their Rolls-Royces. It may have been that her landlords objected when they discovered the source of her income; perhaps, too, her increasing alcoholism and addiction to morphine made her an impossible tenant; at all events, the couple moved, on average, once a fortnight. Their thirteenth home, at 44 Park Crescent, proved to be unlucky for both of them.

It was an unfurnished basement flat. They picked up bits and pieces of furniture in second-hand shops and markets. Mancini did the cooking and housework, and their day was punctuated by the arrival of clientele who tramped down the narrow, worn steps, and left after half an hour or so. Violette seems to have been genuinely dependent on Mancini; when he considered taking a job, she dissuaded him on the grounds that he would be away from her all day. But on 5 May 1934 he took a job as a cook, waiter and general handyman at the Skylark Café, facing the sea.

Violette seems to have missed him, or perhaps she was jealous of the waitresses and female customers. She had met Mancini when he was working in a restaurant near Leicester Square. On Thursday 10 May she arrived unexpectedly at mid-afternoon, obviously a little the worse for drink. Mancini cooked her a meal then sat and talked to her while she ate – it was a slack period. Then he went away to get the staff their tea. Among these was a young waitress named Florence Attrell, who had started to work at the same time as Mancini. When Mancini handed the girl her tea with the comment, 'Here you are, mate', it seems to have aroused Violette Kaye's worst suspicions. She said in a loud voice, 'I won't have it. Don't call her mate.' The café fell silent and Mancini told her to pull herself together. What looked like turning into an ugly scene was terminated when she walked out of the café. She sat outside for a while, then went away. Mancini later claimed he got the sack as a result of the quarrel. His memory on this point seems to have been defective, for he arrived for work as usual the following morning, and told his fellow workers that Violette had left him and gone away to Paris. Violette's sister-in-law, who was due to come to Brighton for a holiday the following Monday, received a telgram: 'Good job sail Sunday will write – Vi.'

In fact, by that time, Violette Kaye's body was lying in a cupboard in the basement flat, wrapped in bedclothes. The cause of her death was a number of blows to the head.

That weekend, Mancini took Florence Attrell dancing twice; he also took her back to the flat and gave her some of Violette's clothes, explaining that he had promised to send them on but didn't think he would bother. In fact, he had already taken lodgings elsewhere, in Kemp Street, a mere 200 yards from Brighton station. He told his former landlord, Mr Snuggs, that Vi had walked out on him and that he could not afford to keep the flat on. Mr Snuggs was sympathetic. As they were talking, a large strapped trunk was waiting in the middle of the room; Mancini had bought it in the market for 7s. 6d., and the dealer had delivered it. When Mancini departed, with the trunk on a handcart, he left behind the tray out of the trunk, for which he had no use. His landlord noticed a stain in the bottom of the cupboard, although it was clear that someone had tried to wash it away. Mancini moved into 52 Kemp Street with the corpse of Violette Kaye – and for two months, as the smell increased (his friends asked him, 'Do you keep rabbits?'), he seems to have wondered what to do with it.

Another killer had shown rather more imagination. On 6 June, Derby Day, a trunk was deposited in the left-luggage at Brighton station; 11 days later, an attendant noticed an unpleasant smell coming from it. The police were asked to force the locks and inside they found the torso of a woman, wrapped in brown paper, on which the letters 'ford' were written – obviously half a word. The head and limbs were missing. The legs were found in a suitcase at the left-luggage office in Kings Cross Station, London, the following day. The killer was obviously a man capable of foresight and planning; he had deposited the trunk at Brighton during the rush hour on Derby Day, when it was unlikely that he would be noticed. In spite of a massive police investigation that extended to four countries, the body was never even identified.

But the Brighton trunk caused Mancini some inconvenience, for the police began door-to-door investigations in the area of the station. They also heard about the disappearance of Violette Kaye, and asked Mancini to come to the station to make a statement. He was allowed to leave afterwards. On Sunday, 15 July he left Brighton for London by an early train, and a few hours later, the police called at Kemp Street, entered the basement flat, and forced open the trunk, whose smell now left little doubt what it contained.

It took the police 48 hours to catch up with Mancini. He had spent the two days eating in cheap East End cafés and sleeping in the Salvation Army hostel. He had fled on Sunday; on Monday morning the newspapers were headlining the discovery of the second body in a trunk in Brighton. At one point Mancini had picked up a 17-year-old waif, taken her for a walk and asked her to provide him with an alibi for the murder. She had agreed – because he looked so formidable a character with his scarred face. Then Mancini's fear got the better of him, and he decided to leave London. The police picked him up as he trudged towards Maidstone in Kent. When they told him he fitted the description of a man who was wanted for the murder of Violette Kaye, Mancini wearily agreed, 'I'm the man. But I didn't murder her . . .'

The case caused a sensation. The notion of keeping a woman's body in a trunk for two months touched a strain of morbidity in the national character, and Mancini – one of the most incompetent crooks of all time – was regarded as a monster. A brutal-looking, scar-faced photograph did nothing to improve his image. Fashionably dressed girls booed him and threw things as he was taken to court in Lewes.

Mancini, however, had had one supreme stroke of luck. The task of defending him had been undertaken by one of the most brilliant advocates of the period, Norman Birkett. Birkett was not, like so many advocates, an actor *manqué*; he seldom descended to court-room fireworks or the bullying of witnesses. He was quiet, courteous and kindly – and as a consequence, he impressed juries as a man of complete integrity.

Birkett's task was not easy. Yet in this case, there was one basic fact in favour of the accused: no one could prove that it was his hand that had killed Violette Kaye. She was a prostitute and the killer could have been one of her customers. This was Mancini's story – that he had returned to the flat after his day's work in the Skylark to find her already lying dead. This was a plausible defence. The afternoon they had quarrelled, a man named Kerslake had called at their flat to tell Violette that one of her regular customers had just been certified insane. Violette had come to the door; she looked upset and shaken, and seemed to be drunk. Kerslake could hear voices in the back room. So Violette had had visitors after her quarrel with Mancini; one of these could have been her killer. Mancini's story was that he had panicked; a man with his record could not expect a fair trial.

Birkett built up his case carefully, like a great novelist setting a scene. Each witness was questioned until he had established one single point in Mancini's favour. A police inspector was made to admit that the stairs down to the basement were narrow and worn; and later, pathologist Sir Bernard Spilsbury was made to concede that the injury to the dead woman's forehead could have been caused by a fall down these steps. Another pathologist, Dr Roche Lynch, was made to admit that he was not sure whether Violette Kaye had died from morphine. Birkett even took the amazing step of insisting that Mancini's previous convictions should be read in court – two for stealing and one for loitering with intent. Birkett wanted to establish that Mancini had never been convicted for violence. If the jury had known about the episode with the hatchet or meat grinder, they might have been less impressed. The main point of the brilliant defence speech was to insist that the prosecution had not proved that Mancini had killed Violette Kaye.

Mancini was called, and he impressed the jury favourably; he seemed chastened and unsure of himself. He told Birkett that he loved Violette, and perjured himself to the extent of declaring that they had never quarrelled. At one point, he even shed a few tears. Asked why he had not fetched the police when he found Violette's body he asked incredulously, 'With my record?'. It sounded spontaneous and convincing. And in his final speech, Birkett shrewdly pointed out that the 'voices' Kerslake had heard in Violette Kaye's flat on the day of her murder had never come forward. He concluded, 'People are not tried by newspapers, not tried by rumour, not tried by statements born of a love of notoriety, but tried by British juries, called to do justice and decide upon the evidence.'

On 14 December 1934, after one of the most brilliant defences ever heard in a British court of law, the jury brought in a verdict of not guilty, and Mancini walked out of court a free man.

For a year after his trial, Tony Mancini worked in a travelling fair. He was billed as 'The Infamous Brighton Trunk Murder Man', and his stunt involved cutting off the head of a pretty girl with a trick guillotine. In later years there were two broken marriages. In 1976, he suddenly decided to tell the truth about the death of Violette Kaye. The *News of the World* for 28 November appeared with a headline I'VE GOT AWAY WITH MURDER. The story, as reported by Alan Hart, begins:

A man acquitted of killing his mistress, after one of the most famous murder trials in British history, has now confessed to me that he was guilty. Ex-gangster Tony Mancini has lived 42 years with the secret that he was responsible for what became known as the Brighton Trunk Murder.

Mancini told Hart:

When I gave evidence I had carefully rehearsed my lines like an actor. I had practised how I should hold my hands and when I should let tears run down my cheeks. It might sound cold and calculating now, but you have to remember that my life was at stake. I was charged with murder, and in those days the penalty was death.

There are a few respects in which Mancini's story does not tally with the version given at the trial. He says that when Violette found out he had taken a job at the Skylark, 'she started a blazing row'. In fact, he had been there for five days, with Violette calling in daily, before the row. Mancini claims that he was sacked, and that he called a taxi and took Violette home. If that is true, then he himself may have one of the two voices heard by Kerslake – the other probably being a client.

Mancini's story was that Violette was cold and asked him to make a fire. As he was bending over, blowing on the burning paper, he felt a crack on his head; Violette had hit him with a hammer. He took it away from her and started to walk towards the cellar. When she shouted, 'Give me that hammer', he yelled,

64

'I'll give you the hammer all right', and threw it at her with all his strength. It caught her on the left temple, 'and she spun around twice like something on a fairground'. She fell on to the brass fender surrounding the fire. Mancini claims he shouted, 'You stupid bitch, look what you've made me do,' and began banging her head up and down, gripping her shoulders. He thought he was banging it on the floor; in fact, he was banging it on the fender. 'Suddenly blood started to trickle from her mouth and I froze. I realized what I'd done. I honestly didn't mean to kill her – I had just lost control of myself in the heat of the moment.'

In an interview he gave to the journalist Stephen Knight (shortly before the latter's death), Mancini gives a considerably different account of the quarrel and what led up to it. He says he had been working in the Skylark Café 'about three or four months' and Violette had no idea of where to find him. One day she came into the café very drunk and under the influence of drugs, and caused a scene. He picked her up by the shoulders and carried her outside, and she finally went home. When he got home at about 7 o'clock that evening, there was a violent quarrel and 'she came at me with her hands and scratched my face'. Then she picked up the hammer and tried to hit him with it. 'So I hit her.' Violette fell against the brass fender, and when he tried to pick her up, she spat in his face. Mancini insisted, 'I'd never hit her before . . . I don't hit women.' But on this occasion, 'I just got hold of her, of her shoulders, and was banging her head on the floor like that. I said, "Don't you spit at me!" And I don't know how long I was like that. And when I came to out of my rage, she was lying like that . . . quite still you see.'

'So what killed her was not the accidental fall . . . it was you banging her head on the fender?', asked Knight.

'Yes . . . I don't remember really, but that's what I must have done . . .'

A jury who heard that story in court would probably have concluded that this was Mancini's attempt to exculpate himself – the equivalent of the schoolboy's excuse: 'It came apart in my hands.' A modern jury would undoubtedly have brought in a verdict of manslaughter. If the jury Mancini faced at Lewes had known the full truth, there seems little doubt that he would have gone to the gallows.

I can add an amusing footnote to this story. In my book, *Order of Assassins*, I mentioned Mancini's name in a list of twentieth-century killers. It was a careless slip, of the sort easily made – I was confusing Mancini with John Robinson, a trunk murderer who was found guilty. A friend who has an encyclopedic knowledge of crime wrote to me subsequently reminding me that Mancini had been acquitted . . . For the next six months or so, I kept my fingers tightly crossed that no one pointed out my slip to Mancini. Then, in 1976, the *News of the World* came out with its headline: I'VE GOT AWAY WITH MURDER. I heaved a sigh of relief.

A year later, I received a letter from a lawyer. It pointed out that I had included his client, Mr Mancini, in a list of murderers, and that Mr Mancini had been acquitted. Would I, the letter inquired blandly, prefer to settle the libel out of court?

I searched my press-cutting file frantically for the *News of the World* story, and was unable to find it. Then I rang my encyclopedic friend. By the next morning's post, a photocopy of the story arrived. I slipped it into a large envelope, and posted it off to the lawyer, without bothering to enclose a covering letter. That was the last I heard of it.

THE AXEMAN OF NEW ORLEANS

It was 5 o'clock in the morning of 24 May 1918 when Jake Maggio, an Italian cobbler, was awakened by a groaning sound. It seemed to be coming from the other side of the thin partition wall that separated Jake's bedroom from that of his brother Joe. When the groan was repeated, Jake got out of bed, and shook his brother Andrew, who slept in the same room. Andrew was snoring and smelt of alcohol, but Jake finally succeeded in making him open his eyes. As he did so, the groan was repeated, followed by a choking noise. Jake told Andrew, 'There's something wrong in there. Come on with me.'

The first thing they saw as they entered the bedroom was Joe's wife; she was lying on the floor in a pool of blood with her head almost severed from her body. Joe Maggio was lying half in and half out of the bed. As they stood there, too shocked to move, he gave another groan. Then his eyes opened and he saw his brothers. He made a convulsive effort to move, and fell on to the floor. In that position, they could see that his throat had also been cut, and that his face was a mass of blood. They lifted him back on to the bed, then rushed out to call the police.

By the time the police arrived, the brothers had discovered how the intruder had entered the house. A panel in the back door had been neatly chiseled out. And on the steps leading down into the backyard lay a bloodstained axe and a cut-throat razor.

The detective looked at the razor and asked, 'Is this yours?' Andrew was a barber. He shook his head and said 'I don't know.'

'Where were you last night?' asked the detective. A neighbour who had followed the police into the house said, 'I can tell you that. He came home drunk around 3 o'clock this morning.'

The detective turned to Andrew saying, 'I'm placing you under arrest.'

Jake protested. 'Andrew didn't do it. He sleeps in the same room I do.'

The detective said, 'All right, you're under arrest too.'

The news was on the streets shortly after midday. The New Orleans newspaper, *The Times-Picayune*, prided itself on being the first with the story. It had a photograph of the bedroom of the murdered couple, and even a photograph of their wedding 15 years before. The account mentioned that a safe in the bedroom had been found open and empty. Yet $100 had been found below Joe Maggio's pillow and Mrs Maggio's jewellery, including diamond rings, lay untouched on the dressing table. The police were inclined to believe that robbery was not the motive – the safe had been left open only to mislead them. That was obviously why they suspected Jake and his brother Andrew, who had just been drafted into the army. But they were soon forced to release both for lack of evidence.

Detective Theodore Obitz, in charge of the case, was pondering another curious clue. Two streets away from the Maggio's grocery store, someone had chalked on the pavement the words: 'Mrs Maggio is going to sit up tonight, just like Mrs Toney.' Who was Mrs Toney? Then someone recollected that seven years earlier, in 1911, there had been three axe murders of Italian grocers: a Mr Cruti, a Mr Rosetti, and a certain Tony Schiambra and his wife. Could she be the 'Mrs Toney' referred to? The murders had been attributed to the 'Black Hand', a criminal secret society (and predecessor of the Mafia) that demanded 'protection' money from many successful Italian businessmen. New Orleans, city of the Mississippi gamblers, was one of the most crime-ridden spots in the United States.

Before Detective Obitz had a chance to investigate the possible connection of the earlier murders with the latest double killing, he was shot through the heart by a Negro he had arrested for burglary.

The sinister trademark of the murderer continued to worry the Italian community of New Orleans – the panel chiselled out of the back door. Most of those wooden frame houses of New Orleans had open backyards, so anyone could wander in and out. Most people kept chickens and had an axe in the woodshed. The police had identified the axe that struck the Maggios as their own. The Italians of New Orleans felt themselves frighteningly vulnerable.

On 28 June, five weeks after the murders, a baker named John Zanca called to deliver bread at the grocery store of Louis Besumer. As he was about to knock on the back door he froze in horror; one of its panels had been chiseled out. Nervously, he knocked on the door, and sighed with relief as he heard someone unlocking it. Then he almost screamed as the door was opened by a man with blood streaming down his face. Louis Besumer was groaning, 'My God, my God!' Mr Zanca went into the house, and saw that a woman was lying on the bed, her head bleeding from a gaping wound. Zanca called the hospital, then the police.

In this case, both the victims were still alive. *The Times-Picayune* was able to reveal that the woman, known as Mrs Besumer, was not Besumer's wife. Her real name was Harriet Lowe, and she was many years Besumer's junior, being still in her twenties. Besumer himself was apparently regarded by neighbours as a suspicious character. He declared that he was a Pole, but was generally regarded as a German. During World War I all Germans were suspected of being spies. Besumer's story was that he had been knocked unconscious while asleep, and had awakened to find Harriet Lowe outside the bedroom door, bleeding badly. He had carried her back to bed, then had heard Zanca knocking on the door.

Rumours immediately began to spread that Besumer had attacked his 'wife' because she had found out too much about his espionage activities, then had given himself a blow on the head to make it look like an axeman attack. This theory was confirmed when Harriet Lowe regained consciousness, and was asked whether Besumer was a spy. Her reply was that she had long suspected it. He was immediately arrested. But when she was questioned again, she withdrew her accusation, saying it was ridiculous. She had a curious story to tell. She had been walking into the kitchen when she was struck on the head. When she opened her eyes again, she saw a white man standing over her, making threatening motions with a hatchet but not striking her. Then she lost consciousness again.

Mrs Lowe died after an operation, but just before her death she seemed to mumble that Besumer had struck her with an axe.

69

Besumer was charged with murder.

That same night, however, the 'mad axeman' attacked again. Edward Schneider, a young married man, returned home shortly after midnight on 5 August 1918 to find his heavily pregnant wife lying in bed and covered with blood. She was rushed to hospital, where she was able to describe waking up and seeing a man holding an axe above her. One week later, she gave birth to a baby girl. No axe was found on the premises, and no panel had been chiseled out of the back door, and it was presumed that the attacker had entered by an open window.

Five days later, there was another attack. This time the victim was a barber, Joseph Romano. His nieces, Pauline, 18, and her sister Mary, 13, woke up soon after 3 o'clock in the morning; noises were coming from the next room where their uncle slept. Pauline had been nervous for weeks about the 'axeman', and now she crept fearfully to her uncle's room, turning on her own light as she opened the connecting door. What she saw made her scream. A man she later described as 'dark, tall, heavy-set, wearing a black slouch hat' was standing by her uncle's bed, holding an axe. Mary also screamed, at which the man 'vanished as if he had wings'. Their uncle had staggered into the parlour; when they propped him in a chair they could see that he had two large cuts on his head. He groaned, 'Call the Charity Hospital,' then fainted. Two days later, he died in hospital. A panel of a rear door had been chiseled out and the bloody axe was found outside in the yard. Nothing had been stolen, although Romano's room had been ransacked.

Now, at last, there could be no doubt that there was an axeman in New Orleans. The panic was not unlike that which had swept London 30 years before, when Jack the Ripper had killed 'fallen women' in Whitechapel. One grocer reported finding an axe and a chisel outside his back door in the morning; another found that a panel had been chiseled out of his door when he was absent for the day. Yet another grocer, who lived close to Romano, told of finding a panel chiseled out of his door in the previous June, and an axe lying nearby. No one felt safe in their beds. When someone reported seeing a man with an axe jumping over a fence one evening, the neighbourhood was suddenly alive with angry people armed with home-made weapons. A shot was fired, and a young man claimed he had fired his shotgun at the axeman. Police arrived and advised everyone to go to bed.

On 30 August a man named Nick Asunto heard a noise in his house and went to the head of the stairs; near the front door he saw a heavily built man holding an axe. When Asunto yelled, the man fled by the front door. Such reports became a regular item in the newspapers. As people began taking extra precautions, the number of sightings of the axeman seemed to diminish. Perhaps he had decided it was too dangerous to show himself.

On 11 November 1918 World War I ended; there had been no attacks for three months. When Christmas and the New Year passed without incident, people began to hope they had heard the last of the axeman. But on 10 March 1919 Iorlando Jordano, a grocer who lived in Gretna, just across the river from New Orleans, heard screams from a house on the other side of the street, where another grocer called Cortimiglia had his business. He went into the house and found Mrs Cortimiglia sitting on the floor, blood gushing from her head, and a dead baby in her arms. Her husband Charles lay nearby. The Cortimiglias were rushed to the Charity Hospital. When the police arrived they found the now-familiar axeman signatures: the panel chiseled out of the back door and the abandoned axe. Nothing had been stolen.

Rosie Cortimiglia told of waking up to see her husband being attacked by a white man wielding an axe with which he gave Cortimiglia a violent blow. Mrs Cortimiglia picked up two-year-old Mary from her cot screaming, 'Not my baby,' The axeman's blow killed the child instantly, and another blow struck Mrs Cortimiglia to the floor.

Yet when Mrs Cortimiglia was able to speak, two days later, she accused the man who had found her – Iorlando Jordano. She also accused his son, Frank. Although Charles Cortimiglia insisted his attacker was nothing like Iorlando Jordano, both Jordanos were arrested. The police had their doubts – for one thing Frank Jordano was too big to be able to squeeze through the door panel – but they had to take account of Mrs Cortimiglia's positive identification.

The citizens of New Orleans now no longer seemed so terrified of the axeman. Somebody wrote a song called 'The Mysterious Axeman's Jazz, or Don't Scare Me Papa', and there were reports of axeman parties. Three days after the Cortimiglia attack, *The Times-Picayune* received a letter signed 'The Axeman'. It was datelined: 'Hell, 14 March 1919', and began: 'They have never caught me and they never will.' He claimed to be invisible, 'a fell demon from the hottest hell'. He continued: 'When I see fit I shall come and claim other victims . . . I shall leave no clue except my bloody axe, besmeared with blood and brains of him whom I have sent below to keep me company.' In his infinite mercy, he said, he was going to make a proposition to the people of New Orleans. 'At 12.15 (earthly time) on next Tuesday night, I am going to visit New Orleans again . . . I am very fond of jazz music, and I swear by all the devils in the nether regions that every person shall be spared in whose home a jazz band is in full swing . . .' The following Tuesday was St Joseph's Day, which was usually celebrated as a welcome break in Lent. That St Joseph's Night, according to New Orleans chronicler Robert Tallant, was the loudest and most hilarious on record. Some students even inserted an advertisement in *The Times-Picayune* inviting the axeman to come and join their party; they said they would leave a window open so that he need not ruin their back door. But the axeman ignored their invitations. In fact, there was no sign that he made any appearance in New Orleans that night.

At the end of April, the 'spy' Louis Besumer went on trial, but was acquitted. Everyone expected an acquittal when the Jordanos went on trial in the following month. Charles Cortimiglia flatly denied that the Jordanos had been the attackers, and a stream of character witnesses vouched for their good reputation and honesty. Yet, to everyone's astonishment Mrs Cortimiglia's evidence prevailed, and they were found guilty: Frank was sentenced to be hanged, his father to life imprisonment. There was universal indignation; no one in New Orleans believed they were guilty.

The attacks continued. On 10 August 1919 a grocer named Steve Boca woke up and saw a dark shape above his bed, and an uplifted axe. When he woke up again, he was bleeding from a skull wound. He managed to stagger down the street to the home of a friend, Frank Genusa, who called an ambulance. Boca's back door had been chiseled and the axe was in the kitchen; nothing had been taken. Frank Genusa was arrested but released when Boca insisted that he was not the attacker.

On 2 September a druggist named William Carlson was reading late at night when he heard an ominous scratching sound at his back door. He shouted, then fired through the panel with his revolver. Police found what appeared to be chisel marks on the panel of the door.

On 3 September neighbours became alarmed for the safety of 19-year-old Sarah Lauman, who lived alone, and broke into her house. She was unconscious in bed; several teeth were knocked out and her head was injured. A hatchet was found beneath an open window. She recovered from brain concussion, but could remember nothing.

What was to be the last attack occurred on 27 October. Mike Pepitone, a grocer, slept in a separate room from his wife. She woke up to hear sounds of a struggle, and reached his bedroom door in time to see a man disappearing through another door to the room. Her husband lay dead in bed; the axe blow that had killed him had been so violent that it had spattered blood up the wall. Her six children were awakened by her screams. When the police arrived, they found the chiseled door panel and the bloody axe on the porch.

Then the murders stopped. More than a year passed with no fresh attacks. The Jordanos remained in jail, while their lawyer lodged unsuccessful appeals. But on 7 December 1920 Rosie Cortimiglia, their accuser, burst into the office of *The Times-Picayune*, and fell on her knees. She had become thin and ill – in the previous year she had been an attractive woman – and she was now covered in smallpox scars. 'I lied, I lied. It was not the Jordanos who killed my baby.' She confessed that she had lied because she hated the Jordanos. 'I have suffered for my lie. My baby is dead, my husband has left me, I have had smallpox. St

Joseph told me I must confess.' The Jordanos were quickly released.

Then the New Orleans police learned of something that had happened five days before in Los Angeles. A heavily veiled woman, dressed in black, stepped from a doorway and emptied a revolver into a man who had been walking along the pavement. He was from New Orleans, and his name was Joseph Mumfre. When taken to the police station, the woman at first refused to speak. Some days later, however, she revealed that she was the widow of Mike Pepitone, the axeman's last victim. She had seen the murderer escape from her home and she asserted that Mumfre was the axeman.

Mumfre had a criminal record, and when the New Orleans police checked his history they realized that he could, indeed, have been the axeman. He had been released from prison just before the murders in 1911 but he was then returned to jail, where he spent most of World War I. He had been released just before the first attack of 1918, on the Maggios. In the lull after the attacks of August 1918 Mumfre had been back in prison, being released in March 1919, just before the attack on the Cortimiglias. Soon after the killing of Mike Pepitone, he had left New Orleans.

Mrs Pepitone was tried in Los Angeles; she pleaded justifiable homicide. But there was no evidence that Mumfre was the axeman, and she was sentenced to ten years. She was released after three.

If Mumfre was the axeman, what was his motive? In retrospect, this seems fairly clear. He was in the grip of some kind of sadistic obsession involving axes. We note that in the Maggio case, Joe Maggio was left alive, while his wife's head was almost severed. And someone, probably the axeman, wrote on the pavement: 'Mrs Maggio is going to sit up tonight, just like Mrs Toney.' It was women he enjoyed attacking – their husbands had to be knocked unconscious so that he could carry out the attack. Louis Besumer, aged 59, was only knocked unconscious, but his attractive 29-year-old 'wife' died from her injuries. Mrs Edward Schneider was in the house alone when she was attacked. When the axeman attacked Joseph Romano, he was probably looking for his 18-year-old niece Pauline, but her screams and those of her sister frightened him away. He was evidently a coward for it took very little resistance to make him flee. In the Cortimiglia and Pepitone cases, it again seems likely that he encountered the husband when in search of the wife. Harriet Lowe's evidence is of particular interest – that she woke up after the first blow to see the axeman standing over her, making threatening motions with the axe, yet not attacking her again. It was part of his aim to frighten his female victims.

In *A Glastonbury Romance*, John Cowper Powys, himself a self-confessed sadist, writes of a character called Evans, who is obsessed by fantasies of a 'killing blow with an iron bar'. The axeman's fantasies were of splitting female skulls with a hatchet.

Why Italian grocers? In fact, several victims were not Italian, but most kept shops. A small shop is a place where an attractive wife often serves behind the counter and so can be observed at leisure by a mentally unstable pervert who has fantasies of attacking women with an axe . . .

THE ORDEAL OF JEREMY CARTLAND

It was typical March weather in the Provence area of southern France, with a mistral wind blowing. It was in this beautiful setting that the Impressionist painters created some of their masterpieces, and the area around Pelissanne remains a favourite camping site for holidaymakers.

The two Englishmen who drove a Hillman car towing a caravan looked strangely alike – as well they might. They were father and son. John Basil Cartland, aged 60, ran a language school in Brighton, and his 29-year-old son, Jeremy, was a schoolmaster in the same town. They had enjoyed a holiday mixed with business in Spain, before driving into France. They intended to visit friends in Marseilles, but had decided to park for the night near the village of Salon-de-Provence, where they had filled up with fuel. It was getting late and neither liked the idea of driving in the dark.

They had chosen a quiet, isolated spot to camp for the night, and after supper settled down to sleep. At just after 1 o'clock in the early hours of Sunday, 18 March 1973, Jeremy was awakened by strange noises. He sat upright and saw that his father was not in the caravan – and neither were the noises. They were coming from outside, from the darkness, savage sounds which alarmed Jeremy. Still groggy from sleep, he stepped out of the caravan and stared blankly at the back of a strange man who was trying to open one of the doors of the Hillman car. At that moment, before he could even open his mouth to call out, he was struck over the head from behind, losing consciousness immediately.

Shortly afterwards, a passing motorist, commercial traveller Frederick Delaune, spotted the caravan on fire, the mistral wind causing the flames to leap from the roof. He immediately stopped to render what assistance he could. He ran over to the scene of the blaze, and by the light of the reddish-glare of the flames he saw a sight out of a nightmare. A young man lay slumped near the caravan, blood oozing from stab wounds. Some distance further, about 15 feet from the caraven, lay a much older man, his grey hair matted with blood. He was very obviously dead, with many wounds to his head and stab wounds to the body. Beside him lay the murder weapon: a bloodstained axe.

The Frenchman managed to drag the young man to his car, and on the way to the nearest hospital the man recovered sufficiently to tell him that his name was Jeremy Cartland, and that he and his father had been attacked by mystery assailants. Then he lapsed back into unconsciousness, and it was left to M. Delaune to furnish these scanty details to the local police. By dawn they had examined the caravan, and finding no money or valuables either in the car or the caravan concluded that robbery had probably been the motive for the assault. They set to work with tracker-dogs to scour the immediate area. Meanwhile, the son who had survived the savage night attack lay recovering in hospital.

As soon as his wounds had been treated, and the doctors certified him fit to talk, waiting detectives at his bedside began questioning him. Could he describe the attackers? How many had there been? Jeremy had no answers. It had been dark, he was struck unconscious almost as soon as he saw the back of the strange man. When he was told that his father was dead, he wept quietly. By the simple exercise of deductive logic the French police were able to establish that there must have been at least two attackers – the one Jeremy had seen in front of him, trying the car door, and the one who struck him over the back of the head. Examination of the dead man revealed that he had put up a fierce fight for his life, the degree of resistance measured by the many wounds he had received. He had been struck repeatedly on the head with the axe, and stabbed in the body.

With no immediate leads to follow up, the detectives ordered fingerprints to be taken, and also blood samples. While they waited for the forensic evidence to become available, they concentrated on finding out more about the victim. It was quickly apparent that John Cartland was quite a distinguished victim, one likely to receive demands for a speedy solution to the crime from both the British Consul and the English press. He was Professor Cartland, a well-known scholar, and he had been a secret agent during World War II. Parachuted into Occupied

France as an SOE operative, he had worked with the Resistance, the Maquis, organizing and supplying them in their silent and deadly war with the enemy. It was likely that John Cartland had maintained some kind of link with British Intelligence, for it was an old axiom that once in the 'Firm', you never really left. You might retire, but you would always be available for that 'special job'. Had John Cartland been on a mission for SIS in France? Might that perhaps explain his mystery death – not a common robbery, but an assassination by foreign agents hostile to the British?

Examination of the records revealed some strange patterns, too closely linked to be mere coincidence. For a start, the murder had taken place in the same isolated Provence country-side where, almost 21 years previously, Sir Jack Drummond, aged 52, his wife and daughter, were murdered while on a caravan holiday. Drummond too had been a wartime agent . . . Another coincidence was that a film about those murders had just been released in Paris cinemas. An old peasant farmer, Gaston Dominici, had been convicted of the Drummond murders and sentenced to death. But he was later freed on a Presidential pardon and died aged 87 in 1964. Jean Gabin played the role of the peasant in the film, *L'Affaire Dominici*, which had been released for public showing only weeks before the murder of John Cartland. Could it be that this was an imitative murder?

Other British people murdered in France over the previous 20 years included Miss June Marshall, secretary to Sir Jack Drummond, murdered in Dieppe in 1956. Another wartime agent in the link was Sir Oliver Duncan, murdered in Rome in 1964. More strangely still, just a couple of months previously, on 29 January 1973, a retired British army major died at Cannes, victim of an attack outside his home. Major Michael Lassetter, aged 71, had lived alone since the death of his wife three years previously. Had the Major been involved in Intelligence work? Was it all coincidence – or was there indeed some sinister link? Lacking a swift resolution to these questions, and to the murder of John Cartland, French police were only too aware that with English people being murdered in their area, there would be strong criticism from Britain, and political pressure to find solutions that would satisfy national pride.

It was perhaps as a result of this pressure that Jeremy Cartland, himself the victim of a brutal attack and having lost his father, became dimly aware that he was now the chief suspect in police eyes. His ordeal was not over, but had only just begun. He had stepped into a nightmare scripted by Simenon and directed by the bungling Clouseau. And there would be more than a touch of Kafka about the months which followed . . .

The English press, meanwhile, had published the bare account of the murder of a national in France. They had researched the background of the victim by speaking to his housekeeper, Miss Janet Gibson. She said that John Cartland and his son had been to Benidorm, and were in France to visit friends. John Cartland was a quiet, scholarly man who rarely spoke to neighbours. He had run his language school, catering mainly to foreign students, for several years. The son, Jeremy, was a poet as well as a teacher, having had various poems published. The secretary of the English Poetry Association described him as being 'a very good poet indeed'. At this point it would have seemed inconceivable that French police would label the poet a parricide.

Sir Denis Wright wrote the obituary of his old friend John Cartland, which was published in *The Times*. describing him as a good scholar, soldier and excellent hunter, he summed him up with the phrase: 'He was brilliant and unconventional to the point of eccentricity.' He revealed that Cartland had served with the Political Warfare Executive in London during World War II.

By 22 March, just four days after the murder, the press reported that Jeremy Cartland was 'helping police with their inquiries'. He had, in fact, been questioned for six hours by Grigoire Krikorian of the Aix-en-Provence criminal investigation department. Afterwards, the commissioner emphasized that Jeremy was 'simply a witness, although naturally an essential one'. Police had not revealed the results of the fingerprint and blood tests ordered on the Monday. Jeremy was told he could leave hospital – and France – but the police wished him to remain in order to assist them.

The French legal system – the *Code Napoleon* – is unlike the British process. The examining magistrate has complete power in how he conducts an investigation, and can interrogate witnesses and suspects at will. Essentially, he becomes a policeman investigating a crime – with more powers and less restraints than the policeman. By now Jeremy had become thoroughly alarmed at the line of questioning, and had engaged a French lawyer, Maitre Lombard. On his advice Jeremy lodged an action with the investigating magistrate as *partie civile* against 'X'. This legal procedure was a device whereby Jeremy would become a plaintiff in the case – regardless of any criminal proceedings – and as such he could not be questioned except by the magistrate in the presence of his lawyer. The police could not spring surprise questions on him. He had been questioned the previous evening for nine hours. In a statement issued by his counsel, Jeremy reaffirmed his innocence and emphasized that as a son he was naturally anxious to do everything 'to help the hunt for the murderers'.

Shocked by police suspicions, he gave a press conference at the Marseilles offices of his lawyer, saying 'I am innocent. I am at the disposal of the French police to discover the murderers of my father.' His sister, Elizabeth, aged 24, herself a lawyer, stood by his side, stating firmly that both she and her mother were convinced that he was deeply shocked to learn that police suspected him. The tabloids in both France and England were having a field day with gossip, speculation and innuendo. It was in this climate that Jeremy, depressed by police questioning, announced he would be returning to England.

Jeremy landed at Heathrow Airport to be met by reporters with quick-fire questions. After a few days' rest he flew back to France, again accompanied by his sister. Asked why he had gone to England, he replied, 'I was very tired. I had to see my friends and family.' By the end of March the wartime Resistance background of the case was being publicly linked to the Cartland murder, with Jeremy's lawyers expressing 'great interest' in this angle. The BBC had received two letters signed 'A Friend of Britain' alleging that members of the Maquis had been settling old scores, and had killed John Cartland in revenge because he had deliberately destroyed a list of Frenchmen who had collaborated with the Germans. Jeremy was quoted as saying, 'There could be some truth in it.'

However, the French police remained deeply suspicious of Jeremy, for no apparent reason other than the fact that he had received only minor stabwounds in the attack, and the post-mortem on his father revealed that he had been killed with a single blow of the axe. The other wounds with the axe, and the stabbings, had all been gratuitous, inflicted on an already dead man. By now Jeremy was sufficiently alarmed by police suspicions to attend court before the examining magistrate armed with three French lawyers, and an English barrister, Christopher Heggs. The French press was already critical of the whole affair and its potential effect on Anglo-French relations. Reporters scornfully derided the police for not having sealed off the murder-site immediately after the crime; as it was, many valuable forensic clues had been irretrievably lost. The French police remained sceptical about the alleged Maquis link to the murder, especially when they identified the anonymous letter-writer as one Henrico Polydeskis, a stateless person of Greek origin. He was a notorious 'espionage freak', who showered prominent people with his letters. President Pompidou had been a recipient.

Jeremy shuttled back and forth between England and France, returning on 4 April for further questioning by the examining magistrate, André Delmas. He was questioned for two hours. On 26 April, after a further six hours of interrogation, Jeremy emerged from the court to tell waiting pressmen, 'I am out of the wood. I think it impossible that I will be charged now.' But he complained bitterly about the French police, accusing them of 'falsification of evidence and perversion of justice'. He hinted that the police had acted on a report leaked to them by Scotland Yard, which virtually accused him of being a liar.

The following day Scotland Yard's Interpol office denied that it had ever sent the French police any doctor's report on Jeremy Cartland, which he alleged had been used to 'frame' him. Professor James Cameron, the distinguished pathologist who had examined Jeremy after the attack, said he knew nothing of any report. He said that his notes on the case were still in his desk and had never been shown to any policeman. He denied that his notes stated that the son's words 'could not be relied upon'.

Once again Jeremy flew to England, complaining of police irregularities and saying that the case had cost him some £10,000 in legal fees and expenses. On 5 May Detective Inspector Krikorian flew into London to follow up the British aspect of the case. 'His mission is essentially to find out who might have wanted to kill Cartland,' said the examining magistrate. Scotland Yard assigned a senior Murder Squad detective – Detective Chief Superintendent Ron Page – to assist him. Krikorian said he had no plans to interview Jeremy in England, but his visit served only to fan the flames of rumour once again. The French Ministry of Justice issued a statement 'deeply regretting' the controversy over the investigation into the Cartland murder. Krikorian interviewed the Cartland housekeeper, Janet Gibson, at Brighton police station, before finally returning to France.

On 19 May the French authorities announced that they had virtually found Jeremy guilty of murder, by issuing an international warrant for his arrest. They said they did not intend to apply for extradition, but expected Jeremy to stand trial for murder in England. Jeremy's sister, Elizabeth, tried to halt the proceedings by citing 20 points critical of the evidence, and suggesting that the magistrate had issued the warrant out of a fit of pique when Jeremy failed to attend his court for yet more questioning. On 21 May Jeremy's French lawyers demanded a re-examination of the entire case, after producing two new witnesses. Raymond Blasco and his wife said they were at the scene of the murder at the right time, and saw two men, one blonde, the other dark, near the caravan. Blasco refuted police suggestions that he had confused them with firemen at the scene, saying 'My eyes did not deceive me.' The magistrate refused to hear any new witnesses; in his view the case was over, the culprit identified . . .

When John Cartland's will was published, it was revealed that he had left his entire estate, valued at £30,000, to Janet Gibson, his 57-year-old housekeeper. Thus one possible motive for murder was firmly ruled out.

On 5 July the French sent the 2,000-page transcript of their investigation to the Foreign Office, for forwarding to the Director of Public Prosecutions with a view to putting Jeremy on trial in England. Jeremy's lawyer said, 'Mr Cartland is delighted with this latest move and cannot wait to clear his name. He is willing to meet with a member of the Yard's Murder Squad at any time . . .' Detective Chief Superintendent Ron Page was asked by Sir Robert Mark to start an investigation into the Cartland murder, right from the beginning. The detective flew to France to examine for himself the scene of the crime, and had five more detectives sent out to help him. A satisfied French Ministry of Justice said, 'The situation now is as if the murder had been committed in Britain.' They had washed their hands of an embarrassing affair.

In early August new witnesses were found, a couple who had been driving behind a large black Citroen which appeared to be 'shadowing' the Hillman and its caravan. The Citroen would not let them pass, and when the Hillman parked for the night, the Citroen parked too.

In September, French magistrates refused to grant Jeremy an injunction for the seizure of a book about the case which had been on sale in Paris bookshops for several weeks. The book, *The Enigma of Pelissanne. Jeremy Cartland: Innocent or Guilty?* by Paul Glaude Innocenzi, simply reviewed the evidence and came to no conclusion.

It was at this point, with English detectives busy in France, that Jeremy said bitterly, 'I wish they would charge me! At least I could fight . . . ' On 21 December Jeremy was questioned for 7½ hours at Scotland Yard, and on 4 January 1974 the Director of Public Prosecutions announced his decision not to prosecute Jeremy Cartland for the murder of his father. The evidence, he said, was 'insufficient to prosecute'. Jeremy said he was 'relieved to hear the news' but complained that it had cost him £20,000 to establish his innocence, and he wanted to sue the French police to recover some of that money, if that was possible.

Scotland Yard refused to comment on the end of its six-month investigation, and the French announced that Jeremy could visit France without fear of arrest. On 28 February *The Times* printed an apology for a piece published on 21 March 1973 which may have implied that Jeremy might have been guilty or could reasonably have been suspected of being guilty of the murder of his father. 'We offer our sincere apologies.'

The annals of crime usually lead to definite conclusions of either guilt or innocence. Jeremy Cartland is left in a curious state of limbo, being denied any legal process to clear his name. The stigma of being a named suspect will stay with him for ever. The French effectively condemned him; the British equivocated and said 'the evidence is insufficient'. Thus the ordinary citizen cannot hope to have his name cleared – unlike the madman released from an asylum who can at least claim proof of his sanity.

This case exposed a legal anomaly, but it also left in its wake the essential unsolved mystery. Destined to remain unanswered are the crucial questions: Who killed John Cartland – and why? Who was driving that black Citroen? And who were the two men seen near the Cartland's caravan?

JACK THE RIPPER

The August morning was still dark when a carter named George Cross walked along Bucks Row, Whitechapel, on his way to work. It was a narrow cobbled street with the blank wall of a warehouse on one side, and a row of terraced houses on the other. In the dim light, Cross saw what he thought was a bundle of tarpaulin, and he went to investigate. It proved to be a woman lying on her back, her skirt above her waist. Cross decided she was drunk, and when another man approached, said, 'Give me a hand getting this woman on her feet.' The other man, a market porter, looked down dubiously; his first impression was that she had been raped and left for dead. He bent down and touched her cheek, which was cold, then her hand. 'She's dead. We'd better find a policeman.' He pulled down her skirt to make her decent.

In fact, the beat of Police Constable John Neil took him through Bucks Row, and a few minutes after the men had left, the light of his bull's-eye lantern showed him the woman's body, which lay close to a stable door. It also showed him something the men had been unable to see: that the woman's throat had been cut so deeply that the vertebrae were exposed.

An hour later, the body – which was that of a middle-aged woman – lay in the yard of the local mortuary, and two paupers from the workhouse next door were given the job of stripping it, while a police inspector took notes. It was when they pulled off the two petticoats that the inspector saw that the woman's abdomen had been slashed open with a jagged incision that ran from the bottom of the ribs to the pelvis.

The woman was identified through a Lambeth workhouse mark stencilled on her petticoat. She was Mary Ann Nicholls, a prostitute who had been living at a common lodging house in Thrawl Stret – one of the worst slums even in that proverty-stricken area. A few hours before her death she had staggered back to the lodging house, her speech slurred with drink, and admitted that she lacked the four pence necessary for a bed. The keeper had turned her away. 'I'll soon get the money,' she shouted as she went off down the street, 'See what a jolly bonnet I've got.' She went looking for a man who would give her the price of a bed in exchange for an uncomfortable act of intercourse on the pavement in a back alley. What had happened, the police surgeon inferred, was that her customer had placed his hands round her throat as she lay on the ground, and strangled her into unconsciousness – there were bruises on her throat. Then he had cut her throat with two powerful slashes which had almost severed the head, raised her skirt, and stabbed at the stomach in a kind of frenzy.

Oddly enough, the murder caused little sensation. Prostitutes were often killed in the slums of London, sometimes by gangs who demanded protection money. In the previous April, a prostitute named Emma Smith had dragged herself into the London Hospital, reporting that she had been attacked by four men in Osborn Street. They had rammed some object, possibly an iron bar, into her vagina with such force that it had penetrated the womb; she had died of peritonitis. In July, dismembered portions of a woman's body had been recovered from the Thames. On 7 August 1888 a prostitute named Martha Tabram had been found dead on a landing in George Yard Buildings, Whitechapel; she had been stabbed 29 times with a knife or bayonet. Two soldiers were questioned about her murder, but proved to have an excellent alibi. Evidently some sadistic brute had a grudge against prostitutes. It was hardly the kind of story to appeal to respectable newspaper readers.

This attitude was to change dramatically eight days after the murder of Mary Nicholls, when another disembowelled body was found in the backyard of a barber's shop in Hanbury Street, Whitechapel. It was a place where prostitutes often took their customers, and this is evidently what Annie Chapman had done at about 5.30 on the morning of Saturday, 8 September 1888. A neighbour had seen her talking to a dark-looking man 'of foreign appearance', dressed in shabby, genteel clothes and wearing a deerstalker hat. Half an hour later, a lodger named John Davis went downstairs and into the yard, where the lavatory was situated. He saw the body of a woman lying against the fence, her skirt drawn up above her waist and her legs bent at the knees. The stomach had been cut open, and some of the intestines pulled out. The murderer had placed the woman's rings and some pennies at her feet, and a torn envelope near her head. Medical examination revealed that the killer had also removed the uterus and upper part of the vagina.

Now, suddenly, the press awoke to the fact that the unknown killer was a sadistic maniac. *The Star* that afternoon carried a headline: 'Latest Horrible Murder in Whitechapel'. When Mrs Mary Burridge, of Blackfriars Road, South London, read the story, she collapsed and died 'of a fit'. Sir Melville Macnaghten, head of the CID, would write later in his memoirs: 'No one who was living in London that autumn will forget the terror created by these murders. Even now I can recall the foggy evenings, and hear again the raucous cries of the newspaper boys: "Another horrible murder, murder, mutilation, Whitechapel . . .".'

In our own age of mass violence, we find it impossible to imagine the shock created by the murders. A journalist who reported the crimes later began his account of them in a popular booklet:

In the long catalogue of crimes which has been compiled in our modern days there is nothing to be found, perhaps, which has so darkened the horizon of humanity and shadowed the vista of man's better nature as the series of mysterious murders committed in Whitechapel during the latter part of 1888.

'Shadowed the vista of man's better nature . . .' – this is what so frightened Londoners. It was as if an inhuman monster, a kind of demon, had started to hound the streets. Hysteria swept over the whole of Britain. There had been nothing like it since the Ratcliffe Highway murders of 1811, when two families were slaughtered in East London, and householders all over England barricaded their doors at night.

On 29 September 1888, the Central News Agency received a letter that began: 'Dear Boss, I keep on hearing the police have caught me but they won't fix me just yet.' It included the sentence: 'I am down on whores and I shan't quit ripping them till I do get buckled,' and promised: 'You will soon hear of me with my funny little games. It was signed 'Jack the Ripper' – the first time the name had been used. The writer requested: 'Keep this letter back till I do a bit more work, then give it out straight.' The Central News Agency decided to follow his advice.

That night, a Saturday, the Ripper killed again – this time not one, but two prostitutes. At 1 a.m. on Sunday morning, a hawker named Louis Diemschutz drove his pony and cart into the backyard of a working man's club in Berner Street. The pony shied and Diemschutz saw something lying in front of its feet; a closer look showed him that it was a woman's body. The Ripper was either in the yard at that moment, or had only just left it as he heard the approach of the horse and cart. When Diemschutz returned a few moments later with a lighted candle, he was able to see that the woman's throat had been cut. There had also been an attempt to cut off her ear. She was later identified as Elizabeth Stride, an alcoholic Swedish prostitute.

The killer had been interrupted, but his nerve was unshaken. He hastened up Berner Street and along Commercial Road – this murder had been further afield than the others – and reached the Houndsditch area just in time to meet a prostitute who had been released from Bishopsgate police station ten minutes earlier. Her name was Catherine Eddowes, and she had been held for being drunk and disorderly. He seems to have had no difficulty persuading the woman to accompany him into Mitre Square, a small square surrounded by warehouses, only a few hundred yards away. A policeman patrolled the square every 15 minutes or so, and when he passed through at 1.30 a.m. he saw nothing unusual. At 1.45, he found the body of a woman lying in the corner of the square. She was lying on her back, her dress pushed up round her waist, and her face had been slashed. Her body had been gashed open from the base of the ribs to the pubic region, and the throat had been cut. Later examination revealed that a kidney was missing, and that half the ear had been cut off.

The murderer had evidently heard the approach of the policeman and hurriedly left the square by a small passage that runs from its northern side. In this passage there was a communal

A graphic depiction in *Police News* of the fate of the Ripper's fifth victim

sink, and he had paused long enough to wash the blood from his hands, and probably from his knife. In Goulston Street, a ten-minute walk away, he discarded a bloodstained piece of his victim's apron. The policeman who found it also found a chalked message scrawled on a nearby wall: 'The Juwes are not the men that will be blamed for nothing.' The Police Commissioner, Sir Charles Warren, ordered the words to be rubbed out, in spite of a plea from the CID that they should be photographed first. Sir Charles thought they might cause trouble for the many Jews in Whitechapel.

Macnaghten admitted later, 'When the double murder of 30 September took place, the exasperation of the public at that non-discovery of the perpetrator knew no bounds.' The 'Jack the Ripper' letter was released, and the murderer immediately acquired a nickname. And early on Monday morning, the Central News Agency received another missive, this time a postcard, from Jack the Ripper. It said: 'I was not codding [joking] dear old boss when I gave you the tip. You'll hear about Saucy Jack's work tomorrow. Double event this time. Number one squealed a bit. Couldn't finish straight off. Had not time to get ears for police. Thanks for keeping last letter back till I got to work again.'

The public exploded in fury. Meetings were held in the streets, criticizing the police. Sir Charles Warren's resignation was demanded. The murderer was suspected of being a doctor and men carrying black bags found it dangerous to walk through the streets. The police decided to try using bloodhounds, but to no avail for the dogs promptly lost themselves on Tooting Common.

Yet as October passed with no further murders, the panic began to die down. Then, in the early hours of 9 November the Ripper staged his most spectacular crime of all. Mary Jeanette Kelly was a young Irishwoman, only 24 years old, and she lived in a cheap room in Miller's Court, off Dorset Street. At about 2 o'clock that morning, she was seen talking to a swarthy man with a heavy moustache; he seemed well dressed and had a gold watch chain. They entered the narrow alleyway that led to her lodging: Room 13.

At 10.45 the next morning, a rent collector knocked on her door but received no reply. So he put his hand through a broken pane of glass in the window and pulled aside the curtain. What he saw sent him rushing for a policeman.

Jack the Ripper had surpassed himself. The body lay on the

bed, and the mutilations must have taken a long time – an hour or more. One of the hands lay in the open stomach. The head had been virtually removed, hanging on only a piece of skin; so had the left arm. The breast and nose had been removed, and the skin from the legs stripped off. The heart lay on the pillow, and some of the intestines were draped round a picture. The remains of a fire burned in the grate, as if the Ripper had used it to provide himself with light. But this time, medical examination revealed that the Ripper had taken away none of the internal organs; his lengthy exercise in mutilation had apparently satisfied his peculiar sadistic fever.

This murder caused the greatest sensation of all. The police chief, Sir Charles Warren, finally resigned. Public clamour became louder than ever; even Queen Victoria made suggestions on how to catch the murderer. Yet the slaughter of Mary Kelly proved to be the last of the crimes of Jack the Ripper. The police, hardly able to believe their luck as weeks and months went by without further atrocities, reached the conclusion that the Ripper had either committed suicide or been confined in a mental home. A body taken from the river early the following January was identified as that of a lawyer who had committed suicide, and Scotland Yard detectives told themselves that this was almost certainly Jack the Ripper. But their claims have never been confirmed.

There have, of course, been many fascinating theories. Forty years after the murders, an Australian journalist named Leonard Matters wrote the first full-length book on Jack the Ripper. He ended by telling an extraordinary story: how a surgeon in Buenos Aires was called to the bedside of a dying Englishman, whom he recognized as the brilliant surgeon Dr Stanley, under whom he had studied. Dr Stanley told him a horrifying story. In 1888, his son Herbert had died of syphilis contracted from a prostitute two years before; her name had been Mary Jeanette Kelly. Dr Stanley swore to avenge Herbert's death, and prowled the East End of London looking for the woman. He would pick up prostitutes, question them about Mary Kelly, then kill them to make sure they made no attempt to warn her. Finally, he found the woman he was seeking, and took his revenge. Then he left for Argentina.

Matters admitted that his own search of the records of the British Medical Association had revealed no Dr Stanley, and no one who even resembled him. But there are other reasons for regarding the Stanley story as fiction. If Dr Stanley was only trying to silence his first four victims, why did he disembowel them? In any case, syphilis is unlikely to kill a man in two years – ten is a more likely period. But the most conclusive piece of evidence against the Dr Stanley theory is that Mary Kelly was not suffering from syphilis.

Ten years later, an artist named William Stewart published *Jack the Ripper: A New Theory*. Stewart had studied the inquest report on Mary Kelly and discovered that she was pregnant at the time of her death. He produced the remarkable theory that Jack the Ripper was a woman – a midwife who had gone to the room in Miller's Court to perform an abortion. After killing Mary Kelly in a sadistic frenzy, she had dressed up in her spare clothes and left, after burning her own bloody garments in the grate. The immediate objection to this theory is that Mary Kelly had no spare clothes – she was too poverty-stricken. But the major objection is that there has never yet been a case of sadistic mutilation murder in which the killer was a woman. Stewart's 'Jill the Ripper' is a psychological improbability.

In 1959, the journalist Donald McCormick revived a theory that dated back to the 1920s. A journalist named William LeQueux described in a book called *Things I Know* how, after the Russian Revolution, the Kerensky government had allowed him to see a manuscript written in French by the 'mad monk' Rasputin, and found in a safe in the basement of Rasputin's house. It was called *Great Russian Criminals*, and declared that Jack the Ripper was a sadistic maniac called Alexander Pedachenko, who was sent to England by the Russian secret police to embarrass the British police force. Pedachenko, said LeQueux, was later arrested after he tried to kill a woman in Tver in the U.S.S.R. In fact, LeQueux wrote three books about Rasputin, all full of cynical invention. Although they were written before *Things I Know*, they all fail to mention this extraordinary theory. But the strongest objection to the Rasputin-Pedachenko theory is that Rasputin did not speak a word of French, and that he lived in a flat on the third floor in a house with no cellar.

In the same year as McCormick's book, Daniel Farson investigated the Ripper murders for a television programme, and succeeded in securing an extraordinary scoop. Sir Melville Macnaghten had hinted strongly in his memoirs that he knew the identity of Jack the Ripper, and spoke of three suspects, although he finally dismissed two of these. Farson succeeded in obtaining Macnaghten's original notes, and learned the name of this chief suspect: an unsuccessful barrister named Montague John Druitt – the man whose body was found in the Thames in early January 1889. Farson did some remarkable detective work, and learned a great deal about Druitt's life and death.

Alas, when Macnaghten's comments are examined closely it becomes very clear that he knew little or nothing about Druitt. He calls him a doctor when he was a barrister. He says he believes Druitt lived with his family, when in fact he lived in chambers, like most lawyers. He says he believes Druitt's mind snapped after his 'glut' in Miller's Court, and that he committed suicide the following day. We know that Druitt killed himself three weeks later, and that he did so because he was depressed after going to see his mother, who had become insane – he was afraid that the same thing was happening to him. In fact, Macnaghten joined the police force six months after the Ripper murders came to an end, and it is obvious that his Druitt theory was pure wishful thinking, without a shred of supporting evidence.

When, in 1960, I published a series of articles entitled 'My Search for Jack the Ripper' in the London *Evening Standard*, I was asked to lunch by an elderly surgeon, Thomas Stowell, who told me his own astonishing theory about the Ripper's identity: that it was Queen Victoria's grandson, the Duke of Clarence, who died in the 'flu epidemic of 1892. Stowell told me that he had seen the private papers of Sir William Gull, Queen Victoria's physician, and that Gull had dropped mysterious hints about Clarence and Jack the Ripper, as well as mentioning that Clarence had syphilis, from which he died. When, subsequently, I asked Stowell if I could write about his theory, he said no. 'It might upset Her Majesty.' But in 1970, he decided to publish it himself in the magazine *The Criminologist*. Admittedly, he did not name his suspect – he called him 'S' – but he dropped many hints that it was Clarence. Journalists took up the story and it caused a worldwide sensation. Stowell was so shaken by all the publicity that he died a week later, trying to repair the damage by claiming that his suspect was not the Duke of Clarence.

Michael Harrison, a writer engaged on a biography of Clarence, carefully re-read Stowell's article, and realized that there were many discrepancies between the career of 'S' and that of the Duke of Clarence. He concluded that Sir William Gull had indeed referred to a suspect as 'S', but that it was not the Duke of Clarence; it was, however, someone who was closely acquainted with him. Studying Clarence's acquaintances, he discovered the ideal suspect – James Kenneth Stephen, a poet, lawyer and man-about-town who had become distinctly odd after being struck on the head by the vane of a windmill, and who, like Clarence, had died – in a mental home – in 1892. Harrison had no trouble in disposing of Clarence as a suspect, pointing out that at the time of the Miller's Court murder, Clarence was celebrating his father's birthday at Sandringham. But he was far less successful in finding even a grain of positive evidence to connect Stephen with the crimes. It is almost impossible to imagine the intellectual young aesthete, author of a great deal of published verse, stalking prostitutes with a knife.

The next major book on the Ripper was optimistically entitled *Jack the Ripper: The Final Solution*, and was by a young journalist, Stephen Knight. Knight's candidate for Jack the Ripper was incredibly Sir William Gull himself. But the story behind the murders involved the Duke of Clarence. According to this story, Clarence had met an artist's model at the studio of the painter Walter Sickert. She had become pregnant, and he had married her. The baby's nurse was a young Irishwoman named Mary Jeanette Kelly. When the royal family found out, Clarence was placed under lock and key in the palace, and his wife was confined in a mental home. But Mary Kelly told the secret to some of her prostitute friends in Whitechapel, and they made the mistake of trying to blackmail the government. The Prime Minister, Lord Salisbury, gave orders that they were to be silenced, and the man chosen to do the job was Sir William Gull, who was driven to whitechapel in his private coach . . . Knight admitted that Gull had had a stroke in the year before the murders, but insisted that he was spry enough to disembowel a few prostitutes in the privacy of his coach.

The source of this incredible farrago was Walter Sickert's son, Joseph Sickert, who claimed that his father had married the Duke of Clarence's child, and that he, therefore, was really Clarence's grandson. Unfortunately, a few days after Knight's book appeared in paperback, Joseph Sickert admitted in a newspaper that his whole Jack the Ripper story was a hoax – although still insisting that he was the Duke of Clarence's grandson. And so the most absurd of all the Ripper theories exploded like a bubble.

Does all this mean that we shall never know the identity of Jack the Ripper? Possibly. Yet the investigations undertaken by the various authors underline one fascinating point: that there is still an incredible amount of information lying in various archives, waiting to be unearthed. The identity of Jack the Ripper may yet be revealed to some casual browser in the Public Records Office or the archives of the Lunacy Commission.

'ZODIAC'

America in the 1980s has seen the emergence of a new and terrifying social phenomenon – the serial killer: the man who, for no apparent reason, kills again and again. Of course, there have always been mass murderers, from Caligula to Jack the Ripper. Yet the modern phenomenon is still frighteningly different. Charles Casey, head of the Criminal Intelligence Bureau in California, says, 'These are people who love to kill. We like to tack some deep psychological meaning to it, but really they're just killing for fun – just plain fun.'

In this sense, criminologists of the future will probably regard the unknown maniac known as 'Zodiac' as the first 'serial killer'.

On 20 December 1968, two teenagers – David Farraday and Bettilou Jenson – were out on their first date near Vallejo, California. They had parked near a pump-house up above Lake Hermon Reservoir, and were listening to pop music on the radio. Suddenly, there was a tap on the driver's window, and as the 17-year-old boy wiped away the mist, he found himself looking down the barrel of a gun. A podgy, bespectacled man ordered him to lower the window, then told him to get out of the car. As he started to obey, a bullet entered his head, and he fell dead. Bettilou screamed, flung open her own door and began to run. In the moonlight, five shots struck her, and she collapsed.

Only a few minutes later, a passing woman driver saw the bodies in her headlights; she drove on, and waved frantically at an oncoming police car. When the police arrived at the pump-house minutes later, both teenagers were dead. There was no obvious motive. David Farraday's wallet was untouched, and Bettilou lay where she had fallen, her clothing undisturbed.

The police investigation soon ground to a halt. There were no jealous lovers hovering in the background; no one seemed to have the slightest motive for killing the teenagers. Whoever did it was obviously 'psychologically disturbed'. And the frozen earth had not left tyre marks.

By July 1969 the teenagers were merely statistics in California's alarming list of unsolved murders. Two miles from the pump-house above the reservoir, another young couple sat in their car in Blue Rock Springs Park: they were a 22-year-old waitress, Darlene Elizabeth Ferrin, and 19-year-old Michael Renault Mageau, whose father ran a pest-control agency. Neither was much disturbed when another car drove in beside them in the parking lot. When a blinding light shone in through the window, the couple assumed it was a police patrol car. Then a man stepped out of the 'patrol car' and came towards them. There was an explosion of gunfire; two shots struck Darlene, who was sitting at the wheel, and another entered Michael Mageau's neck. The assailant walked back to his own car and drove off, his tyres screaming. Another nearby car with several people in it also drove away – they were, apparently, determined not to get involved. Michael Mageau, who was trying to crawl towards them, lost consciousness.

At four minutes past midnight, a phone call to Vallejo police headquarters reported a double murder. A man's voice told the operator the precise location of the car park. He added, 'They are both shot with a 9-millimetre Luger. I also killed those kids last year. Goodbye.'

When police arrived, Darlene Ferrin, the mother of an 18-month-old baby, was dead. Michael Mageau, although alive, was unable to speak. But as he recovered in hospital he was able to describe his assailant: a stocky, round-faced man about 5 feet 8 inches tall, with light brown hair that was wavy or curly. His age would be about 30.

Although the gun was not the same one that had killed the teenagers in December, the police knew the man was telling the truth when he said he was also their murderer. Now Detective-Sergeant Leslie Lundblad, who investigated the previous case, knew he had been correct in his assessment: this was a 'nut', a homicidal maniac who killed out of some odd resentment.

Lundblad reasoned that the killer was probably an inhabitant of Vallejo, a small town 20 miles or so from San Francisco. At least, he seemed familiar with the area and in that case, someone might recognize Michael Mageau's description. But no one, apparently, did.

97

One thing was obvious – the killer had a curious craving to be known as a multiple murderer. Otherwise, why volunteer the information about the previous double murder? This argued that he was a man who in his personal life felt ineffectual and insufficiently appreciated. He was trying to make society 'pay attention'. This was the conclusion formed by the police psychologists.

Four weeks after the Darlene Ferrin murder, this was confirmed when the *Vallejo Times-Herald* received a crudely scrawled letter from a man who claimed to be the killer – he added details that had not been made public, so the police had no doubt that he was telling the truth. It was signed with a circle containing a cross, a little like the telescopic sight of a rifle. There was also an enclosure – a torn sheet of paper containing a strange cipher. More of the cipher was sent to two other newspapers, the San Francisco *Chronicle* and *Examiner*. The killer was evidently determined to obtain maximum coverage. The letters were identical to the one sent to the Vallejo newspaper. They also contained a threat that if they were not published that day – 1 August 1969 – the murderer would 'cruse around' [*sic*] and kill a dozen people. The letters also explained that the fragments of cipher would reveal his identity.

All three newspapers published the complete text of the cryptogram, but they withheld the murder threat – there would be no point in causing a panic. They also asked that the writer should provide more proof of his identity. He promptly obliged with a letter that began: 'This is Zodiac speaking', and giving more details of the crimes.

Naval experts attempted to crack the code. But the man who succeeded was an amateur cryptoanalyst, a schoolmaster named Donald Harden, who lived in Salinas. He looked for groups of signs that might fit the word 'kill', and ended with a 'translation' which read:

I like killing people because it is so much fun it is more fun than killing wild game in the forest because man is the most dangerous animal of all to kill something gives me the most thrilling experience it is even better than getting your rock off with a girl the best part of it is when I die I

cipher on your front page by
Fry. Afternoon Aug 1-69, If you
do not do this I will go on a
kill rampage Fry night that
will last the whole week end.
I will cruse around and pick
of all stray people on cupples
that are alone then move on to
kill some more untill I have
killed over a dozen people.

Zodiac's threat published by the *Vallejo Times-Herald* on 1 August 1969

will be reborn in paradise and all I have killed will become my slaves I will not give you my name because you will try to slow down or stop my collecting slaves for my afterlife . . .

It ended in an incomprehensible jumble: 'ebeori et eme thh piti'.

The public offered more than a thousand tips. Every one was checked but none led to new discoveries.

The next murder happened on the afternoon of Saturday, 27 September, on the shores of Lake Berryessa in Napa Valley. Two students from Pacific Union College, 20-year-old Bryan Hartnell, and a dazzlingly pretty blonde, Cecilia Shepard, who was 22, had gone for a picnic. They had just finished eating when a hooded figure advanced on them from the trees; on the part of the hood covering his chest was a circle containing a cross drawn in white – the sign of the zodiac. He had a gun in one hand and a knife in the other. In a gruff voice he asked Hartnell for money; Hartnell said he was welcome to what he had on him. The man then volunteered the information that he was an escapee from Deer Lodge State Prison in Montana and needed their white car. He then produced some plastic clothes line and proceeded to tie them up. As he bent over, Hartnell saw that he was wearing glasses behind the hood. Then he said, 'I'm going to have to stab you people.' The man plunged the knife repeatedly into Hartnell's back. Then he attacked Cecilia. This was what he had been looking forward to; after the first stab he went into a frenzy. Eventually he turned her over and stabbed her in the stomach. Finally, he went over to their car, wrote something on the door, and left.

A fisherman on the lake heard their screams and rowed over

The cipher that accompanied the letter to the *Vallejo Times–Herald*

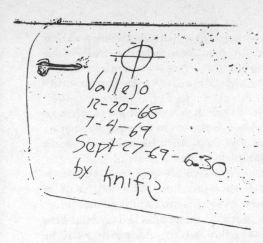

Student Bryan Hartnell recovered from his brutal attack but his girlfriend died shortly afterwards. Zodiac wrote this inscription in black felt-tip pen on Hartnell's car after the stabbings.

to the headquarters of the park ranger. Within half an hour, ranger William White was kneeling by both victims, who were still alive. Soon after, the Napa police arrived; they had been alerted by a gruff voice on the telephone that told them he wanted to report a double murder, and described the location.

Cecilia died two days later in hospital; Bryan Hartnell recovered slowly. By then, the police knew they were dealing with Zodiac – he had written his sign on the passenger door with a black marker pen, adding also the dates of the previous two attacks. The police also located the telephone from which the killer had rung them; it was only six blocks from police headquarters, and it was still swinging loose. But it had no fingerprints on it.

A check with Deer Lodge Prison revealed, as the police expected, that there had been no escape. Zodiac had told this story to give his victims the impression that they were in no danger while he tied them up.

What was to be Zodiac's last recorded murder took place two weeks later, on 11 October 1969. A San Francisco taxi-driver named Paul Stine picked up a fare near the Fairmont Hotel on Nob Hill – a stocky, brown-haired man with horn-rimmed glasses. A quarter of an hour later, the taxi pulled into the kerb at the intersection of Washington and Cherry Streets, and two youths standing nearby heard a gunshot. A man climbed out of

101

the back seat, and leaned in through the driver's window. There was a tearing sound, and the man began wiping the cab with a piece of cloth, evidently to remove fingerprints. Then he saw the youths, and began to trot away towards the open space called the Presidio.

Paul Stine, a 29-year-old student who was a part-time taxi-driver, was slumped over the wheel, shot in the back of the head. His wallet was missing, so was a piece of his shirt, which had been used to wipe the taxi-cab.

Four days later, the San Francisco *Chronicle* received a letter that began: 'This is Zodiac speaking. I am the murderer of the taxi-driver . . .'. It enclosed a bloodstained piece of Paul Stine's shirt. The letter went on to jeer at the police: 'They could have caught me last night if they had tried . . .' Then he went on: 'School children will make nice targets. I think I shall wipe out a school bus some morning . . .'

From then on, armed deputies began to ride on all school buses. But the precaution was unnecessary, for Zodiac would never try and kill where he might be caught – he preferred stealth. And now the heat was on. The police had a good description and were able to issue photofit pictures of a crew-cut man with horn-rimmed glasses. There was a notable drop in courting couples in lovers' lanes. Moreover, the police had one clue that seemed to guarantee that the killer would eventually be brought to justice – they had his fingerprints, taken from a telephone.

But if Zodiac had decided it was too risky to go on killing, his craving for publicity was still unsated. Ten days after the murder of Paul Stine, a gruff voice spoke on the telephone to the Oakland Police Department, and made a number of remarks that left no doubt he knew unpublished details about the five murders. But the caller's most astonishing message was that he had decided he wanted to give himself up. His condition, he said, was that he should be represented by some famous lawyer like Melvin Belli of F. Lee Bailey. He would also like to speak on a famous television talk show – the Jim Dunbar programme.

It sounded absurd, but the 'Zodiac Squad' decided it was worth a try. They asked Melvin Belli, who had an office in San

Francisco, if he was willing to try and help them capture Zodiac; he agreed immediately. Next, they asked Jim Dunbar if he would reserve space for a telephone call on his breakfast chat show. They then contacted the three people who had heard Zodiac speak – victim Bryan Hartnell, and the two switchboard operators.

When the show went on the air, at 6.45 a.m., it had a good audience. At 7.41, a soft, boyish voice came on the line; he rang off, but called back five minutes later. This time he identified himself as Zodiac but said he preferred to be called Sam. In the studio, Bryan Hartnell and the switchboard operators shook their heads. Unless Zodiac had been lowering his voice when they heard him, this man was a fake.

'Sam' rang back in all 15 times. He explained that he had been suffering from headaches since 'I killed that kid last December', and he punctuated his remarks with groans of pain, which he explained 'were the headache speaking'. Belli tried hard to persuade the caller to give himself up but 'Sam' refused. Finally, when the conversation was taken off the air, Belli persuaded 'Sam' to meet him in front of a store in Daly City, south of San Francisco. Predictably, the caller failed to arrive. But the policemen who were hidden around corners told themselves that they did not believe the caller was Zodiac anyway.

Yet they could have been wrong. Just before Christmas, Belli received a letter signed 'Zodiac'. It began 'Dear Melvin', and asked for help. And, to prove his identity, the sender enclosed another piece of Stine's bloodstained shirt. If the television caller had been a hoaxer, surely the real Zodiac – assuming he was the letter writer – would have denounced him?

The letter seemed to indicate that Zodiac's mental state was deteriorating; the spelling was worse than usual, and the note of desperation sounded genuine. 'I cannot reach out for help because of this thing in me won't let me. I am finding it extremely difficult to hold myself in check and I am afraid I will lose control and take my ninth and possibly tenth victim. Please help me I am drownding . . .'

The implied claim that he had killed eight people led to frenzied activity in the San Francisco Police Department. They could find only one likely case: of a girl named Cheri Jo Bates, who had been found dead in her car in the college car park. But the killer had cut her throat and that was a departure from Zodiac's known methods.

Police now began to receive many 'Zodiac' letters, most undoubtedly from hoazers. One letter taunted them for being unable to catch him, and added the figure '17 plus' implying that there had been a dozen more victims. In fact, a 'Zodiac' letter of 1974 – four years later – claimed that the total had now reached 37. Internal evidence suggests that this letter was genuine. As far as is known, this was the last authentic communication from the killer.

Many psychologists studied the Zodiac material, and produced interesting commentaries. One of these, Dr Laurence Freedman, wrote: 'He kills senselessly because he is deeply frustrated. And he hates himself because he is an anonymous nonentity. When he is caught, he will turn out to be a mouse, a murderous mouse . . .'

Freedman's remarks sound like an anticipation of another mass killer, New York's 'Son of Sam', David Berkowitz, who terrorized the city in the mid-1970s, strolling up to courting couples and shooting at random. He killed six and wounded many more before he was caught, by accident, through a parking ticket. Berkowitz also proved to be a 'mouse of a man' who was mentally retarded.

What is perfectly clear about the Zodiac case is that the killer was, as Freedman said, a nonentity who hated himself for being a nobody. Like the bad behaviour of a naughty child his crimes were a cry of 'Look at me!'. And also, as absurd as it sounds, 'Love me!'. What he would now like is to be publicly chastised, then forgiven and taken to everyone's heart.

With the murders, he had achieved what he always craved: public recognition, a kind of fame. Yet the fame is self-defeating. He can walk along the street and think, as he sees the newspaper headlines, 'Yes, I am famous' – yet no one knows him. He can address the famous lawyer as Melvin, yet he does not dare to give his own name. All he dares to do is try to stay in the centre of the stage by writing more letters threatening violence. And even so, there comes a time when the public is bored with him; he has cried wolf too often. He is finally forced to face up to the irony of the situation. If he had gained notoriety in a hundred ways that were publicly acceptable – from betraying government secrets to streaking at a football match – he could enjoy his fame; as it is, he is condemned to the same obscurity that drove him to the crimes in the beginning. He does not even dare to do anything that might draw too much attention, for now the police have his fingerprints and he may be captured at any time. The Zodiac case is the classic demonstration of the ultimately self-defeating nature of murders of this type.

WHAT HAPPENED TO THEM?

FREDDIE MILLS: A PUZZLE

Any visitor to London's West End can easily find Goslett Yard.
All you have to do is walk along Charing Cross Road towards
Oxford Street and there, just at the top on the left-hand side, is
the small L-shaped cul-de-sac.

You turn into the long part of the L and, neatly tucked away
round the corner is the exact spot close to a solitary street lamp
where, early in the morning of Sunday, 25 July 1965, Freddie
Mills, perhaps the most famous boxer Britain has ever known,
was found dead in the back of his own car.

Twenty-one years later, his widow, Mrs Christine Mills, still
remembers the scene vividly, 'Freddie was on the rear seat,
behind the front passenger seat. His head was down and his
hands were on his knees, as if he was asleep. I opened the offside back door, got in and sat next to him. I had a white suit on. I
put my arms around him. They had told me he was sleeping and
they couldn't wake him up. "Come on Fred, what's the matter?"
And then I realized that I couldn't get close enough. There was
something between us, and I thought it was a starting handle. I
lifted this thing across the front of my knees and laid it beside
me; as I did so I saw blood on my white jacket. I turned round
and the penny dropped.

I said to my son, standing outside, "Donny, it's a gun! Get the
police!" I went berserk.'

The ex-light-heavyweight champion of the world, television
star, night-club owner and popular entertainer had been shot
through the eye by the .22 fairground rifle that his wife had
found propped on the seat beside him. He had died almost

instantly. But why? Who would want to kill Freddie, whom everybody loved, and what possible reason could there be for this tough, hungry fighter ever to have killed himself?

Even the scene of his death adds to the mystery to this day. Tucked away from the main road, it is an ideal setting for a man to choose to kill himself – *or* for a murderer to hunt down his victim.

Frederick Percival Mills was born in Bournemouth in 1919. His father gave him a pair of boxing gloves on his eleventh birthday. Later as he grew into a stocky, good-looking youngster, he began to throw punches for 'nobbins' – the coins spectators threw into the ring after a good scrap – in the smokey, fairground boxing-booths of the West Country. It was a tough, blood-spattered, poorly paid training ground. As he once told my colleague, Alan Hoby, 'It was a good night if you made £3.'

He was a rampaging bull of a fighter with just one basic idea – to batter his opponent into submission. There was never any doubt that boxing was going to be his career. On August Bank Holiday weekend 1941, Ted Broadribb, the famous boxing manager, went to Leicester to see this new contender fight. Broadribb took his wife and daughter Chrissie with him. Chrissie was to become the future Mrs Mills.

Some years later, after her marriage had failed, she and Freddie got married. Chrissie's son from her first marriage, Donny McCorkindale, lived with them and they had two daughters of their own. At the time of their marriage, Freddie was world light-heavyweight champion.

He won the title in 1948, but lost it – and five teeth – two years later when he was knocked out in ten rounds by American Joey Maxim. Still only 31, the career that had made him clamber into the ring more than 100 times was over. He announced his retirement. He had wanted to continue but his wife had persuaded him to the contrary.

Unlike some professional boxers, the ex-champion had no financial worries. In the latter days, Freddie had earned good money in the ring. Besides, in 1946, with three partners, he had opened Freddie Mills's Chinese Restaurant in London's Charing Cross Road.

The business was a success and so was Freddie's new career, as a television entertainer. People today still remember his weekly appearances in '6.5 Special' with Pete Murray and Jo Douglas. Freddie's cheery, extrovert nature bubbled away with the sheer enjoyment of living, and he and his family enjoyed the material fruits of success as well. Their large comfortable house in Denmark Hill in south London had a swimming pool. As the 1950s gave way to the 1960s, life continued to be good.

Then, in 1962 when Chinese restaurants had become two-a-penny, Freddie's restaurant became a night club called Freddie Mills's Nite Spot. Freddie now had only one of his original partners, a man named Andy Ho. To the outside world, he was still the same old Celebrity Freddie, but Mrs Mills now tells me: 'Turning the restaurant into a night club was the worst thing we could ever have done. We were not night-club people, and instead of being a working pleasure, the club became a nightly routine.'

Freddie was not really a late-night sort of person. He got into the habit of going for a sleep in his car parked at the back of the club, in Goslett Yard, for half an hour or so every night, before he was called on to give a performance and be the cheerful host, shaking hands and chatting. 'He would go to the club at about 10 o'clock,' remembers Mrs Mills, 'and then at about 12.00 or so he'd say, "I'm going for my little egg and dip" – his kip. He would go out to the car, and then they'd call him down to introduce the floorshow or talk to the customers.'

That was exactly the routine on the night of Saturday, 24 July 1965. It had been a perfectly normal day, and shortly after 10 p.m. Freddie left for the club saying to his wife, 'I'll see you at midnight.' They had arranged that when her son, Donny, had returned home that evening after borrowing her car, she would drive up to town and have a late-night supper with Freddie at the club. Donny and his wife, Kate, were delayed in getting back to Denmark Hill with Chrissie's car. Nevertheless, she invited them to join her at the club.

It was sometime after midnight when they arrived, to find an anxious Andy Ho waiting for them. He told them that Freddie was sleeping in his car round the back as usual, but they could not wake him. Mrs Mills and her son went to investigate – and found that scene of silent horror in the stationary Citroen.

What had happened after Freddie had arrived at the club that evening?

The senior police officers who investigated the ex-champion's mysterious death have long since retired or left the force. I am told that the papers at New Scotland Yard are no longer available. However, I have been fortunate enough to obtain copies of the witnesses' statements made to the detectives operating out of London's West End Central Police Station.

This then is their account of Freddie Mills's last hours. At about 10.30 p.m. a man, whom the doorman had never seen before, came up to him and said that Freddie was in his car at the back of the club and would he go and see him. The doorman went round and saw Freddie sitting in the driving seat. Freddie told him he did not want to go into the club, that he was going to have a sleep, and the doorman should wake him up in half an hour.

At about 11.10 p.m., the young doorman went back to the car where Freddie was still in the driving seat. He said, 'You told me to wake you up.' But Freddie replied, 'No, come back in half an hour.' At 11.45 the doorman again went back into Goslett Yard. The car was still in the same position, but Freddie was now in the nearside rear seat. He was sitting upright with his head slumped forward. The offside rear window was wound down. So the young man went to it and called, 'Mr Mills', several times and banged on the car door.

Freddie did not respond. So the doorman opened the door, leant in and pushed Freddie's right shoulder and patted his right cheek. He still did not respond. There was what appeared to be saliva round his mouth and nostrils. The young man felt uneasy but did not think that anything was really wrong. He shut the car door, went back into the club and told the head waiter what he had seen. At about 1 a.m. the head waiter went to wake up Freddie, and concluded he was ill. He informed Mr Ho, who telephoned Mrs Mills at her home. But she, of course, had already left for the club.

Was it suicide or murder? The police later discovered that

Freddie had obtained the .22 fairground rifle that killed him and which was found lying beside his body from an old lady who owned a fairground rifle-range at the Battersea Fun Fair. He had known her for years, and within the past few days had asked her to lend him the rifle. He was attending a charity fête at Esher and would be dressed as a cowboy. It was only after he had left that she realized he had also taken some ammunition from a box on her mantelpiece. It transpired that there was no charity fête at Esher.

Even so, Jack Solomons, who knew Freddie well, told Chrissie Mills the very next day, 'If Freddie stood here and said to me, "Jack, I shot myself", I wouldn't believe it. But I'm warning you, be prepared. They may try to bring this in as suicide.'

Indeed, that was the official verdict at the inquest, held without a jury, at Westminster Coroner's Court on 2 August 1965. From that day to this, Mrs Mills and her son, Donny, have not believed it for one munute. 'If I live for a million years I will never accept that Freddie killed himself,' Mrs Mills told me. She and Donny McCorkindale are convinced that Freddie was murdered by one of the gangs that in the mid-1960s were extorting a fortune in protection money from restaurateurs and night-club owners in the West End – allegedly under the benign eye of certain policemen.

'If he had been threatened, Freddie would have refused to pay for protection,' says Donny. 'He would have told them exactly what they could do with themselves!' Freddie never mentioned any threats to Chrissie, but she says, 'He would not have told me. He knew what a worrier I was.'

Mother and son know of an ex-wrestler (now dead) whose club was destroyed only two weeks before Freddie died because he refused to pay protection money. They are sure that Freddie was killed as an example to deter any others similarly minded to defy the villains. Sitting asleep in his car at the back of his club, as was his habit, he would have been an easy prey for any killer. But ex-Commander Leonard 'Nipper' Read, who, three years later, led the team that put the Kray brothers and their confederates behind bars, is adamant that, if this were true, he would have heard something about it.

A major obstacle in the murder theory is the evidence of the elderly rifle-range owner at the Battersea Fun Fair who said that Freddie borrowed the weapon that killed him from her, and that he also stole three rounds of ammunition. Surely that must knock on the head any murder theory?

Not necessarily. For, as a good friend has told Chrissie Mills, the fairground people at Battersea Fun Fair were having their own problems with the protection gangs. It is not impossible that the evidence supplied to the police was false, given under duress by an elderly woman who feared that 'the boys' would come in and 'rough up' her place. She is now dead so I cannot ask her myself.

Certainly, Mrs Mills insists that she never saw the rifle until she found it in Freddie's car that night.

The insistent question remains: what possible motive could have been strong enough for a man like Freddie Mills who never quit in the ring to end his own life?

In a book published in 1977, Jack Birtley revealed that Freddie had fallen in love with a girl nearly 20 years younger than himself. Mrs Mills tells me, 'Yes, he did have an affair with a girl, but that was all finished the year before. It had nothing to do with his death.'

Undoubtedly, Freddie was having serious money troubles. He grossed over £100,000 from boxing, yet died with only £387. Before his death he had, unknown to Chrissie, sold off all his properties to meet pressing debts, and at the end some £12,000 could not be accounted for. No one to this day has any idea where the money went – or why. Yet surely financial worries, however onerous, were not enough to make a man like Freddie kill himself?

The police investigation into his death seems to have been remarkably apathetic. It is amazing, to my mind, that the ambulance summoned to the scene took Freddie's body away before the police arrived. I have never known of such an event in a firearm fatality. Mr Read says, 'I agree that it was unfortunate that the ambulancemen removed the body before the arrival of the police. This precluded the taking of photographs, which in the event would have been most helpful in determining precisely

111

what happened. I cannot account for this.'

What makes this all the more intriguing is the persistent, nagging worry in the minds of the family, and in my own mind, about the position of the rifle. Mrs Mills and her son find it difficult to believe that Freddie could have killed himself with the rifle and than have placed it neatly beside himself in the back of the car. They think it far more likely that he was shot with the rifle from outside the open window and that the weapon was placed beside him by the killer.

What really happened, and why, remains a baffling mystery.

THE PRIME MINISTER DISAPPEARS

Shortly before midday on 17 December 1967, two cars arrived at Cheviot Beach, about 60 miles south of Melbourne in Australia. The beach was forbidden to the general public, since it was part of an Officer Cadet Training School; but the driver of one of the cars was the Australian Prime Minister, Harold Holt, and he could go anywhere he liked.

The sea was rough, and Cheviot Beach is known to be one of the most dangerous in the state of Victoria. Holt showed no hesitation as he changed into swimming trunks and walked straight into the surf. Most of the others in the party – a neighbour of Holt's and her house guests – were disinclined to follow him. However, a young businessman named Alan Stewart remarked, 'If Mr Holt can take it, I'd better go in too,' and followed the Prime Minister.

Holt seemed to be swimming dangerously far out. Alan Stewart stopped swimming when he felt an undertow dragging at his legs but the Prime Minister seemed to be swimming, as calmly as a seal, in the general direction of Tasmania. His neighbour, Mrs Marjorie Gillespie, stared after him with anxiety, wondering why he was going so far. Suddenly, the water around the Prime Minister seemed to boil and bubble, and his head disappeared. That was the last time he was seen.

Within hours, dozens of skin divers were searching the sea, while helicopters flew as low as they dared. The search continued for six days, but no body was ever found. Many distinguished statesmen attended Holt's memorial service, including Lyndon Johnson, Harold Wilson, Edward Heath and Prince Charles.

Inevitably, there was speculation that Holt may have committed suicide. He had been Prime Minister for two years, and had been in trouble from the beginning. Young Australians demonstrated vigorously against his commitment to the war in Vietnam – Holt had trebled the Australian contingent to 8,500 troops. He had been accused in parliament of using airforce planes as a personal taxi service for himself and his family. His party lost two by-elections under his leadership, and also suffered in elections for the Senate. There were persistent rumours that his own Liberal Party wanted to get rid of him, and nothing would have humiliated Holt more deeply – he was a man who was very sensitive to snubs and setbacks. When he left Canberra that weekend to travel to his seaside home in Portsea, Holt looked tired and depressed. His opponents in parliament felt he showed signs of cracking under the strain.

However, those who had seen him that weekend scoffed at the idea of suicide. Harold Holt had a remarkable capacity for relaxing and forgetting his worries, and to his housekeeper, his stepson and his various friends, he had seemed to be a man without any serious problems. At 59, after more than 30 years in politics, Holt had become accustomed to the ups and downs of the life of a statesman.

Fifteen years after his disappearance Harold Holt became the centre of a scandal that eclipsed anything that had happened during his lifetime. A book by a highly respected journalist, Anthony Grey, accused him of leading an extraordinary double life. The title tells its own story: *The Prime Minister Was a Spy*. Grey claimed to have reliable information from Chinese sources which revealed that Holt was not drowned on that December afternoon. He had swum out to a Chinese submarine and been taken to the People's Republic of China.

The story sounds incredible, and most reviewers of the book were scathing. The story told by Anthony Grey with its wealth of detail needs to be absorbed slowly. Anyone who does this will agree that Grey has made a strong case for the notion that Australia's Prime Minister was a Chinese spy.

Harold Holt was the type of politician more often found in America than England: the charming, flamboyant spellbinder. He once stated that if he had not been a politician, he would have been an actor – an admission that no doubt led many of his opponents to retort, 'You are.' He was certainly born under the right astrological sign for an actor, that of Leo, in the year 1908. Holt's background was theatrical: his father was a self-made impressario, while his mother was a member of a well-known family in the theatre. When he was still a child, his parents moved to England, where his father had become the representative of J. C. Williamson, Australia's biggest theatre group. Holt and his brother were educated at a private school, Wesley College, with a minimum of parental affection or interference. When he was only ten his parents divorced.

At Queen's College, Melbourne, Holt studied law. It was not that he found the subject particularly attractive but it seemed to offer opportunities to exercise his considerable theatrical talent – at college he proved to be a brilliant orator and debater. He also played in the cricket team, acquired fashionable left-wing opinions, and showed himself to be an ardent enthusiast of the opposite sex. He lacked money to entertain his girlfriends, but at least his theatrical contacts provided him with endless complimentary tickets to the theatres and cinemas of Melbourne.

It was in July 1929, when he was 20 years old, that Holt delivered, at the college debating society, a paper advocating a closer relationship between Australia and China. China was at that time in turmoil, with Communists and Nationalists, under Chiang Kai-shek, struggling for supremacy. Young Australian Liberals had mounted a 'Hands off China' campaign. Holt went to see the Chinese Consul to request information for his paper. The Consul asked if he could see a copy of his paper when it was finished. Holt obliged. And, according to Anthony Grey, Holt was later asked to tea by the Consul, who told him that a small publishing firm wanted to print his paper on China, and gave him £50 for it. He was urged to write more articles on China and was delighted to oblige. He needed the money and the payments of £50, rising soon to £100, were extremely generous.

In 1931, Grey (who claims to be quoting official Chinese sources) reveals that Holt was asked by his Chinese contact if he would become a member of the Chinese Intelligence Service. His brief seems to have been vague, simply 'to help China's cause'. Holt promptly agreed. After all, there was no hostility between China and Australia, and he was working for Chiang Kai-shek's Nationalists, not for the Communists who might well have been regarded as enemies.

In the following year, Holt set up in a law partnership that quickly prospered, largely due to his old theatrical contacts. His father, now back in Melbourne, also did his best to push

115

business his son's way, in spite of the fact that Harold was refusing to speak to him. The reason for this behaviour sheds an interesting light on Harold's character. When his father returned to Melbourne, he invited Harold to a dinner party, where he found himself sitting next to a beautiful young actress named Lola. Being a fast worker, the young man was soon making advances only to be rebuffed and told that she was in love with his father. The humiliation was like a slap in the face; he walked out of the party and never spoke to his father again. When invited to the wedding of his father and Lola, he ignored the invitation. Later he went so far as to tell new acquaintances that his father was dead.

In December 1931 Harold Holt met Robert Menzies, the distinguished right-wing politician who had attended the same school. They liked one another, and the result was that in 1934 Holt was invited to contest a by-election in Melbourne. His chances seemed minimal for his opponent was an ex-Labour Prime Minister. Holt's charm and spellbinding oratory came close to gaining him the seat. In the following year, at the age of 27, he again stood for the United Australian Party (Liberals) at Fawkner, and gained the seat. On Monday, 23 September 1935, he swore the oath of allegiance.

Holt's socialist sympathies were widely known, but his party was liberal in spirit as well as name. A month after entering parliament, he received a dressing-down from the Prime Minister, Menzies, for attacking the Italian invasion of Abyssinia in terms that sounded distinctly Communist. The young politician learned his lesson and subsequent speeches showed tact and restraint, as well as a thorough grasp of his subject.

Grey states that Holt's activities as a 'spy' did not involve the kind of betrayal of his country that we associate with the names of Kim Philby or Alger Hiss in the U.S.A. He was merely a kind of glorified information officer. His position meant that he had access to information from all over the world. In the 1930s, when the world was seething with political turmoil, such information was worth having. Holt could openly ask questions in parliament on matters that might affect China – such as whether Britain would sell Australia old airforce planes which China urgently wanted to purchase. The answers could play an important, if indirect, part in the complicated chess game of world politics.

A few weeks after the outbreak of World War II, Holt acquired a position that made him even more valuable to the Chinese – he became Minister without Portfolio to the Ministry of Supply and Development. He was still only 31 and known to his friends as something of a playboy – a keen race-goer, a friend of theatre and film personalities, and a frequenter of night clubs (where his preference for wearing a top hat earned him the nickname 'Topper' Holt). His political success made him one of the most desirable bachelors in Australia. Moreover, he was appointed Minister of Air and Civil Aviation in 1940.

Then came an episode that disturbed his Chinese friends. After a snap election, the Liberal Party was returned with a majority of only one. Menzies had to form a coalition and Holt (as the youngest Minister) lost his post and was returned to the back benches. Most politicians would take such a demotion in their stride, but it seemed to shatter Holt. He announced that he was leaving the government to join the army as a private. His Chinese contact, who called himself Mr Wong, tried hard to dissuade him but when Holt insisted he told him to regard himself as temporarily 'deactivated' as an agent. To report on military matters as a soldier would be far more dangerous than as a minister.

In fact, Holt was soon back in government: three ministers were killed in a plane crash and he was subsequently offered the post of Minister of Labour and National Service. He accepted with delight and relief. But the Chinese must have felt that his fit of pique revealed a certain weakness of character.

In 1948, Holt was again 'deactivated' as a result of the new political turmoil in China – with Mao Tse-tung now making an all-out effort to overthrow Chiang Kai-shek. He remained deactivated for three and a half years. At the end of that time, in 1952, his old friend Wong contacted him again and asked him to provide more information. Anthony Grey tells us that Holt did not know that Wong had now defected to the Communists (who had been in power since 1949). So although unaware of it, Holt

117

was working for Mao.

If Grey is correct, the rewards for spying were considerable – around £30,000. Holt's value as a spy increased during the Korean War, and even more so when it became clear that Menzies was grooming him to be the next Prime Minister. When he came to England in 1953 to attend the coronation of Queen Elizabeth II he was made a Privy Councillor.

In the following year, Holt told 'Mr Wong' that he had ceased to sympathize with the Chinese Nationalists, and had decided not to spy for them any more. Three years later Wong was told to admit to Holt that he was working for the Communists, and ask for his help again. Holt had, by this time, discovered that 'Wong' was really a Vice-Consul named Y. M. Liu, and summoned him to a meeting to explain himself. 'Wong' took the opportunity to confess the deception. However, when he left the meeting Holt had agreed to become once more an information gatherer for the Chinese. After all, he was a socialist and the Chinese were preparing to break with Soviet Russia.

According to Grey, the Chinese first became seriously worried about Holt in 1964, when a series of political and personal setbacks seemed to have shaken him as deeply as his loss of the ministerial post in 1940. Not for the first time, the Chinese prepared a contingency plan to 'evacuate' Holt by submarine. But the situation stablized, and an evacuation proved to be unnecessary.

Then, in 1966, Sir Robert Menzies unexpectedly announced his resignation, after 17 years; Holt was appointed Prime Minister. For the first month or so, he was immensely popular. Menzies had been a remote, rather aristocratic figure; Holt was a 'populist' who could set the crowds cheering. He had taken to skin-diving and when he was photographed on a beach with his three beautiful daughters-in-law, the press made remarks about James Bond, and showed a disposition to treat him like a film star.

The honeymoon period was soon over, and things began to turn against him. He was accused of lying to parliament about the use of airforce planes as 'taxis'; he interrupted the maiden speech of a new MP, and was booed and jeered by the whole house. When he rose to his feet and stalked out, his Labour opponent, Gough Whitlam, felt that he had begun to 'dig his own grave'. In May 1967, he was shown a secret file on various Soviet spies in Australia, and was shocked to discover his own code name 'H. K. Bors' among them. For a while, he was terrified that the intelligence services knew all about him. It was then, says Anthony Grey, that he decided the time had come to make a getaway to China. The Chinese, observing the signs of nervous tension and exhaustion, were glad he had made the suggestion before it became necessary for them to step in. So, on that December day in 1967, Holt swam out to a prearranged point off Cheviot Beach, where two Chinese skin divers were waiting. Their inverted 'air bubble' almost escaped them, causing the water to boil and bubble (as Alan Stewart and Mrs Gillespie had observed) but Holt was successfully steered into the air pocket, and propelled by a small undersea vehicle to the escape hatch of the waiting submarine.

Anthony Grey believes this is the incredible story of the escape of Harold Holt. It raises the obvious question: where did he get his information and how much of it can be cross-checked? Grey claims that in May 1983, he was approached by an Australian businessman who wanted his help to publish a book on the true story of Harold Holt. The man had been in the navy when Holt disappeared, and had noted inconsistencies in 'confidential reports' that had crossed his desk. In Baghdad in 1973, a comment by an aide to the Iraqi Oil Minister about a 'high Australian government official' who had sought asylum abroad led him to institute inquiries among business associates in Peking.

The most baffling and unbelievable part of the story is that Peking was apparently willing to tell him the story, albeit in fragments and tantalizing hints. What is more, his own researches seemed to vouch for its truth. In the archives of Melbourne University, he found that original debating paper urging closer friendship between Australia and China. He saw the secret file that terrified Holt so much when he found his own code name in it – and was able to check that Holt had initiated an inquiry about the real name of Mr Wong. The businessman also claimed that the Chinese had showed him photostats of the receipts Holt signed for various sums of money in those early days.

Altogether, it must be admitted that it all sounds very convincing. So many parts of the story can be easily checked that it is hard to see why either the businessman or Mr Grey should lie about them. So it seems that the story of how Harold Holt slipped gradually into the role of a Chinese 'spy' (or information gatherer) is highly plausible.

The question remains, however, as to why the Chinese should want to tell the story. Grey suggests that it may be out of a desire to emphasize that, unlike the Russians, they are not given to 'dirty tricks' and underhand activities. That is, indeed, in keeping with the Chinese character and could well be a part of the answer.

Grey's book itself suggests a rather more likely explanation. According to Grey, some of Holt's government colleagues had their doubts about him. Sooner or later, the story of Holt's spying activities was bound to leak out in Australia. If the Chinese themselves 'leaked' the information and declined to supply the precise corroborative details then their story would be only half-believed. In fact, the reception of Grey's book proved the point: very few reviewers took it seriously. If this was, indeed, the Chinese motive, then they have showed a psychological subtlety worthy of Machiavelli. They have allowed the truth to be told, in the certainty that no one will believe it . . . If Harold Holt was alive to read the book – a point on which the Chinese informant declined to comment – he must have felt totally justified in placing implicit reliance in his old allies and co-conspirators.

THE 'DINGO' BABY

It was 8 o'clock on a warm August evening, and most of the occupants of the camping site below Ayers Rock, the mammoth red-stone landmark that rises out of the desert of central Australia, were engaged in preparing supper. This included 32-year-old Alice Lynne ('Lindy') Chamberlain and her 36-year-old husband Michael, a minister in the Seventh Day Adventist Church. Their elder son, seven-year-old Aidan, was still awake; the other two children, Reagan, four, and Azaria ('Blessed of God'), nine weeks old, were already asleep in the tent.

It was Michael Chamberlain who asked, 'Is that Bubby crying?', and Lindy Chamberlain returned to the tent. A moment later she shouted, 'My God, the dingo's got my baby!' Michael rushed to the tent. The baby's blankets were scattered round the empty carrycot.

Within minutes most of the campers on the site were rushing into the darkness with torches. Lindy explained that, as she approached the tent, she had seen a dingo – a wild dog – walking away from it, with its rear towards her. It had been moving its head from side to side, although she had been unable to see whether it was carrying anything. The night was pitch black, without a breath of wind; although 300 searchers scoured through the scrub, they found nothing. Back in the camp, some women were praying. Lindy Chamberlain was trying to quieten Aidan, who was crying, 'Don't let the dingo eat our baby.' Frank Morris, the local police officer, arrived to organize the search. But he suspected that Azaria Chamberlain was already dead.

By dawn, it was obvious that he was right. Lindy Chamberlain had also come to accept it. Over the radio telephone she told her parents, 'Our baby was killed by a dingo last night.' Then she sobbed.

By mid-morning, the Chamberlains had another problem: their story had caused a nationwide sensation – Baby Stolen by Dingo at Ayers Rock and press and television reporters were beginning to arrive. Michael Chamberlain agreed to talk to them — a decision that was later to arouse some criticism. Meanwhile, Lindy told her story to the police: how her elder son had been in bed when he said he was still hungry. Instead of fetching him some food as he lay in bed, she made the fatal mistake of telling him to come with her; and, since he would be returning in a few minutes, she left the tent flap unzipped. Before the day was out, Michael Chamberlain had already noticed that some people were asking questions in an oddly suspicious way, as if they felt that the idea of a baby being stolen by a dingo was preposterous.

This was not the view of the police. The day after Azaria's disappearance, they began shooting dingos and wild dogs in the area of Ayers Rock, hoping to find the child's remains in the stomach of one of them. They shot several dingos but their search was unsuccessful. On Tuesday, the Chamberlains returned to their home in Mount Isa, Queensland. Their religious faith had given them the strength to accept the tragedy. But there were many people who felt they had accepted it a little too stoically.

In fact, they might have received far more sympathy if they had been less religious. As Seventh Day Adventists, they were regarded as a little 'odd'. Seventh Day Adventists have been described as 'Fundamentalists of Fundamentalists'. Like the Jehovah's Witnesses, they believe in the literal truth of every word of the Bible, and in an imminent return of Christ to earth. Their movement was founded in the first half of the nineteenth century by an American, William Miller, who announced that the end of the world would occur in 1843 or 1844. On 22 October 1844, 20 families sat out all night in Phoenixville, Pennsylvania, waiting for the end, and two children froze to death. That night was known as the Great Disappointment. But the Adventists declared that the Second Coming had been delayed by their failure to recognize Saturday as the Sabbath, and that it could be expected fairly soon. In spite of the Great Disappointment, the sect continued to prosper.

Modern Seventh Day Adventists disapprove of alcohol, gambling, jewellery, cosmetics, cinema and television, with the inevitable consequence that there is a tendency among the worldly to regard them as cranks and 'killjoys'. This helps explain why, instead of receiving universal sympathy and commiseration, the Chamberlains found themselves confronted by a curious hostility after the loss of their baby.

Eight days after Azaria's disappearance, a tourist on the west side of Ayers Rock noticed some clothing; it proved to be a bloodstained stretchsuit, napkin, singlet and booties. Yet there was not the slightest trace of flesh. It looked as if the dingo had removed the baby from the stretchsuit and taken it to its lair. Oddly enough, the singlet was inside out. How could a dingo do that? One local theory was that the dingo had dropped the baby, which had then been taken home by a camp dog, and that the owner of the camp dog, worried about being implicated, had removed the clothes and buried the body. But that still failed to explain why such a person had not simply buried the baby with her clothes on.

The Chamberlains were questioned several times by the police. A rumour began to circulate that she had fallen from a supermarket trolley and become spastic, and that her parents had decided to kill her for this reason. Another rumour was that Azaria meant 'the sacrifice', and that she had been sacrificed on top of Ayers Rock in some gruesome ceremony.

Forensic evidence seemed to throw some doubt on the story about the dingo. A stuffed stretchsuit was dragged across the ground from the camp site to the base of Ayers Rock, then examined by botanists. There were fragments of charcoal in the experimental stretchsuit, as might have been expected, since there had been bush fires in the area. Yet there was no charcoal on Azaria's suit. Forensic tests seemed to indicate that Azaria's clothes had been rubbed in the dust at the base of the rock. A dead goat was put into the baby clothes and thrown into the dingo pen at Adelaide Zoo. The dingo buried the carcass and clothes in various parts of the pen. Forensic experts concluded that the damage caused to the clothing – particularly the teeth-marks – was quite unlike the damage to Azaria's stretchsuit. Moreover, the blood that soaked the stretchsuit seemed to suggest that the baby had been in an upright position during the bleeding. Michael Chamberlain, pursued by journalists who wanted to know what he thought about this suggestion that his baby had not been taken by a dingo, admitted that it was possible that a human being had carried Azaria off, 'but he or she would have been a maniac'. But where was the baby? It seemed unlikely that a dingo had eaten every morsel of a 9lb baby.

The inquest opened in Alice Springs in December, and moved to Ayers Rock. By that time, the Chamberlains were living in an atmosphere of continual hostility – there were even death threats. Many people simply doubted that a small wild dog would steal a nine-week-old baby. And when the police forensic laboratory announced that the holes in the garment had been made with an instrument like a pair of scissors, the Australian public began to feel that there was more in this case than met the eye. On Wednesday, 18 February 1981 Coroner Barritt startled everyone by announcing that because of the widespread interest in the case, he had granted permission for television to film the findings of the inquest. But Australians who hoped for some sensational revelation, or accusation, were disappointed when the coroner found that Azaria Chamberlain had met her death through a wild dingo. He added that it was untrue that Azaria meant 'sacrifice in the wilderness'.

The debate continued. In September that year the police were ordered to reopen their investigations. In November, a supreme court judge ordered a new inquest. It opened on 14 December 1981. Just before the inquest, the police received a letter from an anonymous couple who claimed that they had seen a dingo carrying what they thought was a doll, and that when one of them threw a stone at the dog, it dropped its burden, which they found to be a badly mutilated child. The couple decided to bury the baby, so the parents would not see it in this condition; they undressed it, and later got rid of the clothes at Ayers Rock. But the writers could not be located.

At the inquest, Michael Chamberlain was asked whether he had cleaned blood out of the car. He agreed that he may have cleaned 'some blood', but insisted that it was not much. Lindy was asked why she had sent a bloodstained tracksuit – which she had worn on the night of the baby's disappearance – to the cleaners. When a policeman told how he had unbolted the front seats of the car and found bloodstains on the cross section, the court sensed that this inquest was, in fact, a trial of the Chamberlains. This became even clearer when Joy Kuhl, a forensic biologist, told how she had discovered fetal bloodstains on a pair of nail scissors, and on the inside of a yellow container found in the car. But the most sensational evidence came from a British expert in legal medicine, Professor James Cameron. He had been sent the baby's clothing at the London Hospital Medical College, and his examination had led him to conclude that the blood on the stretchsuit suggested that it had flowed down from above. He also commented that the holes in the stretchsuit had been made with scissors, and that he had been surprised at the absence of teeth-marks or of animal saliva around the neck of the suit. And when he added that ultra violet light had revealed a bloodstained handprint on the stretchsuit – a print too large to be a child's but too small for a man – it was obvious that the finger of guilt was now pointing at Lindy Chamberlain.

When the inquest resumed after Christmas 1981, Mr Desmond Sturgess, the barrister appointed to help the coroner, finally made the accusation that everyone was expecting. He believed that Azaria had been killed in the family car, and her body concealed in a camera bag. The coroner then committed Lindy Chamberlain for trial on a murder charge, and Michael Chamberlain was charged as an accessory after the fact.

The trial of Lindy Chamberlain began on 13 September 1982, and the prosecuting counsel, Ian Barker QC, announced that he would attempt to prove that Azaria Chamberlain died of a cut throat while Lindy Chamberlain was in the front passenger seat of the car. The prosecution case was that Lindy Chamberlain had taken the baby from the tent and into the front seat of the car, where she had cut Azaria's throat. The case depended largely on forensic evidence. It lacked one vitally important element – a reason why Lindy Chamberlain, mother of a happy family, should have murdered her own baby.

The defence called experts who disagreed that the stains found in the car were fetal haemoglobin, and a dental expert

125

argued that the holes found in the stretchsuit were caused by an animal's teeth. Lindy Chamberlain's doctor testified that she was not suffering from post-natal depression after the birth of Azaria. A mother testified that a dingo had tried to grab her 12-year-old child by the elbow at Ayers Rock on the evening before Azaria disappeared. A Geelong pathologist flatly denied that the bloodstains on the tracksuit could have been caused by a head injury or a cut to the throat. And he denied that there was a bloodstained handprint on the suit.

The one point that emerged very clearly from the trial was that the evidence of the various experts could not be accepted as scientifically unshakeable. The defence made the telling point that if Lindy Chamberlain had murdered her baby, surely she would have claimed that the child had been carried off in the dingo's mouth? From the beginning she had stuck to her story of only seeing the dingo moving away into the darkness.

The trial lasted for seven weeks. When the jury returned from six and a half hours of deliberation, the foreman announced that their verdict was unanimous: the Chamberlains were guilty as charged. Thereupon the judge, Mr Justice Muirhead, told Lindy Chamberlain, 'There is only one sentence I can pass upon you – hard labour for life.' She was taken away to Berrimah Jail where, within a few days, she would give birth to another daughter. Michael Chamberlain was sentenced to an 18-month suspended sentence.

When, in April 1983, the Federal Court rejected Lindy Chamberlain's appeal, it seemed that the Dingo Baby Case was finally over. But soon Lindy Chamberlain support groups were formed all over the country. In February 1984 the High Court of Australia rejected Lindy Chamberlain's appeal. But soon after that a family described how, eight weeks before the disappearance of Azaria, a dingo at Ayers Rock had dragged their child from the car. The chief ranger from the Ayers Rock district, Derek Roff, wrote to the *National Times* saying he was convinced the dingoes might well attack a child. Thirty-one scientists signed an open letter protesting about the conclusions drawn from Joy Kuhl's evidence. A psychologist who had examined Lindy Chamberlain in prison stated on television that he was unable to account for criminal behaviour on her part, and affirmed his conviction that she was totally innocent.

Although these pleas had no effect on the authorities, Lindy Chamberlain was released from prison on 7 February 1986 on the grounds that she had paid her debt to society. She had served just over two years of her life sentence. After her release, she announced that she and her husband would continue the fight to establish their innocence. Part of that campaign was a long television interview with reporter Ray Martin, in which she spoke frankly about the charges against her, and of the reasons why so many had felt her to be guilty – her apparently cool demeanour during the inquests and in television appearances. She pointed out the obvious – that if a mother who has lost her baby is then faced with a campaign of rumour and innuendo, her reaction is bound to be one of anger, and she is not likely to look bereaved and miserable. During the course of the programme, one of the jurors who had been responsible for the guilty verdict announced that she had since become convinced that Lindy Chamberlain was innocent. She went on to admit that many of the other jurors had felt doubts but said that the forensic evidence had seemed conclusive.

In retrospect, it is difficult to see why Lindy Chamberlain was ever suspected of murder. No one disputed that the Chamberlains were a happy and affectionate family unit, and no one was ever able to allege any kind of motive. It seems fairly certain that the Lindy Chamberlain case will be regarded as Australia's most tragic miscarriage of justice.

It was later announced that Lindy Chamberlain had been pardoned. This followed the tabling in Darwin of the Inquiry conducted by Mr Justice Morling in which he found that the evidence was such that he could not rule out the child having been taken by a wild dog.

Mrs Chamberlain said she would now seek complete exoneration by the quashing of the conviction.

DONALD CROWHURST

Donald Crowhurst was 15 when he and his parents returned to England from India in 1947. He was bright, mathematically inclined, and 'on the pushy side' according to a school chum at Tilehurst, on the fringe of Reading, where his family settled.

His favourite people seem to have been those who refused to accept defeat. Men like Hillary and Tensing were his heroes, and when Everest was conquered on Coronation Day 1953 he said he felt frustrated because he believed there was nothing left of comparable achievement to be tackled. He was in the RAF then and accepted a challenge of dubious merit from fellow officers – to ride a motorcycle at speed through a Nissen hut full of sleeping aircraftmen in the middle of the night. Dangerous havoc naturally resulted and he resigned his commission as a consequence of the escapade and transferred to the army. Again he took up a foolish challenge and tried to steal a car after a long pub crawl. He was caught and once more resigned the service – this time for married life in a 'semi' in the river port of Bridgwater, Somerset, where he got a job as an electronics engineer.

'We all thought marriage would take that aggressive look off his face,' said his Tilehurst chum. Indeed in 1957 he soberly settled down and concentrated on the invention of a new navigational aid to shipping – the Navicator – which his mother, now a widow, helped to finance. Another apparent sign of his abandonment of youthful indiscretions was his adoption of the tranquil leisure pursuit of 'messing about in boats', for which he'd acquired a 20-foot dinghy named *Pot of Gold*.

The New Elizabethan Age had begun with the conquest of Everest. As the 1950s reached into the 1960s the challenges and triumphs came thick and fast, giving the lie to Crowhurst's gloomy prognostication. Olympic Games produced new records; a new 'fastest crossing' of the Atlantic by the liner *United States* was achieved; the International Geophysical Year promised the launch of satellites into space and Yuri Gagarin became the first man to orbit the earth in a spacecraft; and on terra firma Jack Brabham captured the driving championship of the world in a car of his own construction. On the oceans tremendous enthusiasm was raised by the yachtsmen Francis Chichester and Alec Rose, both of whom circumnavigated the globe in tiny craft and were rewarded with knighthoods – Chichester's at Greenwich, whither the Queen made her way specially for the dubbing, as her namesake had made her way to Deptford in 1581 for the knighting of Francis Drake after his circumnavigation in *Golden Hind*. Long-distance sailing made a special appeal to a wide public because radio linkage and aerial sightings could keep track of the sailors, keeping them in touch with the world at large.

In 1968, *The Sunday Times* promoted a contest that was at once a circulation spinner and a tribute to the spirit of the age. Citing Chichester and Rose as exemplars, the newspaper agreed that there was little left of the world to explore, but pointed out that there were still increasingly daring ways to encircle it. They offered a prize of £5,000 for the fastest circumnavigation of the globe by a singlehanded yachtsman, and a Golden Globe trophy for the first sailor to return regardless of speed. There were, of course, conditions – among them that there should be no help accepted from other vessels and that there should be no putting in to any port for repairs. It was to be a loner's race.

Donald Crowhurst had been fortunate in finding a market for his Navicator device through Pye Radio, which bought up the Crowhurst firm and gave him some capital for the new enterprise that now seized his imagination. Novice though he was at sailing he got it into his head that he could win the *Sunday Times* contest. Not, of course, in *Pot of Gold*, which was scarcely bigger than a rowing boat, but in a craft that he would have designed and built specially, leaving nothing to chance in either the design or the construction.

He did not realize until he started to cost the venture that he would need a great deal more capital than he had available, bearing in mind that he had the domestic problem of providing for his wife and four children and the mortgage during his absence (which he optimistically estimated at eight months) as well as fitting himself out for the voyage. Somewhat deflated, he tried to save the cost of the boat by borrowing Chichester's

129

yacht *Gipsy Moth IV*, but without success. Meanwhile, time was running out.

The start had to be made in British waters between the beginning of June and the end of October 1968. Compromise and a philanthropic businessman, Stanley Best, came to the rescue. Best and the BBC led the sponsors who had been sold on the idea of backing a cheeky challenger competing with experienced yachtsmen such as Chay Blyth, Robin Knox-Johnston, and Nigel Tetley. Rodney Hallworth, who handled PR for Teignmouth in Devon, saw a great deal of publicity coming the town's way if he acted as Crowhurst's agent. He chipped in with the sort of news stories and gossip paragraphs that built up the image of the tough little fighter against formidable odds.

The nationals picked up the press releases and headlines like WHACK 'EM, DON! proliferated. For weeks there were 'work in progress' photographs of the building of the boat in the Norfolk yards, and features about comparable heroes who had overcome all to achieve fame and glory. It was the stuff dreams were made of for Donald Crowhurst.

He had decided that in the matter of design he would go all out for speed, since that would give him two chances – to be either first home or fastest; or, with an inordinate amount of luck, both. 'Nothing daunts Donald' was the headline message.

Expert sailors were invited to give their views on the trimaran ketch that gradually took shape. The consensus was that a triple-hulled boat was a daring venture for an inexperienced sailor. There could well be problems caused by the lack of a keel to give the boat stability. Also, there was much head shaking over the completion date to ensure meeting the deadline for the start of the race. Boat building is not an activity that should be hurried. But hurried it had to be – and with alarming consequences: some of the hatches leaked, and on the trial runs excessive vibration necessitated several returns to the boatyard for trimming and adjustments.

The three days Crowhurst had budgeted for the maiden voyage to Teignmouth stretched into a fortnight. He arrived there putting on a show of debonair calm for the press that must have belied his inner state of tension, for he had only a day to

Above left: Dr John Bodkin Adams, the prosperous Eastbourne doctor suspected of murdering many of his patients. He was however charged only with the murder of Mrs Edith Morrell, and the trial opened at the Old Bailey on 18 March 1957.

Above right: Mrs Edith Morrell. She had promised to leave Adams a Rolls Royce and a case of silver cutlery.

Below right: Janice Weston, at 36 already a wealthy and outstanding company law specialist, was brutally murdered on 10 September 1983.

Left: A police reconstruction at the scene of the murder on the A1.

Below left: Janice Weston's silver-coloured Alfa Romeo was found in north-west London, but yielded no incriminating evidence.

Above left: **Charles Lindbergh became the idol of America after his flight across the Atlantic in *Spirit of St Louis* in May 1927.**

Above right: **Bruno Richard Hauptmann, the 35-year-old carpenter charged with the Lindbergh baby murder, seen here in court on 10 January 1935.**

Left: **Charles Junior, the adored child of the Lindberghs, aged 19 months. These pictures were taken shortly before his abduction in March 1932.**

Right: **Hauptmann, convicted in February 1935 of the kidnapping and murder of the Lindbergh baby, in the death cell at Flemington, New Jersey. Hauptmann vehemently denied his guilt to the end, and his case has continued to attract controversy to the present day.**

Above: **A wooden plank concealing a gun and $860 of the Lindberghs' ransom was found in Hauptmann's garage – a damning piece of evidence. Suspicion remains however that some of the evidence may have been planted.**

Above: William Herbert Wallace was arrested on 2 February 1931 for the murder of his wife. Could this mild-mannered man have committed a bloody murder inside 20 minutes and immediately thereafter have been travelling unconcernedly around the Liverpool suburbs unstained and self-possessed?

Left: Mrs Julia Wallace, whose body was found by her husband in their home. William Wallace became the prime suspect, was tried and found guilty. The conviction, however, was quashed by the Court of Criminal Appeal. Many students of crime have considered the Wallace case to be the perfect murder; but more recent evidence has pointed to the identity of the true murderer.

Below: Wallace leaving court after his acquittal. He was however to die of cancer within two years.

Above: The cross-examination of Mr Bartlett by Edward Clarke. The *left* inset shows Adelaide Bartlett, and the *right* the Reverend Dyson, her best friend who turned prosecution witness.

Below left: Lizzie Borden, accused of murdering her father and step-mother at Falls River, Massachusetts, on 4 August 1892. The brutality of the murders, committed with an axe, has made them legendary in the annals of crime.

Below right: A contemporary drawing of the Lizzie Borden trial shows the defendant with her counsel, ex-Governor Robinson. Robinson proved an excellent defender. Shrewd and worldly, he was nevertheless able to address a jury of his own state in the homespun terms that won their confidence. A verdict of Not Guilty was returned.

Above: Professor John Cartland, murdered while on holiday in France.

Right: Jeremy Cartland and his sister fly to Marseilles for further questioning.

Above: A graphic description in *Police News* of the fate of the Ripper's fifth victim. The Whitechapel murders in the autumn of 1888 caused unprecedented panic and formed the basis of a continuing legend.

Above: Harold Holt (left) with Harold Wilson, and their wives, at No. 10 Downing Street during the new Prime Minister's visit to Britain in July 1966.

Right: Holt soon became a personality, taking up skin diving and other pursuits. He was a powerful swimmer, yet he disappeared suddenly on 17 December 1967 while swimming in the sea off Cheviot Beach near Melbourne. The astounding yet well authenticated claim is now made that he was picked up by a Chinese submarine.

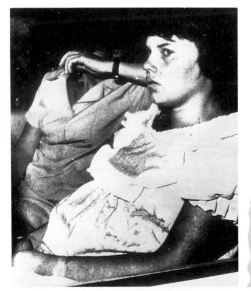

Left: Lindy Chamberlain, heavily pregnant, was found guilty of murdering her daughter, Azaria. She was subsequently pardoned however, and is now seeking complete exoneration.

Left: Rudolf Hess, prisoner no. 6 in Spandau Jail in 1982. There had been doubts about whether the prisoner was in fact Hitler's deputy, and further mystery now surrounds him as a result of the circumstances of his death.

Above: Hess's Me 110 after it crashed in Scotland in May 1941. The pilot had bailed out 30 miles from his target – the Duke of Hamilton's estate.

Above: To Robert Maxwell the external trappings of being a very rich and powerful man meant a great deal, and in his often tasteless posturings he was perhaps compensating for the poverty of his youth. One of his prized possessions was the <u>Lady Ghislaine</u>, a 155-ft yacht named after his youngest daughter, which he had bought from the Khashoggi brothers for £15 million. True to his precept that possessions only become status symbols after they are seen, he poses in this picture with his 'toy' in the background.

makc final preparations, load his stores, and check his radio, tape recorder, camera, and Navicator.

The press, of course, loved it, and built up the drama of the preliminary race against time. The hero was pictured in nautical rig, a book called *The Great Yacht Race* on the chart table (it was the story of millionaires racing their yachts across the Atlantic in 1866), and confidence brimming in his eyes as he pointed proprietorially to the name painted on the prow: *Teignmouth Electron*. They were the last pictures he posed for. He was towed across the bar and set sail with only nine hours to go before the deadline of midnight on 31 October. He was now alone with the world before him.

Radio transmissions gave cheering reports of his progress. In early December he announced that he had sailed 243 miles in a single day, and Rodney Hallworth's publicity began to whisper of the possibility of Crowhurst being a winner, five of the original nine entrants having withdrawn for one reason or another. Only Robin Knox-Johnston, the French yachtsman Bernard Moitessier, and Commander Nigel Tetley (also in a trimaran) remained as competitors. Hopes of possible success seemed to be reinforced in January, when the news was that Crowhurst was southeast of Gough Island in the south Atlantic and had logged 1,086 miles in the previous week. Radio stations in the vicinity of Cape Horn, he said, should prepare to listen for his transmissions – though for the moment he was closing down his transmitter to effect some repairs to the generator.

There followed a prolonged silence.

Tetley rounded the Horn on 20 March and Robin Knox-Johnston was sighted on the homeward leg of the voyage on 6 April. Moitessier had abandoned his attempt, so there were only the three entrants left. Of Crowhurst nothing more was heard until the end of April, when he reported being in the area of the Falkland Islands.

The long silence had caused much anxiety, and some suspicion. Chichester, who was chairman of the judges, said publicly that a lot of explaining had to be done to account for it. Nevertheless, Teignmouth was preparing for a hero's welcome even before it was learned that Tetley had been forced to abandon ship on 21

May and that, it was presumed, Crowhurst and Knox-Johnston were racing for a neck-and-neck finish. This was the stuff of real drama. 'May the best man win' was the 'in' cliché of the day.

But drama of a more tragic kind was to be the payoff.

On 10 July the mailboat *Picardy*, heading for Florida, found *Teignmouth Electron* abandoned in mid-Atlantic. No sign of Crowhurst, but nothing else untoward. The life raft was intact, the radio in working order; there was no shortage of food or water, the logbooks were displayed – with the last entry date nine days earlier.

'It was like the *Mary Celeste* over again,' said Captain Box of *Picardy*.

What clues there were to Crowhurst's disappearance had to be pieced together from the logbooks, the tape recorder, the camera, and the damning evidence that was submitted by the coastguard station at Montevideo, where Crowhurst had been logged on 19 March as heading for Buenos Aires for repairs – an act that alone would have disqualified him.

It was a depressing picture that resulted – a picture of a man beset by vainglory who had entered a contest in the preparation for which care had been sacrificed to haste, and which was right out of his league so far as seamanship was concerned. As the log revealed, cursory attention had been given to the most important matters, and he had found himself lacking essential spares and without even a working pump to rid the boat of the water that constantly leaked into the 'watertight' compartments. (The boxes containing spares had been forgotten; they were found later in the boathouse at Teignmouth.) 'With so much wrong with the boat,' he had written, 'it would perhaps be foolish to continue. I will . . . think about the alternatives open to me.' And that was only two weeks after leaving Teignmouth.

The logs, which had to be accurate to ensure proper navigation, also told a very different story of the miles sailed from that of the boastful broadcasts. For weeks his average had been no more than 50 miles a day. This revelation was followed by another indication of mind-wracking indecision: 'Racked by the growing awareness that I must soon decide whether I can go on in the face of the actual situation . . .'

The honourable alternative would, of course, have been for him to quit. There would have been no disgrace in throwing in his hand; but Donald Crowhurst could not bear to be a loser – not even a gallant one. He continued to cook up the glowing reports of his progress in the hope that some miracle would aid him. Indeed the hint of such a miracle came when he detected nothing in the worldwide broadcasts of the contestants' progress to indicate that it was known that he had put in to Buenos Aires for repairs. Evidently the coastguards had failed to notify their inland headquarters. Perhaps some gods were on his side after all . . . Lie low, keep radio silence, and log weather reports as if he had received them from radio stations on his homeward-bound course while he was really lying becalmed with numerous technical troubles to contend with: that was the cheating tale the logs seemed to tell. But it was a desperate move, one that he must have known would be discovered as false on inspection of the logs by the judges. So, it was conjectured, in his approaching mental breakdown he started keeping a false log as well as the true one, perhaps to conceal his failure even from himself, and in the confusion of his mind could not distinguish between truth and falsehood.

He evidently sailed on as best he could, in his lucid moments encouraging his own and the public's belief in a neck-and-neck finish when he was still 1,000 miles from home in mid-Atlantic. It remains a mystery to this day why he did not radio for help. His fraud would have been discovered, but the race was lost anyway. It seems uncharacteristic of his audacious nature that he should not have tried to turn his deception into a sort of victory with stories of hazards risked and perils triumphantly overcome.

It was assumed that, burdened with guilt and failure to satisfy his ego, he abandoned ship and life too. His body was never recovered, and theories were advanced suggesting that he might have been picked up and taken perhaps to South America to begin a new life. Whatever his fate, a charitable view of his attempted cheat was taken, and an appeal fund was launched for his family. The unrivalled winner, Robin Knox-Johnston, contributed his £5,000 prize money.

IDENTITIES: TRUE OR FALSE?

THE RIDDLE OF RUDOLF HESS

The mystery surrounding Rudolf Hess is not just a question of whether the old man who lingered for so long in Spandau Prison, last of the Nazi war criminals, was or was not the real one-time Deputy-Führer of the Third Reich. It goes much deeper than that, to the problem of what may have happened to Rudolf Hess, which in itself leads to many other questions.

Hess was born in 1894 in Alexandria, where his father was a businessman. He spent the first 14 years of his life in Egypt and went to a local German school. When the family returned to Germany he was sent to a boarding school at Bad Godesberg on the Rhine, and as soon as World War I began he volunteered for service in a Bavarian infantry regiment. He became a lieutenant and was wounded three times: by shrapnel in his left hand and upper arm in June 1916, in the left upper arm in July 1917, and finally, in October 1917, he was seriously wounded by a bullet through his left lung. Although this put an end to his active infantry service, after four months in hospital he recovered sufficiently to join the Flying Corps and complete his training as an officer pilot just before being demobilized in December 1918. The bullet through his lung left entrance and exit scars and thereafter he suffered from shortness of breath and attacks of bronchitis.

In the general confusion after the war, Hess became deeply involved in politics. In May 1919 he was wounded yet again, this time in the leg, during the street rioting that drove the Communists out of power in Bavaria. In 1920 he became an undergraduate at Munich University, and in April of that year joined the National Socialist German Workers' Party (NSDAP) – the Nazis – as one of its founder members under the leadership of an Austrian named Adolf Hitler.

Hess fell completely under Hitler's spell and became his loyal and devoted lieutenant. On one occasion in a Munich beer cellar, someone threw a beer mug at Hitler. Hess deliberately stood in its path and received a permanent scar on his head. He marched beside Hitler in the abortive Munich Rising in November 1923, when the Bavarian State Police opened fire and killed a number of National Socialists. Hitler was arrested and imprisoned in the fortress of Landsberg. Hess escaped, but returned and gave himself up when he heard what had happened to Hitler. He joined Hitler in Landsberg, and being well educated gave the future Dictator of Germany invaluable assistance in the writing of *Mein Kampf*, which became the Nazi bible.

These historical details have their place in the riddle because the scars left by war wounds and differences of political opinion provide positive identification, and it is important to establish the elationship between Hess and Hitler. Hess was a gifted administrator and organizer, the true architect of the Nazi Party, a skilled negotiator and one of the few men in whom Hitler confided.

In 1927 Hess married Ilse Pröhl, and their son, Wolf-Rüdiger, was born ten years later. By making Hess the head of the Central Party Commission in 1932, Hitler put him in charge of all political activities, and when Hitler became Chancellor in 1933 he appointed Hess as his Deputy. Hess now had enormous power in every field of State affairs, yet he lived frugally and without ostentation. He neither smoked nor drank, was a vegetarian and very careful about what he ate. Although he took homoeopathic drugs there is no doubt that in May 1941, the critical month in the story, he was in excellent physical and mental health. He had various obsessions: a hatred of Jews and Communists, but to him, Soviet Russia was the real enemy.

He came to the conclusion that if peace could be made with England, Germany would be free to deal properly with the Russians. His close friend Albrecht Haushofer knew various prominent people in England, and Hess began to investigate the possibility of meeting one or more of them on neutral ground. One of Haushofer's acquaintances was the Duke of Hamilton who, though distinguished in many ways, did not possess any political influence at that time. In September 1940 Hess wrote to the Duke of Hamilton, through an intermediary in Portugal, suggesting a meeting in Lisbon, but the letter was intercepted by the British Security Service and was not seen by the intended recipient until March 1941. In the meantime, other negotiations were in train with Dr Carl Burckhardt, President of the Swiss Red Cross, to bring about a meeting with the British in a neutral country. There was, therefore, no apparent need for Hess to do what he did on 10 May 1941.

On that day, accompanied by one of his adjutants, Karlheinz Pintsch, he drove the 35 miles from his house in Munich to the airfield at Augsburg, beside one of the Messerschmitt factories, wearing Luftwaffe (airforce) uniform. During the previous six months he had flown a considerable number of training sorties from this airfield, and was well known to everyone there as a skilful and experienced pilot. He found that someone had removed his leather flying suit from its hook in the changing room, so he borrowed one clearly marked with the name of its owner, Helmut Kaden. He climbed into a Messerschmitt 110D which was not fitted with additional long-range fuel tanks, and took off.

A fighter aircraft of that type had a range of about 850 miles in optimum conditions; the distance from Augsburg to Glasgow in a straight line is about 850 miles. But a direct flight would mean crossing the east coast of England in the area of Hull and risking attack by fighters for the next 200 miles. If it was Hess's intention to fly to Scotland to see the Duke of Hamilton, he would have to make a detour over the North Sea – and probably run out of fuel.

He left Augsburg at 5.45 p.m. and was tracked by German radar all the way to the coast northeast of Amsterdam, which he crossed at 7.30 p.m. Two hours and 40 minutes later, at 10.10 p.m., radars on the Northumberland coast picked up a single aircraft approaching from the east. Flying due west and identified as a Messerschmitt 110, it was tracked on a somewhat strange

136

course over Scotland until it crashed about an hour later near the village of Eaglesham, south of Glasgow. The pilot came down by parachute, was arrested by a local farmer to whom he gave his name as Hauptmann (Captain) Alfred Horn, and then later said he was Hitler's Deputy, Rudolf Hess, and wished to see the Duke of Hamilton. He had intended to parachute into the grounds of Dungavel House, the Duke's seat, but had missed his target by 30 miles.

After deep research and meticulous checking, the story of Hess and the pilot who landed in Scotland has been set down by Mr Hugh Thomas, a consultant surgeon, in his fascinating book *The Murder of Rudolph Hess*. In 1973, when serving in the British Military Hospital, Berlin, as an officer in the Royal Army Medical Corps, he was required to make two examinations of the man known as Rudolf Hess, Prisoner No. 7 in Spandau. His painstaking, five-year investigation and his book were the direct result of those two examinations.

As a surgeon with considerable experience of gunshot wounds — gained in Northern Ireland — Mr Thomas makes the point that the scars of wounds such as those suffered by Hess, and confirmed by his army record of service, do not disappear, and there was no trace of them on the body of Prisoner No.7. His careful comparison of what was known of Hess before 10 May 1941, and the physical and mental characteristics of the man in Spandau, revealed discrepancies so obvious as to leave him in no doubt that the man who took off from Augsburg was not the man who landed in Scotland.

Hess was a fussy vegetarian: Prisoner No.7, code-named Jonathan while a prisoner of war in England, ate anything and everything voraciously. Hess was a neat, fastidious man, one of the few so-called 'gentlemen' (implying reasonable manners and education) in the Nazi hierarchy: Jonathan ate like an animal. Hess was fit and mentally stable: Jonathan was excessively thin and had to remain in the care of psychiatrists. Hess had a gap between his two front teeth: Jonathan had no gap. Hess's lung wound caused him respiratory problems: Jonathan, when allowed to go on escorted country walks, could out-distance his companions up steep hills and never suffered from bronchitis.

137

Admittedly, Frau Ilse Hess said that the handwriting of the man in Spandau was that of her husband, but added later she had no specimens dated before May 1941 because Rudolf always telephoned during any period of separation. It is significant that Jonathan refused to see her or her son for 28 years after his landing in Scotland, that he suffered from attacks of amnesia when questioned about the past, and when he finally agreed to see his wife she commented at once on the change in his voice – it was so much deeper. Increasing age has exactly the opposite effect on vocal chords.

The man who parachuted into Scotland had no identification papers of any kind. He produced some photographs which he said were of himself as a child; he also had two visiting cards in the names of Albrecht Haushofer and his father Karl Haushofer; and he had an envelope, postmarked Munich, and addressed to Alfred Horn. He also had a Leica camera later identified as belonging to Frau Hess. There was no name inside his leather flying suit.

As a result of Mr Thomas's research, it would seem that the real Rudolf Hess vanished into the North Sea and that Jonathan, his physical but by no means his mental double, in a different aircraft, possibly from Norway, took his place. He had no identity papers because they had gone down into the sea with Hess.

But how and why did Hess disappear, and why did his double, assumed at his death to be about 93, continue to play the part of Hess and endure more than 40 years of imprisonment? Why didn't he say who he was? The lack of scars on Jonathan's body would appear to be conclusive. Why did Hess try to fly to Scotland in the first place? Why did Göring, known to have been a bitter enemy of the real Hess, appear to be so friendly when sitting beside 'Hess' during the long Nuremberg Trial? Why didn't the British ever take advantage of the arrival of Hess for propaganda that could have been immensely damaging to the Third Reich?

There are many questions left unanswered, although Mr Thomas has tried to tackle most of them. To take the last question first: if the impostor was subjected to the standard interrogation by MI5 experts, his cover would have been blown in about five minutes. It may be that MI5 and the Government knew he was not Hess – certain relevant files have been carefully 'weeded', others are not available and, significantly, precautions were taken to ensure Hess was never photographed while he was in England.

The only clue to the disappearance of the real Hess is in a book called *The First and the Last*, the memoirs of Adolf Galland who commanded fighter squadrons in Holland at the time. He says Göring rang him up 'early in the evening' of 10 May 1941, told him the Deputy Führer had gone mad, was flying to England and must be brought down. According to Galland, he scrambled a few aircraft without giving them a mission; they failed to find anything and returned. Galland took steps to avoid seeing Mr Thomas when he tried to check this. The inference – and it is no more than that – is that Hess was seen and shot down. The substitution of a double presupposes the existence of a carefully prepared plot, because the double had to be briefed, learn Hess's background, practise his handwriting, and so on. So what lay behind this plot?

Mr Thomas suggests it was all inspired by Himmler, author of numerous plots against Hitler. The removal of Hess would in effect be the removal of the brains behind the Nazi Party – and anyone who reads the memoirs of Walter Schellenberg, the man responsible for Nazi Intelligence, will know that nothing was too fantastic for a Nazi plotter. But why go to such lengths in dealing with Hess? It was so easy to arrange fatal accidents in the Third Reich; why go to all the bother of sending Hess's double to Scotland? Presumably because Himmler had some good reason for prolonging the belief that Hess was still alive.

But the theory of Himmler's plot raises all sorts of other questions: how could Himmler have had the foreknowledge of Hess's intentions in time to find, brief and train a double, and transport him to another country so that he could take Hess's place at such short notice? Furthermore, in 1941 Hitler's standing in the German nation was higher than it had ever been, so why should Himmler, whose general appearance was so mild and inoffensive, plot against him, especially when there were

139

rivals like Heydrich and Göring to compete with?

There is a possible answer to the first question in the part that may have been played by Karlheinz Pintsch, the adjutant Hess trusted. He could have been one of Himmler's many agents. Pintsch could have obtained the photographs, the visiting cards and the camera belonging to Frau Hess that were in the possession of the double when he arrived in Scotland. He could also have taken Hess's flying suit from the changing room in Augsburg. In the foreword to Mr Thomas's book, Rebecca West makes the point that the Nazis kept a stable of doubles, for use when the need arose. A man closely resembling Hess physically could well have been spotted before the war began and it would have been a matter of routine for him to acquire the skills and attributes of the man he might have to impersonate at very short notice. Amnesia provided the excuse when he could not answer questions.

Himmler was responsible for the security of high-ranking Nazis. He moved in a mysterious way, and it is more than likely Hess never knew he had a double. But did Himmler plot against Hitler before the tide had turned? After the defeat of the Afrika Korps and the disaster at Stalingrad in 1942 the tide flowed strongly against Hitler, and there was more than one attempt to assassinate him. But were there any plots before that? We do not know for certain, but we do know that for all his apparent mildness, Himmler was a ruthlessly ambitious man as well as a mass-murderer on an unprecedented scale. He had very little time for Hitler and thought he was mad. Himmler controlled the Schutzstaffeln, the SS, which made him the most powerful man in Germany. Walter Schellenberg implies in his memoirs that he was a compulsive plotter.

Sir Winston Churchill in *The Grand Alliance* devotes half a dozen pages to the story of Hess in which there is no suggestion of doubt about his identity. Churchill had made up his mind on the subject and would not be persuaded otherwise.

Why didn't the double speak up, say who he really was and reveal the plot? Himmler had killed himself before the Nuremberg Trial began, and at any time during imprisonment in England, or during the trial, this *doppel-gänger* could have told the truth to the British or Americans, saying he was the victim of a Himmler plot, and asked for asylum. This, perhaps, is the real riddle of Rudolf Hess – the enigma of his double. Mr Thomas explains it by referring to *Sippschaft* – meaning literally 'kin' or 'kindred' – Himmler's system of exterminating a whole family when one member of it was disloyal to the Party. He feels this threat hung over Hess's double and ensured his silence.

Perhaps he is right. Perhaps the old man in Spandau was not Hess, but if he wasn't, surely there must have been some more powerful reason for his silence. Surely, by the time of his death he had outlived his would-be executioners – or had he? We shall probably never know.

Even in death Hess has managed to add to the riddle; did he hang himself or was he helped out of this world: and what has happened to his body?

To say he hanged, or was helped to hang, himself is not strictly accurate since hanging implies suspension from a rope, cord or wire round the neck – the Nazis hanged Admiral Canaris, wartime head of the German Intelligence Service (*Abwehr*), with piano wire in Flossenberg Prison. Hess was garotted with a length of flex, and his death was announced officially on 17 August 1987. His body had been found in the garden pavilion of Spandau Prison, in Berlin, where he had been the sole inmate for the past 21 years. A length of flex had been looped round his neck and tied to the handle of a window. He had been sitting in an armchair and the flex had strangled him when the chair was tilted to one side. Two autopsies failed to establish whether he actually killed himself or was helped to do so, and there were stories, at the time, that Hess at the age of 93 was incapable, physically, of killing himself.

There is, however, the evidence of Pastor Charles Gabel, the French military chaplain at Spandau, who had known Hess for 9 years and had talked to him privately for three hours every week, to the effect that Hess had a deep-rooted fear of lapsing into senility. It is also known that when Pastor Roehrig succeeded Gabel as prison chaplain it used to take Hess several minutes to realize who the new pastor was when he came to visit. Perhaps

141

Hess regarded this as an indication of the symptoms he dreaded. Thus it is neither unlikely nor impossible that Hess did in fact kill himself, but we don't know for certain.

But what has happened to Hess's body?

Some years before his death, during one of Gabel's visits, Hess gave him a handwritten note which constituted his will. In it, Hess nominated his son, Wolf-Rüdiger, his solicitor Alfred Seidl and Gabel himself as his executors, and stated that he wanted to be buried beside his parents and his brother in the churchyard at Wunsiedel in Bavaria, and the service was to be a simple one, conducted by Gabel.

The time and date of Hess's funeral was fixed for 2 p.m. on Wednesday 26 August, 9 days after his death on the 17th. Pastor Gabel arranged with Hess's family to go to Munich on Monday, spend the night in a hotel, go to Wunsiedel on Tuesday to make the final arrangements, spend the night there and take the funeral service on the following day.

Matters were somewhat complicated by the fact that Wolf-Rüdiger had just had a stroke, had been taken to hospital and was in no state to attend the funeral of his father. Gabel waited in his room for a message from Hess's widow or sister, but the telephone did not ring; and then, while watching the 7 p.m. news on television he learned that the funeral of Hess had already taken place. No details were given.

Next day, the family told him he could return home because there was nothing for him to do at Wunsiedel, and the mystery deepened a few weeks later, in October, when Wolf-Rüdiger asked him if he would come back one day to conduct a proper burial service for his father.

It is obvious that the funeral of Rudolf Hess, the Prisoner of Spandau, would have been an event swamped by journalists, cameramen and television crews, as well as acting as a focal point for neo-Nazis. It is equally obvious that this would have been extremely distasteful to the family and to the West German authorities in Bonn. In the light of Wolf-Rüdiger's remark to him in October, Pastor Gabel believes that Hess's body is in cold storage in some place known only to the family and the West German authorities, awaiting a suitable time for quiet

142

burial in Wunsiedel.

This, too, is neither unlikely nor impossible.

THE TICHBORNE CLAIMANT

The dignified, aristocratic old lady crossed the floor of the room in a Paris hotel, and approached the bed. The man lying on it was vastly more bulky than the slim one she had expected – but so many years had passed . . .

His face was turned to the wall. She bent to look at him: he was not only gross, but coarse-featured, yet there was something about the ears, the way the eyelids under the heavy brows twitched recurrently.

It was enough. 'Like his father!' she declared, and stooped further to kiss him. One of the onlookers, a lawyer, turned to another, a servant, and demanded that she bear witness that, in her sight and hearing, the Dowager Lady Tichborne had acknowledged her long-lost son, Roger.

Had the old lady's gesture and statement been enough to satisfy the rest of the family, the saga of 'the Tichborne Claimant' would have ended then and there. The gross man would have accompanied his mother back to England to take up his inheritance of the fine house, park, lands, ancient church, and exquisite village in the Itchen valley of Hampshire.

For a dozen years, since hearing of the loss of the ship bearing him from South America to the West Indies, Lady Tichborne had kept a candle burning in Roger's room, convinced that he had survived and would come home. Against the advice of her family, she had kept more or less open house at Tichborne House for merchant seamen who might bring a clue or rumour to keep that belief alive. She had advertised extensively in English and Colonial newspapers, offering a handsome reward for information.

He sailed from the port of Rio de Janeiro on the 20th of April 1854, in the ship *La Bella*, and has never been heard of since, but a report reached England that a portion of the crew and passengers of a vessel of that name was picked up by a vessel bound to Australia – Melbourne, it is believed. It is not known whether the said Roger Charles Tichborne was amongst the drowned or the saved. He would at the present time be thirty-two years of age, is of a delicate constitution, rather tall, with very light brown hair and blue eyes. Mr Tichborne is the son of Sir James Tichborne, baronet, now deceased, and is heir to all his estates . . .

That advertisement was printed in Australian newspapers in 1865, and among those who read it was a New South Wales solicitor, Mr Gibbes, of Wagga Wagga. Gibbes had recently acquired a new client, a butcher named Tom Castro, who was seeking his advice on the delicate procedure of bankruptcy. Castro had mentioned that he had some property in England, and wondered whether it might have to be taken into account.

Gibbes called his client again. In casual conversation, he remarked that he would sooner be sailing his boat on Sydney Harbour than sitting in his office on so fine a day. Castro responded that if Gibbes had ever known what it was like to be shipwrecked, he might prefer to stay ashore. As he spoke, he produced his pipe to accept a fill of the lawyer's tobacco. Mr Gibbes's sharp eyes widened when they saw the initials carved on the pipe's stem – RCT.

He determined not to beat about the bush, and, with further leading questions, persuaded Castro to admit that the initials stood for Roger Charles Tichborne, and that he was indeed the missing heir, who had chosen to stay on in Australia and make a new life after being saved from the shipwreck.

On Gibbes's prompting, Castro answered the advertisement. The Dowager's joy on receiving his letter was in no way diminished by its spelling mistakes – her son's Stonyhurst education had not made much impression on him. She recalled his letter:

My dear Mother,
The delay which has taken place since my last letter dated April 22nd, 1854, makes it very difficult to commence this letter. I deeply regret the truble and anxiety I must have cause you by not writing before . . .

There inevitably followed a request for money, but the Dowager remained cautious. Sir Roger had better come home and show himself.

145

Mr Gibbes was hedging his bets, too. If all went well, he could expect a worthwhile reward in return for lending his client a few hundred pounds. But the fat, uncouth-looking butcher far from resembled the advertised description. Against that, two genuine former servants of the Tichborne family, now living in Sydney, had come forward as a result of press stories that the missing heir had been found. They were a gardener and a West Indian valet, named Bogle, and each said he recognized Tom Castro as Roger Tichborne, though changed by time and hardship.

Gibbes lent some £700, and the claimant, as he had become known in both Australia and England, moved to Sydney, to be in the limelight and raise more funds to enable himself and his wife and child to travel home in style. He had no difficulty in achieving this, throwing money about as fast as it was pressed on him, engaging a secretary, nursemaid, and valet – the old family retainer, Bogle. When there was some difficulty over paying their hotel bill, he bought the hotel with a cheque of a London bank, signed 'Roger Tichborne'.

It turned out later that the missing Tichborne had never banked at that London bank. By this time he had sailed with his entourage for England, where an excited reception awaited him from press and public, if not the Tichbornes. The Dowager herself was away in Paris, where he duly went, accompanied by a man he had met in a billiard parlour, and a lawyer whom the man happened to know. They and the servant were present when Lady Tichborne accepted Castro as her son.

The news provoked a sensation, especially when artists' impressions of the claimant appeared. The Tichbornes, remembering Roger as frail and slight, with sloping shoulders and a little beaked nose, were derisory.

Meanwhile, agents acting for the interested parties were hard at work in England, Australia and South America. The claimant, advised by his knowing valet and lawyers, sought out anyone and everyone who had known Roger Tichborne at Stonyhurst College and during two years as an officer in the 6th Dragoon Guards. Of their own accord, or with prompting, they signed affidavits identifying him. In due course, he had over a hundred men and women prepared to testify in his favour.

It was, however, expensive being a claimant. His supporters' donations dwindled before the onslaught of bills and writs from hoteliers and tradesmen, and the bankruptcy which had started the whole train of events became reality, making his situation a win-or-lose, all-or-nothing affair. All of 18 months passed before a formal hearing was convened, to prepare the way for a full trial of the claim.

Nothing overtly sensational emerged – apart from the claimant himself, who had been keeping out of public sight, and who could now be wondered at in the fullness of his 24 stones. A casual piece of evidence came up which was to have considerable consequences: when questioned about his assumed name of Castro, he was asked if he had known a man called Tomas Castro in South America. He answered, 'Yes, he was a man I knew at Melipilla.' It was observed that no reference to Melipilla had been made in the submissions but the claimant retorted, in his brusque manner, that he had not mentioned every town or village he had travelled through on the journey that was in question, from Valparaiso to Santiago. Nevertheless, his lawyer, spotting the possibility of further useful affidavits, quickly made inquiries in Melipilla about a visiting English milord who had passed that way, and might be remembered. He did not get what he hoped for. The only English visitor at the relevant time, remembered by many, was a poor boy in his 'teens, whom they had called Arturo, but thought was named Arthur Horton or Orton.

The Tichborne family lawyers had also not been slow to follow up this line of inquiry, with the same result. In their case, it caused excitement. They had the claimant watched from the moment of his arrival in London. That very first day in England had been Christmas Day 1866, and he had gone to Wapping, in the London's East End dockland area, and visited a house there. It belonged to a butcher and his family, and their name was Orton. The Tichbornes lost no time in hiring a private detective to visit Wapping again to find out more about the Ortons, in particular a son named Arthur, who had gone abroad a good few years before.

In March 1868 the claimant lost the one witness on whom

147

above all he depended – the Dowager Lady Tichborne, who died suddenly. Her affidavits, however, were already safely sworn, and there remained all the other witnesses too. He was going to need them more than ever by the time the case came to trial on 11 May 1871.

The trial was bound to be long and costly: as a measure of its importance, it was to be heard before a special jury of men of property. Should the claimant come out loser of such a marathon, it was bound to cost him dearly.

The judge was Sir William Bovill, Chief Justice of the Common Pleas. Mr Serjeant Ballantine, one of the leading counsels of the day, appeared for the claimant, while the Tichborne family was represented by the Solicitor-General, Sir John Coleridge, later Lord Chief Justice. The whole of England hung upon the proceedings and split into factions favouring either side.

The claimant's counsel paraded that long assemblage of generals and colonels, J.P.s, Deputy-Lieutenants of counties, clergymen, ladies, servants and others, all of whom had known Roger Tichborne at various ages and in differing capacities, and were certain that the man claiming to be he was genuine, though admittedly much changed. Having questioned him in their own way, at their initial interviews, and received answers which, on the whole, it seemed to them that only the real Sir Roger could have given, they were satisfied. His eyes were the most memorable feature for most of them.

The eagerness of some of them to be believed led to some exchanges which produced laughter in court. Roger Tichborne had been bad at English and spelling. Judging by the claimant's virtual illiteracy, he had lapsed further with the years. But the late Lady Tichborne had been French, and had brought up her son to speak it fluently, so that even his English had a French accent. When, at last, to everyone's eager anticipation, the claimant himself was put into the witness-box, and was asked about his knowledge of French, he claimed to have forgotten it completely. The subject of Roger Tichborne's three years at Stonyhurst College was debated as follows:

SOLICITOR-GENERAL: Is there more than one quadrangle?

CLAIMANT: What do you mean by quadrangle? You may have a different meaning.

SOLICITOR-GENERAL: What did *you* mean by it?

CLAIMANT: I meant the staircase at the side of the house.

SOLICITOR-GENERAL: Do you really mean to say you do not know the meaning of 'quadrangle'?

CLAIMANT: I mean to say I am explaining to you where it is, and you will not understand.

SOLICITOR-GENERAL: Did you ever go to the Seminary at Stonyhurst?

CLAIMANT: To what?

SOLICITOR-GENERAL: To the Seminary.

CLAIMANT: Do you mean the cemetery?

The claimant said he had studied Hebrew, Latin and Greek.

SOLICITOR-GENERAL: Did your studies in Greek go as far as the alphabet?

CLAIMANT: I don't remember how far they went.

SOLICITOR-GENERAL: Could you read a line of Latin now?

CLAIMANT: No, I'm certain I could not.

SOLICITOR-GENERAL: Is Caesar a Latin writer, or a Greek?

CLAIMANT: I don't remember, but I should think he was Greek.

SOLICITOR-GENERAL: That was the Stonyhurst edition, I suppose.

Sir John, having shown up the claimant's ignorance of his childhood in France, his schooldays, French and any other language, his experience in the army, and other areas where memory could not possibly have been totally expunged by time and travel, then asked him about Wapping, and Arthur Orton. The claimant admitted he had often met him in Australia, and that his agents had been unable to find him to produce him as a witness. Sir John continued:

SOLICITOR-GENERAL: Are you not yourself Arthur Orton?

CLAIMANT: I am not.

SOLICITOR-GENERAL: Are you the son of George Orton, of 69 High Street, Wapping, a butcher?

CLAIMANT: I am not.

SOLICITOR-GENERAL: Were you born in June 1834?
CLAIMANT: I don't think a man can know when he was born.

The trial dragged on for over three months. Serjeant Ballantine had had enough and asked to be allowed to withdraw the suit. The jury agreed, and the judge heartily endorsed its view, adding that the claimant had been shown to be deserving of trial for perjury. He ordered his arrest for trial at the Central Criminal Court. The charges were based on forgery.

The subsequent trial lasted 188 days. When it ended, the Lord Chief Justice, Lord Cockburn, addressing the claimant as 'Thomas Castro, otherwise called Arthur Orton, otherwise called Roger Charles Doughty Tichborne, Baronet', sentenced him to two consecutive terms of seven years each. It was a long sentence, but so had been the trials in the face of much conflicting evidence.

The culprit was released after ten years, returning to Australia, where he published a signed confession of his imposture in the Melbourne *People*. He subsequently retracted this confession before dying in poverty.

The claimant had caused a lot of people much trouble and expense. There are several mysteries which still attend this much-debated case. How could so many people, mostly of impeccable character, have been truly convinced that he was the missing heir? How had he managed to answer correctly many questions about Tichborne's life, yet display appalling ignorance of the most elementary matters?

It has been suggested that the Dowager Lady Tichborne must have known at once that he was not her son, but pretended he was out of spite for the family, with whom she was at loggerheads. Did she die in the happy belief that she had regained the son whom she had always believed would come home – or triumphing at having, so to speak, set a Castro among the Tichbornes?

If he was not Tichborne, was he Castro, or Orton, or neither? A great jurist of more recent years, the late Lord Birkett, wrote: 'The jury in the civil case decided that the Claimant was not Roger Tichborne, and that was undoubtedly the right decision.

150

The jury in the criminal case . . . said the Claimant was not Roger Tichborne, but a man named Arthur Orton, and in this last finding they were almost certainly wrong.'

Birkett's view was that a 'coarse and unlettered butcher' would not, and could not, have embarked on an imposture of such magnitude, and been able to keep up 'an attitude that for a time staggered the faith of thousands, baffled the force of argument, and seemed to hold in temporary abeyance the very laws of evidence themselves'. It is a view which many lawyers – who may not care to think of their profession having been hoodwinked – are still inclined to share.

WAS CHESSMAN THE RED LIGHT BANDIT?

On the evening of 19 January 1948, a man and a woman were sitting in a Chevrolet, enjoying the view of the lights of West Pasadena, California, which stretched below them. A car pulled up behind them and, since it had a red spotlight beside the driver's door, both assumed it to be a police car. A man with a flashlight approached them and asked to see their identification. Naval veteran Jarnigan Lea fumbled for his wallet, and suddenly found himself looking down the barrel of an automatic pistol as the man pronounced, 'This is a hold-up.'

The man grabbed Lea's wallet, and asked his companion, Mrs Regina Johnson, for her handbag. In the dark, Mrs Johnson quietly dropped a diamond watch and some rings on to the floor. As she reached out to hand him the bag, the man snapped, 'All right, keep your faces turned the other way.' They heard a click as the gun was cocked, and, for a moment, both suspected he was about to shoot. Instead the man said to Mrs Johnson, 'Keep your purse. I'm taking you with me.' He pointed his gun at Lea's head. 'Stay where you are and don't make a move, or I'll let you both have it.' Then at gunpoint, he forced Mrs Johnson to get into his car. His face was hidden by a handkerchief mask.

Once in his car, he ordered her to remove her panties; he threatened her with death until she complied. As she struggled out of her underwear, he unzipped his fly. In tears, the woman told him she was menstruating, and begged him not to rape her. 'All right', said the bandit, 'you can do it this way', and forced her face down into his lap.

Although paralyzed with fear and disgust, Mrs Johnson was also infuriated by the way this brute had humiliated her. When the headlights of a car came up behind them, she said, 'Better drop your mask – it might be the cops.' The man did as she suggested, and she was able to see his face. The passing car proved to be full of teenagers. When its tail-lights had receded, the bandit made her give him $5 from her purse; then, with more threats, allowed her to go back to the other car. The robbery and sexual assault had taken about ten minutes.

When the couple reported the incident at the sheriff's office, the police had no doubt that the robber was the man who had become known as the Red Light Bandit. In the past 24 hours, there had been two other hold-ups committed by a man driving a car with a red spotlight; in both cases he had demanded to see the driver's identification, then taken his wallet. A countrywide bulletin on the Red Light Bandit had gone to police stations. When Jarnigan Lea and Mrs Johnson had been robbed, the newspapers had not yet picked up the story, so they had no reason to be suspicious of the car with the red spotlight.

Less than three hours after the assault, the bandit struck again, in the Hollywood Hills, driving up in front of a car containing a young couple and taking a few dollars. The girl was a pretty airline hostess. Fortunately, the bandit did not seem interested in further attempts at rape. During this robbery, his handkerchief mask slipped, and the young man, a truck salesman named Gerald Stone, was able to see his face. He was convinced that he would recognize him again if he saw him.

Three days later a young man, Frank Hurlburt, was sitting in his car with a pretty 17-year-old girl whom he was escorting home from a dance in a church hall. A car with a red spotlight pulled up in front, and a man wearing a mask ordered him to hand over his money. When Hurlburt said that he had none, the bandit said, 'All right, I'll take the girl.' Mary Alice Meza was forced into the gunman's car. Then the man ordered Hurlburt to pull down the road, on to the hard shoulder, and drove away fast.

Dozens of police cars combed the area. But when they arrived at Mary Alice's home she was already back. She was in tears and badly shaken, but was able to give an account of her ordeal to a policewoman.

The bandit had driven around for several hours, until he found a quiet place. Then he ordered the girl to strip and to climb into the back seat; he removed all his own clothes, except his shoes and socks. Like Mrs Johnson, Mary Alice was menstruating, but this did not deter the bandit. He ordered her to

153

lie, face down, on the seat and tried to enter her; an obstruction convinced him that she was a virgin. This seemed to cause him to change his mind; instead, he ordered the girl to commit fellatio. She pleaded, 'I never did anything to you – why should you do this to me?' The bandit ignored her pleas, and pointed the gun at her head. The girl did as he asked. After this, the man asked her where she lived, drove her to within a short distance of her home, and allowed her to go.

At 6.30 the following evening, on 23 January 1948, two men walked into a clothing store at Redondo Beach, 20 miles away from Hollywood, and pulled out guns. The owner, Melvin Waisler, and his clerk, Joe Lescher, were forced into the back of the store and made to hand over their money. Then the robbers took over $200 from the till, helped themselves to a quantity of clothes, and left in a hurry. Although Waisler was suffering from a head wound, where one of the robbers had struck him with his gun, he hailed a cab and chased the bandits' car, but he soon lost it in the traffic.

This time, however, the bandits were not to escape. An hour and a half later, two policemen in a patrol car saw a vehicle that fitted the description of the robbers' car. When they tried to stop it, the car drove off at top speed. They radioed for help, and other police cars joined the chase. Finally, the vehicle was rammed as it tried to make a wide turn; two men jumped out, and one of them immediately raised his hands; he had a moustache, and sounded like the man who had struck Waisler on the head. The other man made a run for it, and police officer Robert May chased him, firing shots after him. The man turned into a back yard, and found he was trapped; May closed with him, hit him on the head with his gun, and handcuffed him.

There could be no possible doubt that these two men were the robbers of the clothes store for their car contained the stolen money and clothes. At the police station, they identified themselves as David Knowles, aged 32 – he was the man with the moustache – and Caryl Chessman, aged 26. The police looked at Chessman with considerable interest. He was a 'tough-looking egg' – a description given by one of the victims of the Red Light Bandit. He had a long face with a pointed chin and a

154

bump in the middle of his nose, characteristics of the Red Light Bandit observed by his victims, including Regina Johnson and Gerald Stone.

Both the bandits were, according to Chessman's later account, severely beaten by the police. Chessman agreed that it was a 'fair cop', and that he had been one of the robbers of the clothes store. But when the police told him that his description fitted that of the Red Light Bandit, he looked astonished and said, 'I wasn't on the sex jobs, and I don't work late at night.' Pressed about other robberies, Chessman admitted to one near the Rose Bowl in Pasadena. This was the second stick-up of the Red Light Bandit. The victims had been a man called Floyd Ballew and his girlfriend, Elaine Bushaw. Ballew had described the bandit as having a pointed chin.

According to the police, the most damaging admission of all came when Chessman was asked about the red spotlight he had used. He replied that he converted an ordinary spotlight with the use of red cellophane. Chessman was then taken to the house of Mary Alice Meza. As a result of her ordeal three days earlier, her face had swollen so that her eyes were narrow slits. Chessman stood on the sidewalk, while Detective-Sergeant Colin Forbes went into the house and brought the girl to the window. She pointed at Chessman, 'That's the man . . . The one with the crooked nose.'

Forbes had decided that the best way to get a confession out of Chessman was to treat him with sympathy. (This is a well-known interrogation method – a brutal beating, followed by warmth and sympathy from a fellow officer, which induces such relief in the prisoner that he breaks down.) They took Chessman for a T-bone steak in a nearby diner.

'I tell you I'm not a sex maniac,' Chessman insisted.

'Then who committed the assaults?' asked Forbes.

'A guy called Terranova,' Chessman is alleged to have answered. But he declined to say more. The relentless questioning continued at the police station. Finally, Forbes asked him, 'How long did you have the Meza girl in your car?'

Chessman answered, 'About two hours.' He went on to admit the assault on Mary Alice Meza, and to robbing Jarnigan Lea –

although he denied assaulting Mrs Johnson. These were the admissions that would finally bring Chessman to the gas-chamber under the 'Little Lindbergh' law that makes kidnapping a capital offence.

Carol Whittier Chessman – he later changed the spelling to Caryl because he felt Carol looked 'cissy-ish' – had been in trouble since he was in his mid-teens. His childhood had been plagued with illnesses, the most serious of which was brain fever – encephalitis – which left him tone deaf and subject to temper tantrums and moods of violence.

His mother was a quiet, withdrawn woman, a dreamer; his father, a carpenter, was weak and inadequate, a born failure. And at the age of ten, fate struck another blow that must have left Caryl shattered. A neighbour invited him and his mother for a drive, but as the vehicle turned into a traffic stream it was struck by a heavy touring car. Chessman's nose was flattened, giving him the 'tough egg' look, and his mother was paralyzed from the waist down. She was a religious woman and told Caryl it was the will of God; Caryl's reaction was rage, frustration and, later, atheism. At 15 he almost died of diptheria. His father tried twice to commit suicide and the family had to live on poor relief. One day, a schoolfriend saw Chessman's father walk into the house with a poor-relief package, and commented, 'Gee, you must be poor to eat that stuff. I feel sorry for you.' One week later, Chessman committed his first crime – stealing milk and fruit from someone's doorstep.

At school, he was unpopular, being small, puny and bookish, and his schoolfellows called him 'hooknose'. But then he began to acquire a reputation as a criminal, and suddenly, he found people seemed to regard him with a sneaking admiration. He stole cars for 'joy rides', provoked police cars into wild pursuit and committed burglaries. After his first arrest, for auto-theft, he escaped. The next morning he was arrested in a drug store, caught in the act of emptying whisky over a pile of cigars.

After each term in reformatory, he went back to crime, graduating to hold-ups. In 1940, at the age of 19, he married and promised his bride to reform. But after a week or so, he decided that robbery was easier than work, and held up a fuel station. He saw himself as a romantic rebel and liked to imagine that he was the French robber-poet François Villon. Again and again these fantasies landed him in jail; he was in custody almost continuously until a month before the Red Light crimes. He was paroled in December 1947, and immediately joined a criminal gang who extorted money from bookmakers. Then, in January 1948, the Red Light crimes ended his freedom for ever.

His trial began on 4 May 1948, and from the beginning Chessman did not stand a chance. His prospects were not improved by his decision to conduct his own defence. The first witness was Mrs Regina Johnson, who described how she was forced to undress, then perform fellatio. She confirmed that Chessman was her assailant. When Chessman cross-questioned her, he asked, 'How long were you in the bandit's car?' she asked demurely, 'In the car with you?'. Chessman became angry, so much so that the judge had to caution him. No one was surprised when, on 21 May Chessman was found guilty of 17 out of 18 charges, and sentenced to death.

However, for the first time in his life, luck was now with him. Two days before the end of the trial, the court shorthand reporter dropped dead. By law Chessman was supposed to be supplied with a complete daily transcript of his trial, but the hostile judge, Charles Fricke, had denied him this right. Now Chessman seized on this legal loophole and demanded a retrial. He demanded law books and set out to overturn the verdict.

At first, the fight seemed hopeless. After a three-year struggle, the Supreme Court of California confirmed Chessman's sentence, so an execution date could be set. It was to be 28 March 1952. An appeal succeeded and the date was postponed to late June 1952. At this point, Chessman decided to write a book about his struggle. With advance money from the publisher, he hired a private detective to find proof of his innocence. When *Cell 2455 Death Row* came out in May 1952, it became an immmediate bestseller, and turned Chessman into a *cause célèbre*. Surely he could never be executed now? His appeal was turned down the day after publication.

Yet he continued to fight. He made more appeals, which delayed his execution, and wrote two more books. On 2 May

1960, as he was being escorted to the San Quentin gas-chamber, yet another stay of execution was granted. The secretary of the judge who granted it dialled the wrong number when she rang the prison, and by the time she got the right number, the cyanide pellets had been dropped, and Chessman was dying.

It seems almost superfluous to ask: was he guilty? Surely he had to be guilty? He admitted to being the robber of Floyd Ballew, using a red spotlight. It follows, therefore, that he was the man who held up Mrs Johnson 24 hours later. This logic is hard to deny.

However, Milton Machlin and William Woodfield, the authors of *Ninth Life*, the major study of the Chessman case, raise one very serious doubt. They succeeded in examining an early report on the case which included depositions by Mrs Johnson, Gerald Stone and Mary Alice Meza. Oddly enough, Mrs Johnson said that two bandits might have both been present in the car – the second, presumably, in the back. Stone stated positively that there were two bandits, one of whom remained in their 'red light' car. Mary Meza gave the interesting information that she had asked the bandit if he was Italian, to which he replied that he was.

Moreover, the authors tracked down police documents showing that 'red light' crimes were committed before Chessman left prison in December 1947, and after his arrest in January 1948. In one of these, the bandit made a girl get out of the car and forced her to undress.

Witnesses also spoke of the Red Light Bandit as being of slight stature and having a scar on his face. Neither of these descriptions fitted Chessman.

Then who did they fit? The answer is an Italian criminal named Charles Terranova. We may recall that, soon after his arrest, Chessman said that the Red Light Bandit was a man named Terranova. In court, the prosecutor announced that Terranova was a figment of Chessman's imagination. He was not. He was, in fact, a close acquaintance of Chessman's and probably a member of the same criminal gang that he joined on leaving prison in 1947.

When Chessman was first in prison, his father visited him,

and told him that he had received a threat from one of Chessman's friends. His father continued, 'He told your mother to send you word to keep your mouth shut. He said that if you didn't, he'd blow your mother and me sky high some night . . .' This friend could not have been David Knowles, the man who was arrested with Chessman and imprisoned at the same time. It was almost certainly another member of the gang. And *what* was he so anxious that Chessman should not divulge? Almost certainly the identity of the 'other man' in the car.

If Machlin and Woodfield are correct, Chessman himself was that other man, and the man who committed the sexual assaults was Charles Terranova. The two men were so much alike that when Terranova's wife saw a 'mug shot' of Chessman, she asked, 'Where did you get that picture of Charley?' They told her that it was not Terranova, but Caryl Chessman. 'That's funny – he looks just like Charley.'

So in the event it seems that the state of California may have executed an innocent man. They certainly executed a man who possessed remarkable intelligence, pertinacity and courage.

OSCAR SLATER

In most famous miscarriages of justice, the blame can be laid on the imperfections of the legal system. There are, however, a few instances in which fate itself seems to conspire against an innocent victim. Such was the case of the unfortunate Oscar Slater.

It should have been impossible for a thief to get into the home of Miss Marion Gilchrist. The door of her first-floor flat in West Princes Street, Glasgow, had not only an ordinary lock, but two spring locks and a bolt and chain. The back windows were kept fastened. The downstairs street door could be opened by pulling a handle inside the apartment. Inside that flat, Miss Gilchrist should have been as safe as in a fortress.

Moreover, she was seldom alone. Her maid and companion, 21-year-old Helen Lambie, was with her most of the time. Helen had been working for Marion Gilchrist for three years. She found her rather mean – 'She made one kipper do for two' – but they got along well enough.

Why had the 83-year-old woman turned her flat into a fortress? Her main concern was for her remarkable collection of jewellery, which she kept in the flat. Her rings and brooches were in all kinds of hiding places – in clothes in the wardrobe, in secret pockets, in drawers in the spare rooms. Malicious neighbours said she trafficked in stolen goods; in fact, her considerable fortune was the result of shrewd management and frugal habits.

On 21 December 1908, the rain fell steadily on the streets of Glasgow, but the shops were still crowded with late Christmas shoppers. At 7 o'clock, Helen Lambie went out for an evening paper, and locked the door behind her. When she returned, ten minutes later, she was surprised to see a man waiting outside the door of the flat. It was Arthur Adams, the ground-floor neighbour. He seemed astonished to see her. 'There must be something wrong if you've been out.' He explained that there was undoubtedly someone in the flat making loud noises. A few minutes earlier, he had heard a heavy crash from the flat overhead, followed by three knocks. It was a code that he had arranged with Miss Gilchrist – if anything was wrong, she would knock three times on the floor. Adams had hurried upstairs and rung the doorbell, noticing, as he did so, that the street door was open. There was no reply. Then he heard a crashing sound 'as if the servant was breaking sticks in the kitchen'. This was why he was so surprised to see Helen Lambie.

Helen took out her keys and opened the door. And as the two of them stood there, a man came walking towards them from the direction of the spare bedroom. He was well dressed, and looked quite calm and self-assured, as if he had every right to be there. He walked past them, and on down the stairs, then he suddenly accelerated and rushed out, slamming the street door.

Helen Lambie had gone to the kitchen to see if the clothes pulley had fallen down – she was convinced that this was the noise Adams had heard. But the pulley was still in place. Then the girl went into the dining room, calling, 'Are you there, ma'am?' She screamed loudly. Arthur Adams, standing behind her, saw Miss Gilchrist lying on her back, her head towards the fireplace. Her face was partly covered with a rug. When this was removed, they could see that her head was a mass of blood. Now Adams could understand the banging noises, 'like someone chopping wood'. She had been attacked so violently that blood was dripping from the coal scuttle and covered the fireplace. The weapon, apparently, had been a chair. One eye had been driven into the brain. She was still breathing faintly, but was dead before the arrival of a doctor summoned by Arthur Adams who also fetched a policeman. The flat was soon swarming with detectives.

Meanwhile, Helen Lambie had rushed a few blocks to Blythswood Drive, where Miss Gilchrist's niece lived. Helen is reported to have said, 'Miss Birrell, Miss Gilchrist has been murdered, and I saw the man who did it.' When asked by Miss Birrell, 'Who?', she replied, 'I'm sure it was . . .'. Helen Lambie went on to name the man she thought she had recognized. We do not know the name of this man, who was almost certainly the murderer. We only know that Margaret Birrell was shocked and told Helen Lambie she must be mistaken. She also advised her not to mention this to the police, for fear of 'smearing the man's reputation'.

Back at the flat, the police had discovered that the murderer's apparent objective was a wooden box of private papers in the spare room. This had been smashed open, and its contents strewn around, as if someone had been looking for something. Whether he found it is not known. It was quite obvious that robbery was not the motive, for Miss Gilchrist's jewellery lay exposed on various tables – a diamond, two rings and some gold objects. When the various items of jewellery had been assembled from around the flat, Helen Lambie maintained that only one thing was missing: a diamond brooch shaped like a crescent.

There were not many clues. The murderer had lit the gas in the spare bedroom and left his matches behind. On the back of the chair that had probably been used to kill Marion Gilchrist, there was a bloody handprint. That alone should have brought the murderer to justice, for fingerprinting techniques had been in use at Scotland Yard since the beginning of the twentieth century. The first murder to be solved by them – that of two old people in Deptford by the Stratton brothers – had occurred in 1905. But the Scottish police were inclined to stick to old and tried methods.

The murder caused a sensation in Glasgow for Miss Gilchrist had been well known. But although the police expended a great deal of energy and manpower, their results were not fruitful. They issued a description of the suspect, based on the glimpse that Helen Lambie and Arthur Adams had caught, as well as on a sighting of a fleeing man reported by a 14-year-old girl named Mary Barrowman. She had described him as tall and slim, about 28 or 30 years of age, with no beard or moustache. But although a number of men of this description were arrested, none was held.

Four days later, on Christmas night, a man asked to talk to a detective dealing with the Gilchrist murder. He identified himself as Allan M'Lean, a cycle dealer. He was a member of a small club in India Street, and had met there a new member named Oscar Slater, a German Jew. This man, he said, had been offering for sale a pawn ticket for a diamond crescent brooch.

The club in question turned out to be a gambling club, and there the police talked with Slater's best friend, and presumably his proposer, a man called Cameron. Cameron was able to tell them that the man they were looking for had probably now left the country. Early in December he had mentioned that he would be sailing for San Francisco and had tried to sell the pawn ticket for a diamond brooch. But that was long before Miss Gilchrist had been murdered, so the brooch could not be the one they were looking for. Nevertheless, Slater sounded a possible suspect. He was obviously a suspicious character, making money from gambling and, according to Cameron, women. He lived just around the corner from Miss Gilchrist and had only been in Glasgow for 18 months. A plate on his door claimed that he was a dentist but he had no dental equipment.

The police rushed to Slater's flat, and found that they had missed him by only a few hours. He had left for London with a lady friend known as Madame Junio. There was still a 17-month tenancy to run on the flat. Why should he leave unless he had some guilty secret?

The brooch itself proved to be a false lead. It had been pawned on 18 November, more than a month before Miss Gilchrist's death. That meant that there was nothing to connect Slater with the murder of Marion Gilchrist. But the Glasgow police were desperate. Slater was their only suspect and they were determined not to let him go. A man who gambled and lived off women must be some sort of a crook . . .

It was not difficult to discover that Slater had sailed on the *Lusitania* under a false name – Otto Sands. In fact, the suspect's real name was not Slater but Leschziner, and he also called himself Mr Anderson, Mr Sando and Mr George. He was born at Oppeln, in Germany, in 1870, so he was about ten years older than the suspect the police were looking for. Nevertheless, Oscar Slater was arrested when the ship arrived in New York. Helen Lambie and Mary Barrowman were taken across the Atlantic to identify him before the Americans would grant an extradition order. Arthur Adams was also taken to New York, although he protested that he was so short sighted he would not have been able to identify the man he saw leaving Miss Gilchrist's flat. By coincidence, the three Scottish witnesses were standing by the court room door when Slater was brought in. Detective-Inspector Pyper of the Glasgow police later claimed that Helen and Mary exclaimed simultaneously, 'There is the man.' But a marshal named Pinckley, who was escorting Slater, declared it was Charles Fox, the attorney appearing against Slater, who said to the girls, 'That's the man.'

Helen Lambie's evidence seems to have contradicted some of the things she had said earlier. In Glasgow she had said the man was wearing a dark cloth cap and a light grey overcoat; now this was changed to a Donegal tweed hat and a fawn-coloured waterproof. She also claimed that she was able to recognize Slater by his walk, because she had not seen his face. Later, at the trial, she changed this, and claimed to have seen his face.

Slater seemed perfectly calm. And when his attorney argued his case, he insisted that there was no sound legal reason why Slater should be extradited. However, since he had nothing to hide, he was willing to return to Glasgow of his own free will. He was apparently convinced that British justice would soon establish his innocence.

When the s.s. *Columbia* sailed up the Clyde, crowds were waiting to see the famous suspect, and as Oscar Slater disembarked, one sailor was seen to kick him. A light hammer and a fawn-coloured waterproof were found in his luggage, and the police took possession of these. Slater was put into an identity parade, and witnesses who had seen a man hanging around outside Miss Gilchrist's flat on the night of the murder were taken into the room. Since they had all by now seen pictures of Slater, and the rest of the men in the line-up were policemen, they had no difficulty in picking out the chief suspect.

The trial of Oscar Slater opened on 3 May 1909 in the High Court of Judiciary in Edinburgh. The man who stood in the dock had dark hair and a dark moustache, and a Roman nose with a slight twist at the end. He was rather heavily built. The case against him opened with 12 witnesses who had seen a man standing outside Miss Gilchrist's flat on the evening of the

164

murder. One lady said she identified Slater by his profile and said he had worn a heavy tweed coat and had a delicate build. She was surprised to see that Slater was undoubtedly a well-fed man. Mary Barrowman identified a soft black hat as the Donegal tweed hat the running man had been wearing on the night of the murder. She was one of the witnesses who said that the man had been clean shaven; Slater's barber was to testify that at the time of the murder, Slater wore the same black moustache that he now wore.

Perhaps more important than the witnesses who were called were the witnesses who were not called. The doctor who had first seen Miss Gilchrist's corpse, Dr Adams, believed that she had been killed by blows from a chair. The crown case was that she had been killed by the hammer found in Slater's baggage. Dr Adams was not called. A Liverpool policeman, Chief Inspector Duckworth, had been asked to check on Slater's movements in Liverpool before he sailed for America, and report if he behaved like a man in flight from justice. He had discovered that Slater had behaved with complete openness, signing his own name in the hotel register and talked openly about sailing on the *Lusitania*. Inspector Duckworth was not called. A man named Duncan MacBrayne, who had seen Slater standing outside his flat at 8.15 on the evening of the murder, when any reasonable person would suppose he would be in hiding or washing off bloodstains, was also not called.

But the witness who undoubtedly convinced the jury that Slater was guilty was Helen Lambie. She declared dogmatically that the fawn raincoat found in Slater's luggage was the coat worn by the man she saw. She now claimed that she had seen the face of the man, and when asked why she had denied this in New York, replied snappishly, 'I'm saying so now.' At the end of four days, the jury found Oscar Slater guilty by a small majority. As he cried passionately, 'I am innocent,' the judge donned the black cap and sentenced him to death.

Oddly enough public opinion, which had so far been against Slater, now began to turn around. If Slater had broken into Miss Gilchrist's flat to steal her jewellery, why did he not do so? And if Miss Gilchrist went to so much trouble to fortify herself behind locked doors, what was she doing to admit a stranger with a strong German accent? The Lord Advocate at the trial had promised to tell the jury how Slater had come to know that Miss Gilchrist possessed jewellery, but he had not done so. These and similar inconsistencies began to trouble the conscience of the British public, and doubts began to be voiced in the press. The result was that two days before the date set for his execution, the death sentence was commuted to imprisonment 'during His Majesty's pleasure'.

If Slater had been tried in England, he could have turned to the recently constituted Court of Criminal Appeal; but this did not yet exist in Scotland. The man who was most responsible for its establishment in England was the novelist Arthur Conan Doyle, creator of Sherlock Holmes. Three years earlier, Doyle had done his best to right a case of flagrant injustice. A short-sighted Parsee barrister named George Edalji had been found guilty of some horrible cattle mutilations at Great Wyrley in Staffordshire. It was obvious to Doyle that this frail, half-blind little man could never have prowled around at night with a razor. Doyle's efforts failed to force officialdom to admit its error, but raised so much public sympathy for Edalji (who had now been released) that the Court of Criminal Appeal was founded.

Slater had been in jail for five years when Doyle received a letter from David Cook, Slater's solicitor, and its contents shocked him. It seemed that a Glasgow police officer named John Trench had searched his conscience and decided that he had to speak out. It was he who told the story of how Helen Lambie had recognized the intruder in the flat, and he insisted that the police themselves had refused to accept her identification, and bullied or cajoled her into identifying Slater. He also believed that Mary Barrowman had been forced to lie when she identified Slater as the man she saw rushing out of the house. Doyle studied the case, realized that there was not the slightest thread of evidence to connect Slater to Miss Gilchrist, and wrote a pamphlet called *The Case of Oscar Slater*. This led to an official inquiry; but the police merely repeated their actions in 1909 and persuaded Helen Lambie and Mary Barrowman to repeat their identifications of Slater. The police denied that Helen Lambie had disclosed the identity of the intruder to them. Slater was once more found guilty; and the courageous police officer Trench was disgraced.

However, the story was not yet over. In October 1927 *The Empire News* printed an interview with Helen Lambie, now living in America, in which she admitted that she had recognized the intruder, and that the police had refused to accept her identification. She also admitted that the police had forced her to identify Slater as the man she saw. After this, Mary Barrowman also stated that she had also been forced to identify Slater as the man. She now said he was definitely not the man.

The Prime Minister, Ramsay MacDonald, ordered Slater's release pending an inquiry. After 18 years in prison, he was freed. Slater broke down in tears when he saw a bed with fresh sheets and a hot-water bottle. Conan Doyle rewrote his pamphlet and sent it to every member of parliament. Relations between Doyle and Slater cooled when Slater wanted to withdraw his appeal because he would not be allowed to give evidence personally. He was persuaded to drop his objection. Helen Lambie refused to come from America, afraid of a perjury charge; the *Empire News* reporter, however, gave evidence. The result was that Slater's sentence was quashed, and he received compensation of £6,000 from the Scottish Office. Ironically, Slater and Doyle now had a bitter disagreement because Slater declined to reimburse people who had spent money getting him out of prison. Doyle probably wished he had been left in jail.

Who did murder Marion Gilchrist? Almost certainly some close relative – in fact, Doyle was certain that it was her nephew. Only Helen Lambie could have named the killer, and she was never heard of again after Slater's release.

ACCIDENTS

THE GREAT BOMBAY EXPLOSION

Sabotage? A lucky hit by a bomb from an undetected Japanese aircraft? Or a mishap in unloading one of the cargo vessels crowding Bombay's docks that hot wartime afternoon of 14 April 1944? These were only some of the rumours which ran through the teeming Indian city as distraught people wondered what had caused one of the most devastating explosions the world had ever known. Even today, though most of the events leading up to it can be identified, an element of doubt remains.

It all began on a chill February day in Birkenhead, when a convoy of 20 ships left port. One was the s.s. *Fort Stikine*, built two years earlier in Canada from Lend-Lease funds and presented to Britain by the U.S. government. She was a single-screw, coal-burning vessel, one of 26 identical cargo ships whose names were all prefixed *Fort*. This one owed her name to the Stikine River in British Columbia.

Her place lay in an outside lane of the convoy, well away from the other ships; closer proximity would have been a danger to all. As well as crated gliders and Spitfires bound for Karachi for the RAF, her cargo was largely explosives – 1,395 tons of assorted shells, torpedoes, mines and incendiary bombs, all destined for Bombay. One direct hit by a torpedo or bomb, and *Fort Stikine* would be blown to kingdom come.

Leaving the convoy in the Mediterranean, she made her way alone through the Suez Canal and round Arabia, to arrive safely at Karachi on 30 March. Three days later, when all the gliders and Spitfires had been off-loaded, there were plenty of empty spaces left in her five holds. A wartime rule was that no cargo ship should sail with anything less than a full load, and soon stevedores were filling up every available gap with goods for Bombay.

Alexander Naismith, captain of *Fort Stikine*, viewed his additional cargo with disgust and anxiety. Rice, timber and scrap iron were all very well, but the fish manure stank. More seriously worrying were the sulphur, resin, hundreds of drums of lubricating oil, and thousands of bales of cotton. It would have been hard to concoct a more inflammable cargo. His protests at the folly of loading it all on to a ship carrying explosives fell on deaf ears. It was vital for the Indian economy that the raw cotton be rushed to the cloth mills in Bombay. The captain could only grit his teeth and obey orders.

He was not alone in his fears. His chief officer, William Henderson, was sure he had read about the danger of mixing cotton and explosives; but he could not lay his hands on any book which would verify it. His and his skipper's worries were not enough to have the cotton taken off the ship, but they were justified. *Modern Ship Stowage*, a standard reference work published two years earlier in America, identified the fire hazard of cotton, which the merest cigarette end could set alight. Also, 'cotton bales which are, or have been, in contact with oil or grease are very liable to spontaneous combustion'. A similar warning was in the regulations of the Board of Underwriters of New York about explosives: 'These should never be stowed in the same hatch with cotton, but must be stowed in a properly constructed magazine erected in the opposite end of the ship from that in which cotton is stowed.'

Both explosives and cotton were together in three of *Fort Stikine*'s holds. In No. 2 hold, 4,100 bales of cotton weighing 769 tons were packed beneath layers of timber and scrap iron, old dynamos and wireless sets. Above them, stacked on tarpaulins which barely covered the deck between upper and lower compartments, stood 1,089 small drums of lubricating oil. (The maximum number of oil drums allowed above cotton by the New York underwriters was 250.) Right on top, level with a steel tank which contained 124 bars of gold worth £1 million, lay

168 tons of category 'A' explosives, the most highly sensitive kind.

When *Fort Stikine* left Karachi on 9 April she was virtually a floating bomb. 'We are carrying just about everything that will burn or blow up,' the captain told his officers. 'The least we can do is to have extra fire drills.' The whole crew responded with extra zeal, familiarizing themselves diligently with the location and use of the fire-fighting apparatus.

The voyage down the west coast of India to Bombay took three days, made extra uncomfortable for all aboard by their anxiety about the cargo, not to mention the foul reek of fish manure. Everyone was relieved when the *Fort Stikine* anchored early on 12 April in the roadstead between Bombay Island and the mainland. An official came aboard and gave the captain a copy of the Port Rules and Dock By-laws. In return, Captain Naismith signed a declaration that his ship was carrying explosives. International Code required all ships with a dangerous cargo to fly a red flag when entering port, but the practice had been abandoned in wartime since the flag would attract the notice of enemy aircraft and saboteurs. The general formalities completed, *Fort Stikine* steamed to a quayside berth in Victoria Dock with no more indication of her contents than the great wooden horse had given when the Trojans welcomed it inside their city walls. All the same, she was granted a certificate of urgency for offloading to begin at once, and the stevedores' foreman was told that the explosives made up much of the cargo.

Ideally, first priority should have been given to the removal of the category 'A' explosives. But regulations stated that, whereas the safer categories, 'B' and 'C', could be unloaded direct on to the quay, category 'A' must be transferred only into lighters coming alongside the ship. No lighters turned up until almost the following afternoon, so the most dangerous explosives had to be left where they were. The stevedores concentrated instead on the drums of oil. Some of these were found to be leaking. Although it was noticed that the tarpaulines on which they had stood, above the cotton in No. 2 hold, were quite damp with oil it seemed hardly worth bringing to the attention of anyone in authority.

The ship's officers had a more urgent concern: they wished the stevedores would hurry up and take off all that abominable fish manure, lying heaped in No. 1 hold. The Indian dockers jovially agreed. An extra gang was set to helping them clear it, working through the night. What happened that night may have had a crucial bearing on subsequent events. Did one of the stevedores slip away for a few minutes' relief from the disgusting atmosphere, to puff a forbidden cigarette in No. 2 hold? Did the smouldering butt fall among the cotton? It was one of the theories advanced for the start of the nightmare that was about to break over Bombay.

All next day, 13 April, the stevedores worked on. The lighters finally arrived at midday, but only a few of the workers were set to unloading the category 'A' explosives.

The following day's progress in No. 2 hold was good. By lunchtime everything had been cleared from it except a huge piece of scrap iron which weighed three tons, about 11,000 pieces of timber, the 4,100 bales of cotton – and the 168 tons of category 'A' explosives above them.

While the stevedores were away eating and resting in the shade, eight watchmen were supposed to be on guard against sabotage and enforcing the no-smoking rule. Two were sailors, the rest civilians – and on this occasion there was a misunderstanding. The sailors thought the civilians were supposed to be on duty during the lunch hour, while the civilians believed the lunch hour was for their benefit as well. No one was keeping watch.

Could a saboteur have seized this opportunity to slip aboard and into No. 2 hold? It is not beyond the bounds of possibility, and it was during the next hour that the first signs of impending disaster showed. Independently of one another, several men on ships berthed nearby noticed wispy smoke curling up from one of *Fort Stikine*'s ventilators. Convinced that if anything had been wrong someone aboard would have raised the alarm, none of them thought any more about it. In fact, no one in *Fort Stikine* had seen the smoke at all.

The stevedores came back at 1.30 p.m., descended into No. 2

171

hold – and then clambered up again, talking excitedly. One of the seamen looked for the cause of the commotion, saw the smoke, and raised the alarm at least.

It was over an hour since the smoke had been seen by others. Even so, there should have been plenty of time to put out the fire before it reached the explosives. What followed instead was a series of mishaps, mistakes and misunderstandings which reacted together to bring cataclysmic disaster. If the original cause of it all was never explained fully, no less hard to credit is the way in which events conspired to thwart man's puny efforts.

The first problem was that the fire hoses, rapidly uncoiled and coupled to standpipes, were not long enough to reach into the hold for their jets to be aimed at the seat of the fire. The case was the same with the hoses brought by firemen who manned the dockside emergency trailer pump. Reinforcements were needed quickly, and the fire crew's section leader sent a man to put through an emergency message to the Bombay Fire Brigade. In his confusion, he failed to make the call, only breaking the glass in an ordinary fire alarm. That brought just two engines to the dockside, instead of the required fleet.

The next person on the scene was Captain Brinley Oberst, the ordnance officer in charge of explosives in the docks, who needed only to look at *Fort Stikine*'s stowage plan to realize the gravity of the situation. Warning Naismith that the whole of the docks would be destroyed if the fire reached the explosives, he recommended that the ship be scuttled. It was an impossibility; the sea-cocks in all *Fort* ships had non-return valves, to let water out but not in.

Naismith was still confident that the fire could be put out. The emergency message was at last telephoned to the Fire Brigade. Eight more appliances rushed to the scene, with Bombay's chief fire officer, Norman Coombs, to take charge of operations. Soon 32 hoses were pouring water into No. 2 hold – yet the smoke and heat grew mysteriously. The reason, only discovered with hindsight, was that the water, while still missing the seat of the fire, was flooding the hold. The burning cotton bales were starting to float, rising ever nearer to the explosives above. Far from putting out the fire, the millions of gallons of water were bringing catastrophe closer.

At 2.50 p.m. the general manager of the docks, Colonel Sadler, arrived. His solution to the crisis was to tow the ship out into the harbour and sink her. The idea horrified Coombs, the fire chief. He pointed out that it would mean withdrawing the hoses, which were fixed to dockside pumps. Without their jets to keep the fire in check the ship would blow up before she could reach deep water.

Things might have been better if one person had been in undisputed authority over the rest, and able to issue decisive orders. No one had this power. No one even acted to clear the docks of all other people. Sailors, stevedores, carpenters, engineers and lightermen all went about their usual business. Those who had to pass the hubbub around *Fort Stikine* paused at the spectacle of other people's problems.

There was one last chance to avert disaster. Just before 3 o'clock the trailerpump's driver felt heat on his face. Looking up, he saw the grey paint bubbling over a small patch on the ship's side. The paint suddenly began to fly off in hardened flakes. The man gave a shout – he had found the seat of the fire.

Coombs sent at once for a gas-cutting appliance from the Fire Brigade's emergency tender. If a hole could be cut in the ship's side, a hose could be fed through at last to direct water at the fire's heart. The gas-cutter was brought so promptly that someone else, who had also sent for a gas-cutter from another course, saw it and cancelled his request.

It was the last tragic mistake; the gas-cutter which had been brought was faulty. No searing flame came when a match was put to its jet, only black smoke. Coombs sent for another gas-cutter – but too late.

As 4 o'clock approached, thick black smoke billowed out of the hold, lit by tongues of flame. The firemen on deck staggered back, choking. Recovering for a last heroic effort, they ran forward again and aimed their hoses at the ammunition cases in the hold. It was hopeless. Five minutes later a huge flame shot up, rising higher than the top of the ship's mast. Coombs ordered his men to get clear. They scattered, as Naismith gave the command to abandon ship. The crew, who had stayed on

173

board to a man, were quick to obey. Captain Naismith made a last tour of his ship; then, satisfied that no one remained aboard, he walked down the gangway to join his chief officer on the quayside.

Seconds later, *Fort Stikine* exploded. No trace of Naismith or his chief officer, Henderson, was ever found.

It was like an earthquake and a volcanic eruption combined. Searing metal fragments, bursting drums of oil and blazing cotton bales hurtled through the air, starting new fires wherever they fell. A tidal wave lifted the stern of the *Jalapadma*, a steamer berthed close by *Fort Stikine*, 60 feet into the air and dropped it on the roof of a dockside shed. Hundreds of people were killed or maimed instantaneously; others with them did not suffer a scratch, though some had their clothes blown completely off.

The worst was still to come. *Fort Stikine* had stayed obstinately afloat, and the fire in her raged on. Just over half an hour after the first explosion it reached the 790 tons of explosives in the after hold. A second and far more devastating explosion occurred. Debris was flung up as high as 3,000 feet, to rain down in a lethal shower over a largely residential area inflicting terrible injuries.

Rescue work in the docks was hampered by continued lack of organization. Though some officers set themselves up as a general staff to deal with the situation, they had no guidelines for coping with so widespread a calamity on such a scale. Thousands of volunteers rushed to help, but the acts of individual heroism were offset by many costly mistakes. As the Bombay *Free Press Journal* summed up later: 'Symbolic of the way the city met the disaster is the solitary figure plying his hose without knowing exactly how.'

Army officers requisitioned spare pumps from fire stations for soldiers who had little idea how they worked. When the water pressure soon fell the men decided the pumps were faulty and abandoned them. Any one of the experienced firemen who had been deprived of the pumps would have known that floating cotton had got into the suction hoses and blocked the water flow from the pumps. With the hoses uncleared, the unlimited water supply, only yards from the raging fires, was useless.

Immediately after the first explosion a port offical had sent home all the Alexandra Dock shed supervisors and most of the stevedores. They had gone before it was found that nearly 40,000 heavy boxes of ammunition were in the sheds. Soldiers were sent to shift them urgently, only to be refused entry by docks police because they had no passes. They had to force their way in.

The worst blunder was the decision to abandon both Victoria Dock and the adjacent Prince's Dock to their fate, after several Army and Navy officers agreed that rescue workers could not hope to reach them. Later evidence showed that this was simply not correct; a concerted effort could have saved many ships from destruction.

The volunteers worked on all through the night and into the following day. By now, a shattered Bombay public was clamouring for explanations. Hundreds were dead and injured, thousands were destitute. The explosions had rocked every building in the city. Something terrible had happened; but what? All that the government of Bombay would say was that an accidental fire had broken out on a ship in the docks, resulting in two violent explosions. The military and fire services had soon got the situation under control.

Everyone in Bombay could see that the government was covering something up. Rumours of sabotage spread rapidly, with others claiming that a Japanese aircraft had bombed the docks. Offical denials, coming too late, only added to the rumours, which were believed in Bombay up to years afterwards. The true cause of the fire which set off the explosions was never to be explained to everyone's satisfaction.

The final estimate of those known to have died was 1,376, but the real figure must have been much higher. Thousands were severely injured. Huge stocks of grain were destroyed, and thousands of tons of seeds, spices, butter and oil. Fifty thousand people lost their jobs. Three thousand lost everything they owned. The Allied shipping loss added up to 34,639 tons.

If the disaster itself was exacerbated by incompetence and disorganization, the reverse was true of the rebuilding of the docks. Under Army control, 8,000 men achieved wonders. Incredibly, the docks were restored and working again only seven months later.

THE MOORGATE CRASH

At 8.45 on the morning of Friday, 28 February 1975 passengers waiting on Platform 9 at Moorgate Underground Station in London could not believe their eyes and ears as the incoming train approached.

Platform 9 serves an end-of-the-line tunnel blocked off with buffers and a wall of sand. There were not many passengers awaiting the arrival of the train. The dozen or so who heard its crescendo approach and readied themselves in anticipation of boarding it were casuals rather than regular commuters; they were waiting for this shuttle service to stop, reverse, and take them south to Bank Station where they would get the City Line line, the 'drain', to Waterloo. But though the waiting passengers were few the approaching train was packed, its six coaches carrying probably rather more than 600 commuters, most of them straphanging or crushed into the vestibule ends of the coaches. These were the regulars arriving for the day's work in this, the banking and insurance heart of the City.

What was unbelievable was that the train, instead of slowing down as it entered the station, gathered speed and hurtled towards the blind end of the tunnel. The three or four seconds that elapsed before the front coach hit the buffers were, in the words of one platform passenger, 'Like that moment in a nightmare when you're on the edge of screaming and then you wake up. But this time there was no waking up.'

The cacophony of impact, of ripped steel, shattered glass and falling debris from the roof of the tunnel could have been that of a high-explosive bomb exploding in the middle of the city. The second coach had telescoped into the first, and the top half of the third, split asunder lengthwise, rode over the top of the second.

The first emergency call for help was logged at 8.53 a.m., and ambulances and fire-brigade rescue tenders with heavy lifting gear filled the streets round the station – Moorgate, Finsbury Circus, London Wall – for the rest of the day, and indeed for the rest of the nightmare weekend. The nearest hospital, St

Bartholomew's, seems to have been misinformed as to the extent of the disaster, but it prepared for casualties – the first of which were those passengers who could be extricated through the windows and buckled doors of the rear three coaches. Most of these had broken limbs or were suffering from multiple cuts and bruises and, of course, shock.

The subterranean location caused many additional difficulties, not least for the firemen, whose heavy rescue gear had to be taken down escalators and along tunnel passages that were in many cases too small to admit it without its being stripped down. Oxy-acetylene cutting equipment was the first priority; in the low-powered emergency lighting (the track current was off) firemen started to cut away at the indescribably twisted mass of wreckage of the first three coaches.

By mid-morning a railway-breakdown gang had managed to get within winching distance of the wreck and the rear coaches were being winched back at the rate of 1 inch every ten minutes. Apertures little more than 3 feet square were cut in the wreckage and through these torn and broken bodies were squeezed, those beyond help being set aside with cursory deference to be transported to the mortuary for identification. Of these the number mounted rapidly as the hours passed. The known death toll was to be 23 before the day's end, and nearly twice that number by the time the rescue work was completed. On the platform an emergency operating theatre was set up in the glare of portable arc lights, and the heat of these and the lack of oxygen doubled the difficulties for the rescue teams. The one press man who was allowed on the scene to represent the whole of Fleet Street (he was from *The Daily Telegraph*) reported:

Platform 9 was like something out of a wartime film. The platform was choked with helmeted firemen, police, ambulance men, doctors, nurses, and welfare workers. The *up* escalator was working, bringing up blackfaced and tired rescuers. Everybody was sweaty, ghastly haggard, and filthy; and amidst the sounds of rescue I could hear the sound of people laughing hysterically. The heat was intense – it must have been 120 degrees.

177

Relays of doctors arrived as and when they could be spared from the nearest hospitals, and supplies of blood for transfusions were rushed from the blood banks. Volunteers donors queued for hours and the midday editions of the papers pictured them and the grim burdens that were being carried on stretchers to the surface. Hurriedly written leaders demanded immediate full-scale public inquiries.

Rumours were rife as to the cause of the crash – the most heavily subscribed being that the driver had had a heart attack. This was contradicted by the semi-knowledgeable, who spoke of the Dead Man's Handle and the fact that this device had been contrived for the very purpose of ensuring safety in the case of the sudden collapse of the driver. Others flourished the opinion that there should always be a second man in the driver's cab in case of emergency. Others again laid the blame fully at London Transport's door for keeping rolling stock far beyond its reliable life. The fact was, of course, that no one knew; and the inspecting engineers who were soon on the scene had very little chance of making their examination while the rescue work was going on.

The evening editions of the newspapers, though also edging toward the censorious, balanced their muted criticism with stories of courage and endurance gathered by reporters waiting above ground in the drizzling rain. Typical was the story of the 19-year-old policewoman who was trapped in the wreckage for many hours and had had to have a foot (and subsequently a leg) amputated and had been asked if she would like one or two of her WPC colleagues to be with her and had spiritedly replied that she'd 'rather have a few men'.

It was not until late Saturday morning that inspecting officers could begin to piece together the grim evidence in the driver's cab. The recovery of the body was of vital importance. It had sustained terrible injuries; but as the pathologist who conducted the first examination said, 'we can deduce a lot from a little'. (The macabre edge to the remark earned him a newspaper comment as 'unfeeling'.) The mutilated corpse had his on-the-spot report attached to it and was taken to the pathology laboratory while the engineers took measurements, made calculations, and cut away the control mechanism for examination by metallurgists and other forensic experts. Perhaps because the impact had been at buffer level it was the undercarriage and bogies that had sustained the greatest damage. What remained of the upper part of the cab would surely reveal, the newspapers insisted, 'vital clues'.

The first vital clue established by the inspectors was that the brakes had not been applied. So, since no man in his right mind would deliberately hurl himself and the hundreds of people in his care toward injury and death, mental aberration or physical incapacity on the part of the driver must have figured; and 'the establishment of one or both of these states', one leader said, 'is the crux of the matter.'

But there were other cruxes, some of them bound up in complex mechanical technicalities that had to be explained by expert witnesses. These were called to give evidence, together with pathologists, analysts, and others at the inquest which opened on Tuesday, 15 April before the Coroner, Mr David Paul, sitting with a jury. The business of the court, he said, was to establish the cause of the tragic deaths of 42 people, and to decide whether the driver himself, or some defect in the train or in the signalling system, had caused the crash.

The signalling system was immediately exonerated. All the signals commanding the approach and entrance to the station had been at clear, and there were in any case safety devices that would have halted the train if a red light had been passed. As for the brakes, there were two systems on every train – the normal one and the Westinghouse emergency non-fail system which the driver could bring into immediate operation if the normal system failed. How? By turning the control beyond its normal stopping point. And the so-called Dead Man's Handle? That was a device to stop the train if for any reason such as physical collapse the driver released his pressure on the main control handle. And had such pressure been released? The indentation of the palm of the hand suggested that it had not.

What about the guard? He had power to apply emergency brakes if he noticed anything unusual, but he admitted to reading a newspaper and failing to notice that the train was entering the station at abnormal speed. 'A feckless young man,' the Coroner remarked.

The questioning went on for two days dealing with technical questions and at the end no positive proof of any fault in the train had been found.

What, then, of the driver?

His name was Leslie Newson, he was 55 years old, a quiet family man with no known emotional or financial difficulties to bother him. He had passed as a fully qualified driver nearly a year previously and his instructor-examiner, Ronald Deedman, confirmed that he was over- rather than under-cautious. Apart from a single occasion when he had slightly overrun a platform his record was unsullied.

Were conditions conducive to safety?

The shuttle run was short and dull and to avoid inattention due to monotony drivers were permitted to do only two hours without a break. On the morning of 28 February, Newson had completed only one hour of his shift at the time of the accident. His wife said he had given her the usual 'peck on the cheek' before leaving home for work, and his colleagues at the depot had noticed nothing unusual in his behaviour.

The Home Office pathologist said that his examination had revealed no sort of disease that would have caused a sudden attack or any hint that Driver Newson was under the influence 'of any substance'. But then came a bombshell. Dr Ann Robinson, a senior analyst, said that Newson's blood had contained 80 mg of alcohol for each 100 ml of blood – an amount equivalent to five single whiskies.

At this Mrs Newson bridled. Through her solicitor she asked for Dr Robinson's evidence to be re-examined. Her husband, she said, was not a pub *habitué* and was most modest in his drinking habits. He liked a glass of brown ale sometimes after his evening meal, but he had not had one on the night before the tragedy. 'There were certainly spirits in the house – Bacardi and things like that for festive occasions like Christmas, but he never touched them. He didn't like spirits.'

'Never a spot to keep out the cold on such a morning as the 28th of February?' she was asked.

'Never,' she replied.

One of Newson's colleagues at the depot confirmed that he had had a cup from Newson's flask of tea and that there had been no taste of alcohol in it. Then another expert witness took the stand and told the court that alcohol levels in the blood can rise considerably through fermentation after death if the blood is not stored in a refrigerator. This way and that, the medical arguments went on for another two days. *The Times* Science Correspondent summed it up:

Though the tiniest traces of alcohol can be detected in the blood and body tissues by new methods of analysis known as liquid-gas chromology, the conditions of the Moorgate crash make the job of interpreting the results nightmarish. Six experts in forensic science, pathology, and public analysis could see no clear way yesterday of guaranteeing how much alcohol was in the body and how much had formed after death.

Dr Paul dealt with the impasse in his summing up to the jury:

If on the evidence you form the view that the level of alcohol, whatever it is, was the result of swallowing drink, and the level contributed or caused Driver Newson to overrun in this tragic manner, you are entitled to look at his conduct in drinking [and] to say if it measures up to the degree of negligence defined as wicked, careless behaviour, deliberately putting at risk the safety of others. This would entitle you to consider returning a verdict of manslaughter.

The jury was out for one hour and 15 minutes. Their verdict was accidental death.

Through her solicitor Mrs Newson thanked the court for the consideration shown her throughout the inquest and wished Dr Robinson to know that she had never borne her any ill will for bringing forward the matter of alcohol content. 'She was only doing her job.'

So there the matter rests. Was Leslie Newson a secret drinker? Or did he suffer some unaccountable mental brainstorm that caused him to drive blindly towards certain death, thus blackening the pages of London Transport's history with the worst disaster ever? The question marks remain.

ENIGMAS OF AIR
AND SEA

KOREAN AIRLINES FLIGHT 007

One day in the late summer of 1985, a Japan Airlines (JAL) Boeing 747 took off from Tokyo for Paris via Moscow. Not long after departure, the aircraft was pushed off its track (known as Romeo 11) by strong westerly winds. There was a good deal of turbulence. In an attempt to make life more comfortable for his passengers, the captain altered course to fly around a large cloud mass. With his attention distracted, and the first officer not sufficiently monitoring his actions, he put his Inertial Navigation System on to the wrong setting. What it amounted to was that he gave it instructions without empowering it to carry them out. The result became apparent some while later, when a couple of Soviet MIG fighters sped into view.

The 747 was 60 miles off course and fast approaching Sakhalin Island – a piece of Russian territory that commands the eastern approaches to Vladivostok. Sakhalin is understandably sensitive from a security point of view. The fighters waggled their wings and went through the rest of the 'get away from here' routine. The pilot realized his mistake, apologized profusely, and sharply altered course. No one was hurt, there was no diplomatic crisis: the only victim was the captain – who was subsequently reduced to the rank of first officer as payment for his error.

Shortly afterwards, Captain Hidermaro Nagano, special assistant to JAL's president, published a paper entitled *Mental Fitness for Duty and Control of Arousal State*. The gist of his findings was that, on a long flight, pilots are apt to be lulled into a state of false security. As the automation in cockpits becomes more and more sophisticated, their dependence upon it is liable to increase.

Their minds may wander; they could become less responsive; and mistakes are possible. The message was emphatic: let the pilot beware.

If we accept Captain Nagano's hypothesis, we may find the solution (or some of it) to a mystery that had occurred about two years earlier – on 1 September 1983. The aircraft concerned was also a Boeing 747, in this case the property of Korean Airlines (KAL). It was shot from the sky by a Russian Sukhoi SU15 interceptor when on a flight from Anchorage, Alaska, to Seoul in South Korea. All 269 people on board died. The place of its destruction was, again, in the region of Sakhalin Island. The pilot of the KAL jumbo, Captain Byung-in, had also made an error of navigation: in this case, he was 365 miles to the north of where he believed himself to be. But, unlike the JAL captain, he either ignored, or else was completely unaware of, the Russians' considerable attempts to attract his attention.

KAL Flight 007 left John F. Kennedy International Airport, New York, on the night of 31 August. It was scheduled to land at Anchorage, after which it would proceed non-stop to Seoul. The weather in New York was appalling. High winds and heavy rain had caused part of the aerodrome to be flooded, and some incoming flights had to be diverted to Baltimore. Among them was one from Georgia carrying Congressman Larry McDonald. Mr McDonald was also chairman of the John Birch Society, an extreme right-wing organization. He was travelling to Seoul to attend the 30th anniversary of the United States-South Korean Mutual Security Treaty. The diversion made him late. He missed the aircraft he had intended to take, and was allocated a seat on Flight 007. Among the other passengers were 81 Americans and 28 Japanese. The rest were mainly Koreans.

The flight to Anchorage was uneventful. Here Captain Byung-in and his crew took over. A flight plan, prepared for him by the Continental Airlines computer at Los Angeles, was sent to Anchorage by telex. There was nothing remarkable about this: it was frequently done. Among its contents was a list of all the waypoints over which the 747 would have to pass on its way to the South Korean capital.

Somebody defined the shortest distance between two points

as a straight line. He was obviously not thinking about navigation. The world, after all, is a sphere. To get from A to B by the most direct course you take the Great Circle route. The section from Anchorage to Seoul is known as Romeo 20. If you have to depend upon a magnetic compass (the 747 in question had two of them, but they were only for emergencies), it involves continually changing course and adds considerably to the workload. But Captain Byung-in, like most other airline captains, had a much better means at his disposal. It is known as INS – inertial navigation system.

Basically, it works by dead reckoning with a very advanced computer at its heart. It can fix the aircraft's position with amazing accuracy; it can reveal the altitude; and it can instruct the automatic pilot. Along the route, there are radio beacons known as waypoints. One minute before a waypoint is reached an amber light comes on in the cockpit. It remains lit until two minutes after the beacon has been passed. By this time, the captain should have radioed his position and his estimated time of arrival at the next. If he fails to do this, an emergency is declared.

The problem about waypoints is their tolerance. If an aircraft is anything up to 200 miles off course as it flies overhead, the reassuring amber light will still light up. It is only when this limit is exceeded that it fails to function. Thus it is possible to make mistakes without being aware of them. Captain Byung-in certainly did.

INS asks only two things of those who use it. The first, and paramount, necessity is that the correct coordinates (the latitude and longitude) shall be punched into its system at the point of departure – it must, after all, be given some clue of its whereabouts. The other is that, when one waypoint has been passed, it should be told the coordinates of the next. It is, of course, also a good idea to inform the automatic pilot that it is to obey these orders. To do this, a so-called mode selector is used. It is easy enough to carry this out, but care is counselled. One click in the wrong direction will put the magnetic compass in control – which is all very well if you wish to use it, but fatal if you believe yourself to be flying by INS.

185

As this may suggest, the risk of selection of mistakes is small but it exists nevertheless.

Captain Byung-in was an experienced aviator. He had begun his career by serving in the air force as a fighter pilot. Now he was 45 years old. Since joining KAL in 1972, he had put in 6,619 hours at the controls of the 747s and this was to be his 88th crossing of the Pacific. Back on his home ground, he belonged to a small élite of pilots selected to fly the South Korean president about his business. The aircraft he was flying that night had been completed in 1972 for Lufthansa. Seven years later, it was sold to KAL. It had now flown for 36,718 hours and made 9,237 landings.

When Flight 007 took off from Anchorage, the radio beacon was not functioning. It had been closed down 12 hours earlier for routine maintenance. But this was thought to be a matter of no importance. The local radar had a range of 175 miles, and, anyway, there was a waypoint at Bethel, 400 miles away.

Beyond any reasonable doubt, Captain Byung-in made his greatest mistake when the aircraft was still on the ground. When the 747 flew out of radar range, it was seen to be 6 miles to the north of track Romeo 20. This was considered to be a small error – doubtless the captain would correct it. There was nothing to worry about. At Bethel, however, it was seen to be 40 miles off track and this might, indeed, have been an occasion for anxiety. The gap was becoming larger: unless somebody told Byung-in, it might very well continue to increase until it became more than 200 miles – and the lack of an amber light would signal the mistake. But nothing was said. Flight 007 continued on its unfortunate way, its flight crew still under the illusion that it would reach Seoul at 5.33 a.m. local time.

So what had Byung-in done wrong? There are two possibilities. Either he fed the wrong coordinates to the INS before taking off (such mistakes are by no means unknown), or else he put the mode selector to the wrong setting. A trace of the distance flown by the 747 shows that it was flying continuously on a bearing of 246 degrees. This is exactly what might have been expected had the autopilot been keyed in to the magnetic compass – and certainly not what a correctly informed INS would have pro-

186

duced. Obviously there was some carelessness. Nor is it to the credit of First Officer Son, whose duty it was to monitor whatever his captain did – to act, as it were, as his guardian angel.

On a less-sensitive route, the errors would probably not have produced a disaster. When he reached a waypoint and no amber light came on, the pilot would have checked his position, found that he was in the wrong place, and done something about it. The flight would have been late on arrival, but it would have arrived. Romeo 20 passed close to some of the more sensitive parts of the U.S.S.R. On the Kamchatka Peninsula, there is a Soviet nuclear-submarine base and an arsenal of ballistic missiles. Visitors are not welcome. Farther on at Sakhalin Island, there is the naval base that is the key to Vladivostok's supply route. This, too, is remarkable for the number of notices bidding strangers to keep out. By an unhappy coincidence, Red Army units at Petropavlovsk on Sakhalin were due to test a new weapon early that morning. Quite often, the authorities at Tokyo are tipped off about these operations. The air-traffic controllers at Anchorage are informed, and a NOTAM (notice to airmen) is put up. But, on this occasion, the Russians said nothing.

Nevertheless, it seems possible that the Pentagon may have had suspicions that something was scheduled to take place. Among the informative devices at the disposal of the U.S. airforce is a Boeing 707 that has been modified almost out of recognition. It is designated an RC135 and is used for operations classified as ELINT (electronic intelligence gathering). It does not need to trespass into Soviet air space – indeed, at night, it flies with its navigation lights turned on – but this is not to underrate its ability to intercept military radio signals. As it happened, an RC135 was in the vicinity as the 747 blundered towards Soviet territory. The two aircraft were flying at the same height (31,000 feet), the same speed (540 knots), and they came so close to each other that, for 10 minutes, their blips on the Russian radar screens merged (despite President Reagan's insistance that they were always at least 75 miles apart).

Consequently, there may have been some confusion down

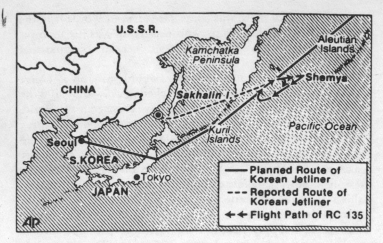

The planned, and reported, route of Flight KAL 007, and the path of the reconnaissance aircraft

below. The Soviet authorities knew perfectly well about these ELINT missions, and they almost certainly knew that one was taking place that night. The trouble seems to have been that they did not realize that two aircraft were involved, and that one of them was a civilian plane.

The RC135, its mission completed, quietly turned away and flew back to its base. The 747, now far to the north of its track, pursued its erroneous course.

Down on the ground at Petropavlovsk, the Russians decided that the game had gone on for long enough. The missile test was cancelled, and a flight of interceptors was ordered to become airborne. With the assistance of radar, it was easy enough to locate the target. Oddly, the pilots reported that it was not showing any navigation lights. As subsequent events showed, this was untrue. The 747, albeit misplaced, was flying quite normally.

There was nothing trigger-happy about the exercise. The Sukhoi SU15 pilots wiggled their aircrafts' wings, flashed their lights on and off, even called up Flight 007 on the distress frequency. For some reason that cannot be explained, the flight deck crew of the 747 appeared blind and deaf to all these demonstrations. The giant aircraft just flew doggedly onwards. Eventually, the fighters reached the limit of their range, and had to turn back for fear of running out of fuel.

As Flight 007 cleared the coastline of the Kamchatka Peninsula, the waypoint NIPPI lay 180 miles to the south – just within the 200-mile limit. The amber light came on in the cockpit.

Sakhalin Island is separated from the northernmost island of Japan by a mere 80 miles. The fighters at Petropavlovsk had been scrambled on the spur of the moment. Consequently, they did not get off the ground sufficiently quickly: the 747 was some way ahead of them, and it took time to catch up. On Sakhalin Island, there are four bomber bases and four interceptor airfields. Presumably, the latter had been warned to expect a visitor: at all events, their reaction was very much more immediate. We know what the pilots said once they were in the air, but there was no way of listening to the instructions from ground control.

One of the fighters certainly fired a burst of tracer cannon shells, presumably to attract attention. We can also be reasonably sure that Captain Byung-in never saw them. In any case, he had other things on his mind. He had decided to ascend from 31,000 feet to 35,000 feet, where the thinner air would reduce his engines' fuel consumption. He was busy telling First Officer Son to inform Tokyo air-traffic control of his intentions, and to obtain permission to carry them out. Tokyo gave the necessary assent, but here is a small mystery. Flight 007 must have shown up on the ATC radar scopes by now, but it does not seem to have occurred to anyone to question its position. Not only was it in the wrong place; it was also, as Byung-in would have realized had he paid more attention to what was going on outside, in a very dangerous place.

One possible answer is that a long night was coming towards its end. The controllers were tired and they did not pay sufficient attention to the situation. Another hypothesis is that civil aircraft were in the habit of overflying this corner of the Soviet realm. It probably clipped a few miles off the route and, once one had got away with it, others followed. If this were the case, the ATC men would have found it unremarkable. It might also follow that Russian patience had at last run out. It was necessary to make an example.

To be fair to the Soviet fighter pilots, they had done everything within their power to attract attention and they had failed. Unlike their comrades at Petropavlovsk, they noticed that the 747 was showing navigation lights. But this did not save Captain Byung-in, his flight crew of three, seven stewards, his 13 stewardesses, and his 246 passengers. At the Dolinsk-Sokol air base on the southern tip of the island, somebody pretty high up in the hierarchy reached a decision. Since it had been impossible to get the message across, the intruder must be destroyed. At this point, the nearest Sukhoi SU15 was 2 kilometres away from the jumbo jet. The pilot noticed that it now seemed to be reducing speed – occasioned, one must suppose, by the start of its 4,000-foot climb. He was given the order to attack: an order that, perhaps, surprised him. At all events, he asked, 'Say again.'

Two heat-seeking missiles tore apart Flight 007 – one of them controlled by radar, the other by infra-red. Both found their targets. From First Officer Son: 'Korean zero zero seven . . . rapid decompression . . . descending to one thousand.' That was rather too optimistic. The 747's descent came to an end in the Soya Strait, just outside Russian territorial waters. There were no survivors; and, when the Japanese authorities attempted to retrieve the flight recorder, a Soviet naval vessel turned them away. Ironically the position was 350 miles to the north of waypoint NOKKA. On this occasion there would have been no amber light.

President Reagan was angered by the loss of American lives – especially that of Congressman Larry McDonald. His invective against the Russians reached new heights of acerbity, and the hands of the 'Doomsday Clock' moved another minute or two towards midnight. But the Russian leaders themselves did not appear to have been pleased with the performance of their men on the spot. Heads fell afterwards: possibly because of the unwanted international incident produced by the tragic episode; or possibly because they would have preferred the trespasser to have been taken alive. They were certainly shedding no tears for Congressman McDonald.

190

There had, indeed, been a previous incident of a civil aircraft that had strayed into forbidden air space being brought down in the U.S.S.R. Nobody was hurt: the aircraft was impounded – but, after interrogation, the crew and passengers were released.

The question in the case of Flight 007, of course, arose as to what, precisely, did the Russians think they were dealing with. Was the 747 seen to be an airliner, or was it mistaken for the RC135 that had gone back to its base? But if the latter were the case, surely an alert military pilot might have been expected to change course and make a run for it – instead of plodding on and getting ever deeper into trouble. Furthermore, greater effort might have been made, not only to attract attention, but also to force it down. The capture of a spy-plane would have served a useful propaganda purpose: the inspection of such an aeronautical oddity would have been richly rewarding. And, then again, its crew would have been useful currency for swopping secret agents. When, in 1960, Lieutenant Francis Gary Powers was shot down over Sverdlovsk flying his high-altitude photo-reconnaissance U-2, he was eventually exchanged for one Rudolph Abel. Before he made one or two fatal mistakes, and was sentenced to 30 years' imprisonment, Abel had been Russia's top spy in the United States. The U.S.S.R. was glad to have him back.

It is not too difficult to deduce the nature of the error that took Captain Byung-in so far off track. It is fairly easy to assume that, down below on Russian territory, someone may have blundered. The real mystery about Flight 007 is why the flight crew allowed so many warnings to go unheeded. Even guesswork contributes little to its solution.

ROYAL TRAGEDY AT EAGLE'S ROCK

On 26 August 1942, the King and Queen were at Balmoral in Scotland. During dinner that evening, His Majesty was called to the telephone. It seemed that Sir Archibald Sinclair, Secretary of State for Air, wished to speak to him. When he returned to the dining room, the monarch looked drawn and sad. He had just learned that, on the previous afternoon, his youngest brother had been killed in an air crash. The RAF Sunderland flying boat, which should have taken the 39-year-old Duke of Kent to Iceland, had smashed into the side of a hill shortly after take-off. He was the first son of a British sovereign to die on active service for 500 years.

Prince George Edward Alexander, second Duke of Kent, was intelligent, well informed, had a good sense of humour, and his easy charm suggested that he was unscathed by the oppressive upbringing his father, George V, inflicted on his sons. His marriage to Princess Marina of Greece was, by all accounts, extremely happy. When in 1936, Edward VIII gave up the throne in favour of Mrs Simpson, there were some who suggested that he should succeed him. The reason was that, unlike the next in line (the Duke of York – later King George VI), he had a son. Kings, it seems, were preferred to queens – at any rate in this corner of the realm.

The first ten years of the Duke's career were spent in the Royal Navy. Afterwards, he held the rank of Rear-Admiral and that of Air Vice-Marshal in the Royal Air Force. When World War II broke out in 1939, he was preparing to set off for Australia to take over the duties of Governor General.

He immediately changed his plans and asked to be excused from the appointment. With Britian pledged to destroy Nazi Germany, he had no intention of departing to the other side of the world. The place for him, he decided, was in the Royal Air Force.

The rank of Air Vice-Marshal was an honorary one: something that involved no executive tasks, a mark of respect that pleased the RAF as much as it did the Duke. It would, he believed, be ridiculous to assume the rank as a working officer. He would, after all, be associating with very much more experienced colleagues. He was, he knew, an amateur; they were professionals. With a nice sense of fitness, he virtually demoted himself to Group Captain. He was appointed to the staff of the RAF's Inspectorate General with particular responsibility for welfare services.

By 1941, he had been promoted to Air Commodore. In the autumn of that year, he embarked in a Liberator bomber for Canada. His mission was to tour airforce establishments set up under the Commonwealth Training Plan. On his way home, he visited New York, where he was a guest at Hyde Park – the home of President Franklin D. Roosevelt. The two men got on famously.

On his return to the U.K., the Duke treated himself to three weeks' leave. His next assignment was to take him to RAF units in Iceland. Departure was scheduled for 25 August. An RAF Sunderland flying boat from 228 Squadron based at Oban would fly him from Invergordon (on the east coast of Scotland) to Reykjavik. On the face of it, Oban might seem to have been a more suitable starting point for the journey. Invergordon was chosen for its proximity to Inverness. It was easier to reach by rail from London.

The commanding officer of 228 Squadron, Wing Commander T.L. Moseley, was an Australian who had graduated at the RAF College, Cranwell. His previous appointment had been at the Air Ministry as Deputy Director of Training (Navigation). His association with flying boats dated back to 1934 – which suggests, rightly, that he was well experienced in their ways. He proposed to accompany the Duke on his trip.

The flying boat in question was W4026 captained by another Australian, Flight-Lieutenant Frank Goyen – 25 years old and with four years in the RAF to his credit. He, too, had considerable experience in the handling of this type of aircraft. Over 1,000 flying hours of his total had been spent in Sunderlands on patrol over the Mediterranean and the South Atlantic. On one occasion in 1940, while keeping a discreet watch on the Italian fleet, his supply of petrol ran low. Nothing daunted, he waited until dark and then came down on to the sea. He and his crew spent the rest of the night watching the distant Italian ships. Then, at dawn and with a flourish, the Sunderland took off and headed homeward.

All told, the crew for the Duke of Kent's trip amounted to ten: two pilots (the co-pilot was also an Australian), two radio operators, a navigator, an engineer, a fitter, and three gunners manning the .303-inch Browning machine-guns. Such, indeed, was the armament, that *Luftwaffe* aircrews used to refer to the flying boats as 'Flying Porcupines'.

The trip to Reykjavik was 900 miles and was expected to last seven hours. However, nothing could be taken for granted. The possibility of bad weather over Iceland had to be accepted: a state of affairs that might make it necessary to abort the landing and to return to Invergordon. With this in mind, it was considered essential that W4026 should set off with her fuel tanks loaded to capacity. The Duke would be accompanied by two aides and his batman. Wing Commander Moseley would be present – making, with the crew, a total of 15 men. The aircraft would be carrying its normal load of depth-charges in case any U-boats were sighted on the flight. What with one thing and another, it would be uncommonly heavy. Once it had settled down at its cruising altitude (5,000 feet for the coming flight), this would pose few problems. The speed would be somewhat reduced, admittedly. The Sunderland is billed as having a maximum of 213 mph. A simple sum makes clear that it would be flying at an average of 128 mph. This, however, was a matter of no concern. W4026 was well able to look after itself – once it had been established in the air. The problem, if such there was, was to get there. Or, to put it another way, the rate of climb would be slow and the distance taken longer than usual.

The most direct route to Reykjavik would have been to follow a northwesterly course after take-off, passing over Sutherland and so over the Atlantic by way of Cape Wrath. The RAF briefing authorities considered and quickly rejected it. As they knew very well, the country is on the hilly side – mountainous, indeed. Two of the peaks exceed 3,000 feet; several more are very nearly that height. With the Sutherland made sluggish by

194

so much weight, such a route would have been foolhardy. Better by far, they decided, to strike off on a northeasterly bearing: to fly over the sea as far as John o'Groats. From there, the pilot would overfly the Pentland Firth and then head directly for Iceland.

Even discounting the possibility of enemy attack, flying in those days was still something of an adventure. The Duchess of Kent was known to worry when her husband took to the sky, but so did many other wives. On this particular occasion, she seems to have experienced no presentiment when, in the late afternoon of 24 August, her husband drove away from Coppins – their country house at Iver, Buckinghamshire – for Euston. She would be seeing him in a week's time, or so she thought: it was something to look forward to.

At the railway terminus, the Duke was met by his private secretary (Lieutenant J.A. Lowther RNVR), an equerry (Pilot-Officer The Hon. Michael Strutt), and his batman (Leading-Aircraftsman John Hales). Strutt was deputizing for the Duke's normal air equerry, who had been taken ill. The train journey to Inverness was uneventful. A car was waiting at the station: at just after 1 p.m. on the 25th, the party walked along the jetty at Invergordon, where a tender was waiting to take them to the aircraft.

Goyen and his crew had flown over from Oban on the previous day. The weather at Invergordon confirmed the good sense of the planners in deciding to resist the tempation of the more direct route. It was pouring with rain and the cloud base was down to 800 feet. On the other hand, the surface of the Cromarty Firth was placid, unruffled by wind. This was not altogether an advantage. A brisk northeasterly and some waves would have assisted W4026's take-off.

Under such conditions, was there a case to be made for delaying the flight: for waiting until the sky cleared and the Sunderland's crew could see what lay beneath them? The authorities decided that there was not. Many flying boats had departed in such circumstances before: there was nothing to suggest that this trip would be jinxed. In any case, W4026 would be passing over the Faroes about midway on its journey.

Up there, or so the meteorological reports suggested, the weather would be likely to improve.

If Goyen and his companions were impressed by the identity of their illustrious passenger, they showed no signs of it. This was just another job of work – probably safer than many of their assignments. The aim, after all, was to deliver the Duke to Iceland and to bring him back again. If a U-boat were sighted, they would certainly engage it, but this was of secondary importance. Transportation, not combat, was the name of this particular game. Nevertheless, their skill at navigation would be tested to the full in such unkind conditions. The Sunderland was fitted with radar, but this was the centrimetric version specifically designed for anti-submarine operations. As an aid to discovering their whereabouts – or for any other purpose, come to that – it was useless.

A few minutes after 1 o'clock, the giant flying boat set off down Cromarty Firth, laboriously trying to get off the water and into the sky. With such a heavy load, it took time and distance, but this was no cause for anxiety. There was plenty of both. And, sure enough, W4026 did eventually heave itself into the air; it climbed slowly and pointed its nose in a northeasterly direction.

We know a little about what happened during the next 30 minutes, but nothing like enough. There was one survivor from the crash, but he was the rear-gunner, snug in his turret at the tail end and some way removed from the cockpit. Almost certainly, Dunrobin Castle, home of the Dukes and Earls of Sutherland, was glimpsed over to port on its remote cliff-top perch. But then the mist closed in and Goyen was flying blind. There is some evidence to suggest that, searching for a hole in the cloud mass through which to catch a reassuring sight of the sea, he brought the Sunderland down to 1,200 feet, but this is mostly conjecture. If it is true, then Goyen cannot have been on top form. Assuming that he was sticking to his planned route, and assuming that he was making the right allowance for drift, no such reassurance should have been necessary. The object, surely, was to gain altitude rather than to lose it.

But strange things were happening on the flight deck of

W4026. A glimpse of the sea, the land, anything, would have been helpful. The Sunderland had indeed strayed from its intended path. At some point after that brief view of Dunrobin Castle, the aircraft must have crossed the coastline and wandered into the air space of Sutherland and then Caithness. Goyen had, by accident, done the very thing his flight plan had been designed to avoid. He was now, unknowingly, in a region full of potential hazards. Not only was he in danger of falling prey to what is described as the 'Rocks in the Sky syndrome' (that is, collision with a mountain), there was also the matter of turbulence.

The action of wind on mountains has been compared to that of waves breaking on rocks. It accelerates, becoming ever more powerful, as it drives upwards towards the peaks. This updraught can continue until it has reached a point well above the summits. Once over the top, however, it breaks downwards, throwing any aircraft unfortunate enough to be in its thrall into a state of utter confusion. The airspeed can increase or diminish by as much as 50 knots. It can pitch; it can yaw; it can slip. It can also be hurled downwards until it makes a disastrous impact with the ground. Given sufficient altitude, of course, it is not difficult for the pilot to regain control. But, in this instance, altitude was a commodity of which the Sunderland was gravely deficient.

Not very far from the Duke of Portland's Langwell House near Berriedale on the coast, there is a 2,313-foot peak named Morven; and, adjacent to Morven, stands a rather less imposing hill, about 800 feet high, the Eagle's Rock. Its lower slopes were grazed by sheep belonging to a farmer, David Morrison. On that Tuesday afternoon, Mr Morrison was going about his business with his son, Hugh, when the two men heard the sound of an obviously low-flying aircraft. Seconds later, or so it seemed, there was the din of a crash: after that, silence.

The younger Mr Morrison hurried down to the foot of Eagle's Rock, where his motorbike was parked. Calling at crofts and farms on the way, he reached Berriedale in admirably short time. He alerted the police and also informed the local doctor – 71-year-old Dr Kennedy.

197

Before very long, a search had been organized, but the weather remained obdurate. Groping through the thick mist, the seekers could find nothing. At nightfall, the operation was called off until first light on the following morning. And, even then and with greatly improved visibility, it was not until the early afternoon that the remains of Sunderland W4026 were discovered. Its path to disaster was marked by a swathe scorched in the heather, about 600 feet long by 300 feet wide. There were no signs of any survivors; the aircraft was considerably fragmented. It was Dr Kennedy who came across a figure, half hidden by the heather, wearing the uniform of an Air Commodore and with a platinum watch on its wrist. It seemed to be strangely peaceful, almost as if the man were asleep. The watch had stopped at 1.20. For a minute or two, Dr Kennedy was perplexed. The man's face made him think of somebody – and then he remembered. It was one that he had often seen in the newspapers: the Duke of Kent.

It seems probable that the Sunderland just about cleared the summit of Eagle's Rock and was then flung by a downdraught on to a shoulder jutting out on the far side. The impact caused the tail to break off, hurling the occupant of the rear turret, Sergeant Andrew Jack, clear of the remainder of the wreck. Sergeant Jack was knocked unconscious, received severe burns to his face and hands, but he survived. He managed to extricate himself and to search the wreckage to make sure that nobody else had come through the disaster alive. Again he passed out. When he came to, his overwhelming ambition was to get off the hill: to find some sort of sanctuary. There was, he noticed, a path that led downwards and he decided to follow it.

A colossal effort of will was needed. All the time, as he stumbled over the rough ground, he was tormented by the desire for sleep. After a while, he could endure it no longer. He curled up in the shelter of a clump of bracken and closed his eyes. When he awoke, it was late the next morning. The mist and the overcast had been replaced by a clear, bright summer's sky. He resumed his trek until, at last, he came upon a cottage. The lady of the house gave him a drink of milk and did her best to dress his injuries.

198

The King was informed that evening. Some days afterwards, he attended his brother's funeral at Windsor and, later, paid a visit to the place where the Sunderland had crashed. 'I felt I had to do this pilgrimage,' he said. Inevitably, there was a Court of Inquiry into the accident. It was, its members concluded, 'due to the aircraft being on wrong track . . . captain changed flight plan for reasons unknown and descended through cloud without making sure he was over water and crashed . . . weather conditions should have presented no difficulties to crew of such experience.'

But did Flight-Lieutenant Goyen change the flight plan – and, if he did, why? Did, for instance, the Duke find fault with it and insist that the more direct route should be taken? To accept such an hypothesis, one has to rethink the characters of both men. As his conduct at the outbreak of war demonstrated, the Duke of Kent respected the professionals. He would certainly have agreed with the recommendations of Goyen – and, come to that, of Wing Commander Moseley. As for Goyen, he was well aware that when he was at the controls of his flying boat he was outranked only by God. He was, indeed, a stubborn man who, when in disagreement, would sometimes say, 'I wouldn't do that if the King told me!' He may not have intended this as more than a figure of speech. Nevertheless, he was unlikely to have been influenced by the prince on a subject in which, he reckoned, he had more than sufficient expertise.

All manner of reasons have been hazarded for the disaster's cause – even the possibility that the crew was drunk. But this, too, seems out of the question. In wartime, aviators are under a lot of stress and they may, on occasion, become excessively thirsty. But this assignment was not an exacting one: it should have been, as they say, 'a doddle'. Furthermore, although Goyen and his crew did not know until shortly before take-off whom they would be taking to Iceland, Moseley did. Without a doubt, his authoritative eye would have been on his subordinates to make sure nobody overstepped the mark. And, finally, they had been carefully selected as men who were stable, skilled and experienced.

The Court of Inquiry attributed the disaster to pilot error, and there seems no reason to doubt this. If you look at a map, you will see that the Sunderland's final resting place is roughly to the northeast of Invergordon. And if, as seems likely from Sergeant Jack's evidence, the crew had glimpsed Dunrobin Castle, this would suggest that the flying boat was not sufficiently far offshore. Wind drift may have nudged it farther to the west, and the turbulence over the hills would have done the rest. The fact that Goyen was flying too low was decisive.

Goyen got it wrong: there can be little doubt about that. How did a pilot of such experience make such a mistake? It is this that remains the mystery of the Duke of Kent's death.

A RED EAGLE FALLING

On the overcast morning of 21 April 1918 a blood-red Fokker triplane, riddled with bullet holes, fell to earth 2 miles inside the British lines near Corbie in the Somme Valley of Flanders. It hit the ground heavily, bounced and lost a wheel, then slid to a halt close to some trenches manned by Australian troops.

The nearest witness to this rough landing was Sergeant-Major J.H. Sheridan of the 3rd Battery, Royal Artillery. He stayed watching and waiting for the pilot to emerge. Seconds passed with no sign of movement. Sheridan ran forward and looked cautiously into the cockpit. The black-helmeted pilot was slumped forward, his head supported by the butt of one of his machine-guns. A thin trail of blood trickled from his mouth, and there was blood seeping from a hole in his chest where the bullet which had gone right through his body had made its exit. Sheridan needed no second opinion to confirm that the German pilot was dead.

The credit for shooting him down went officially to Captain A. Roy Brown, of the RAF. Yet before the day was out several Australian soldiers who had fired at the German aircraft from the ground were vehemently claiming sole responsibility for the kill, and to add to the contest an announcement was made that an RE8 reconnaissance aircraft had brought the Fokker down.

Whose version of events was true and why did this single victory matter so much to the various claimants, when the credit for killing other airmen in similar circumstances was rarely argued? The first question remains unanswered – indeed unanswerable. The answer to the second lies in the identity of the dead pilot. Until that fateful day he had been a living legend, the idol of all Germany, Captain Baron Manfred von Richthofen, the Red Baron himself.

Born on 2 May 1892 at Breslau in Prussia, he was the eldest of three brothers in an aristocratic family. Horsemanship and hunting were second nature to them all. As a horseman, it was only natural for Manfred to join the 1st Regiment of Uhlan cavalry at the outbreak of war, but it was his love of the hunt that inspired him in May 1915 to be transferred into the German Flying Corps. He was accepted, and served that summer as an observer on both eastern and western fronts. During the Battle of Champagne in September he had shot down his first enemy plane, but as it fell unwitnessed in French territory the victory could not be credited officially to him.

It was not long before he applied for pilot training. 'From the beginning of my career as a pilot I had only one ambition,' he wrote later, 'and that was to fly a single-seater fighter plane.' Learning to fly at all proved a nerve-racking business. His first solo flight, on 10 October 1915, ended in a crash landing. Although he failed his first pilot's exam, he completed the course successfully by the end of the year.

Up to August 1916 Richthofen served with a two-seater squadron, based at first near Verdun before being moved for bombing and reconnaissance duties on the Russian front. He might have languished here in obscurity, but for an unexpected visit from the great Oswald Boelcke, whose leadership and tactical appreciation had established Germany as the dominant air power over Flanders. Boelcke had come looking for talented young pilots to join *Jagdstaffel 2*, the fighter squadron he was forming for the new offensive over the Somme. The eager Richthofen made a good impression on Boelcke, and three days later found himself on a west-bound train, heading towards 'the most wonderful time of my life'.

Though Boelcke was only one year his senior, Richthofen idolized him and hung on his every word. Boelcke always stressed that teamwork, not individual brilliance, was the most important element in aerial combat. So long as the team had the victory it did not matter which member of the team won it. Richthofen agreed in theory, even if the streak of arrogance in his character sometimes led him to forget it in practice – as it would on the day he died, when he forgot everything but his love of the hunt and left himself open to attack from more than one quarter.

That day was still far off when he scored his first official victory on 17 September 1916. He was one of four pilots led out by Boelcke from their base at Lagnicourt for a patrol in their new Albatros biplanes. Nearing the front, they came upon a British squadron of eight bomb-carrying BE2cs escorted by six FE2b two-seater scouts. Richthofen singled out an FE and, after one mistimed firing pass, remembered what Boelcke had taught him and slid in beneath his prey in the observer's blind spot. His close-range bullets shattered the FE's engine and mortally wounded pilot and observer. Richthofen exulted over the conquest of 'my first Englishman'.

He wrote that night to a Berlin jeweller, ordering a silver cup, 2 inches high, engraved with the date and the type of aircraft he had shot down. In the next two weeks he ordered a second trophy, then a third, so beginning a matchless, faintly macabre collection which would end only when the jeweller ran out of silver.

Richthofen was in his element now and happier than ever before. He was soon to be stunned, however, by the death of his hero, on 28 October. While flying in close formation, Boelcke's left wing brushed the undercarriage of the plane piloted by his friend Erwin Boehme. Boelcke's aircraft spiralled out of control, and he was killed on impact with the ground.

After they had recovered from the initial shock Boelcke's pupils were inspired to be worthy of their master. Manfred von Richthofen led the way, not least in the race to surpass Boelcke's final total of 40 victories, more than anyone else in the war had achieved up to that point. He was soon into double figures, and his 16th success in January 1917 made him Germany's No. 1 living ace. He was rewarded with his nation's highest military honour, the *Pour le Mérite*, popularly known as the Blue Max. He was also given his own squadron, *Jagdstaffel II*, and proved to be a more brilliant instructor and inspirational leader even than Boelcke.

His new command gave him *carte blanche* to fly whenever he wanted to. His appetite for combat was insatiable and his confidence boundless. His victory tally rose quickly into the thirites. One day, 'for no particular reason', he decided to have his Albatros painted red. 'After that,' as he wrote, 'absolutely everyone knew my red bird. In fact, even my opponents were not completely unaware of it.' The legend of the Red Baron was born.

When the rest of his squadron realized what a conspicuous target he had made of himself they all had their planes painted red as well; but each had a distinguishing splash of some other colour on the rear part of the fuselage, so only the Baron's aircraft was completely red.

April 1917 – 'Bloody April' to the Allies – was Richthofen's golden month. Out of 150 British plances shot down he accounted for 21, taking his total to 52 and racing past Boelcke's record. He felt almost ashamed to have surpassed his hero: 'I am no record-keeper. In the Flying Service records are far from our thoughts. One only fulfils one's duty.'

He went on leave on 1 May, leaving his brother Lothar in command of the squadron. Relieved by the temporary absence from the skies of *le diable rouge*, the British pilots were given new hope by the delivery of two new types of fighter, the Bristol F28 and the Sopwith Camel, which were to turn the tide of the war. The manoeuvrable little Camel would play a crucial part in the final act of the Red Baron's career.

On his return to action on 14 June, Richthofen, by now promoted to captain, found orders which formed part of a new German air strategy. Four of the old *Jagdstaffeln* were to be combined into the first *Jagdgeschwader*, a large mobile unit which, housed in tents and portable sheds, could be moved rapidly by train or lorry to any sector where it was needed most. The *Richthofen Geschwader* was soon imprinted with the stamp of its leader's personality. While the planes which had belonged to *Jagdstaffel II* remained mostly red, other pilots in the expanded squadron had theirs painted all manner of garish colours. They filled the sky like a host of gaudy dragonflies, earning from the Allies the name of 'Richthofen's Flying Circus'. The performances put on by this ruthlessly efficient fighting unit, however, were no laughing matter.

Richthofen had scored a further four victories when, near Ypres on 6 July, he had a close shave with death. A shot from a British plane at 600-foot range wounded him. The bullet drove a furrow across his scalp, splintering the bone. It was all he could do to make a forced landing before he passed out.

It was during his convalescence over the next few weeks that the Sopwith Camel began to give the Allies the upper hand. Richthofen was so concerned that he returned hurriedly to action, his head still heavily bandaged. His hopes rested much on the new Fokker triplanes, designed to climb faster and higher than the old Albatros types. The Fokker was ideal for the Baron, who liked to position himself behind his enemy. He lost no time in having his own new 'bird' painted his customary red.

As summer passed into autumn, however, his comrades saw a corresponding change in him. His talent remained intact, but his appetite for war was lost. At this time he wrote:

The battle now taking place on all fronts has become awfully serious. There is nothing left of the 'lively, merry war', as our deeds were called in the beginning. Now we must fight off despair and arm ourselves so that the enemy will not enter our country . . . I am in wretched spirits after every aerial battle. But that no doubt is an after-effect of my head wound. When I set foot on the ground again at my airfield after a flight, I go to my quarters and do not want to see anyone or hear anything.

He flew less often, devoting time to training pilots. In the six months from September 1917 to the following March he shot down only two enemy planes.

On 21 March, General von Ludendorff launched a full-scale offensive on the Western Front, the last great gamble of a nation on the brink of defeat. Recognizing the urgency of the situation, Richthofen hauled himself out of his depression by sheer will-power. For the next fortnight he was his old self again, raising his tally of victories to 78, as part of a concerted German effort which brought down hundreds of British aircraft. Then, on 8 April, just after his squadron had been moved to Cappy airfield on the Somme heavy rain set in and made flying impossible. In the following week-and-a-half of enforced idleness, Richthofen's depression returned, not helped by the news that the Allies had stemmed the German advance and were counterattacking all along the front.

On 20 April the weather was good enough for him to fly again. He promptly shot down two Sopwith Camels, to lift his score to 80, a figure unsurpassed by any other pilot. His colleagues gave a party in his honour, drinking to 'the one-man army, our leader, our teacher, and our comrade, the ace of aces'.

Richthofen had every reason to be cheerful as he walked out to his trusty red plane the next morning. It was cloudy, but an easterly breeze was keeping off the rain. In three days' time he would go on leave, to spend his 26th birthday on a hunting expedition with friends in the Black Forest. Soon he would be far away from the sights and sounds of war.

Twenty miles away, a squadron of Sopwith Camels was about to take off from Bertangles aerodrome. Its leader was a 24-year-old Canadian, Captain A. Roy Brown, a competent fighter with 12 victories to his credit. He was in a wretched state, suffering constant pain from a stomach ulcer and living on brandy and milk, unable to keep solid food down. A nervous tic twitched at the corner of his mouth. He, too, hoped to be sent on leave soon, far away from the sights and sounds of war.

One of the pilots under his command that day was an old schoolfriend, Lieutenant Wilfred May, making his first flight on active service. Brown told him to stay on the fringes of any dogfight that might develop. He could take a shot if the chance offered, but if he found himself in danger he must break away and head for home.

They had not been airborne long before Brown saw the colourful Fokkers of the *Richthofen Geschwader* attacking two RE8s over the German trenches. He led his Camels to the rescue, and there followed a whirling battle involving a dozen or more planes. Brown knew whose squadron he was up against, and the odds against his surviving the encounter. May, meanwhile, obeyed orders and stayed clear of the mêlée until he saw a stray Fokker. It seemed an easy target. He swooped after it excitedly and opened fire, missing by a wide margin. As he tried to adjust his aim his guns jammed. Furious with himself, but remembering what Brown had said, he veered away and headed for the British lines.

Richthofen, aloof from the battle and biding his time, saw the single Camel break away and decided to give chase. He put his Fokker into a shallow dive, settling in behind, effortlessly closing the gap. May was unaware of him until he heard the dread rattle of the German's machine-guns. Twisting round, he was horrified to see the hunter right on his tail. He sent his Camel into a steep turn, but there was no manoeuvre he could make that would shake off the Red Baron.

Suddenly finding himself free of the dogfight, Brown looked down for May. What he saw made him feel sick: the blood-red Fokker weaving after his friend along the Somme Valley, firing in quick bursts which ripped through the Camel's wings and sent up flurries of spray from the river just 200 feet below. Without a moment's thought, he dived down to the aid of the hapless May.

But surely he was too late? May was exhausted, and certain that his first flight in anger would be his last. 'I was a sitting duck,' he recalled; 'I was too low down between the banks to make a turn away from him. I felt that he had me cold, and I was in such a state of mind at this time that I had to restrain myself from pushing the stick forward and diving into the river, as I knew that I had had it.'

He was wrong. In the thrill of the chase, Richthofen had carried on too far. He was right over the Allied lines. On the ground, two Australians of the 24th Machine-Gun Company, Sergeant C.B. Popkin and Gunner R.F. Weston, fired a long burst as the Fokker flew low over them. Seconds later, Gunners W.J. Evans and R. Buie of the 14th Australian Field Artillery Brigade also opened fire on it with their two anti-aircraft Lewis guns. Simultaneously, Brown pulled out of his dive just above and to the right of the Fokker. Richthofen was so intent on his pursuit of May that he failed to notice Brown, who fired his twin Vickers machine-guns into the triplane's side. Only then did Richthofen look round in dismay. Brown saw his eyes glint behind the goggles for a split second, before he slumped forward in his seat. The Fokker flew on some way before making its rough landing.

Who deserved the credit for shooting down the Red Baron? The Australians, who wanted the glory when they knew the pilot's identity; or the self-effacing Canadian Roy Brown, soon to be invalided to a hospital in England. He himself felt no pride in the official recognition of his 13th victory; his only desire had been to save his friend.

One thing was certain about the Red Baron's death: he who had seemed invincible was no more. His loss, unlike Boelcke's, did not inspire his comrades to greater efforts. It dealt a devastating psychological blow to them and to his countrymen; comparable, Ludendorff thought, to the loss of 30 divisions. The end of Manfred von Richthofen, who had come to be as potent a symbol of the Fatherland as the Prussian red eagle, signified to many minds the beginning of the end of World War I.

THE *LUSITANIA*

Kapitän-Leutnant Walter Schwieger, commander of the German submarine U-20, is accused of torpedoing the Cunard liner *Lusitania*, on 7 May 1915, and thereby causing the death of 1,198 people. Among them were 128 Americans. Britain's official naval historian, Sir Julian Corbett, remarked that, 'Never had there been such a war loss at sea, never one which so violently outraged the laws of war and dictates of humanity.' Schwieger is unable to answer the charges: he was killed on 17 September 1917. Ironically, the agent of his destruction was in marked contrast to his greatest victim. Designated a 'Q-Ship', she was a 1,680-ton freighter named the *Stonecrop*. Outwardly, she looked like any other drudge of the high seas. But, when her disguise was removed, she was seen to be armed with two guns and a quartet of 200-pound howitzers. Schwieger's attack on the *Lusitania* owed little to cunning. His own demise depended upon it.

Inevitably, the German authorities protested that the 31,500-ton Cunarder had been fair game. According to the *Frankfurter Zeitung*: 'The huge steamer now at the bottom of the ocean had, as has been proved, a great quantity of war material and ammunition on board. She was moreover an enemy's vessel, for she was heavily armed. She was an auxiliary cruiser.'

Schwieger may have had similar thoughts. There was, almost certainly, a copy of the 1914 edition of *Jane's Fighting Ships* on board the submarine. In it, he would have seen a profile drawing of the liner. He would also have noted that she was listed as an armed merchant cruiser. If we are to believe the entry in his log, he fired only one torpedo. When he saw that she was carrying a great many civilians, he refrained from discharging a second. In any case, his stock was running low. He intended to conserve them for any targets that might present themselves during his voyage back to Germany.

The explosion occurred at the point just aft of the liner's bridge It did considerable damage in the engine room. On its own, however, it would not have been sufficient to sink the vessel. But the British Admiralty suggested that Schwieger was lying. In Their Lordships' version of the story, two torpedoes were fired. The second delivered the mortal blow.

But why should Schwieger have lied? One torpedo or two: it didn't much matter. His performance would be judged by his sinkings – not by his economy. Furthermore, most of the *Lusitania*'s 754 survivors were in accord with his declaration. There were, they were almost certain, two explosions, but the second seemed to have occurred within the ship.

If, then, Schwieger is to be credited with the truth, what reason had the Admiralty for inventing a second torpedo – and for sticking so tenaciously to the tale? Had they some reason for concealing the real cause of the *Lusitania*'s sinking? Was she not quite such an innocent victim as she seemed?

At the beginning of the twentieth century, it may have appeared to many people that command of the North Atlantic passenger trade was falling into German hands. They were building bigger, faster liners, and Britannia was no longer ruling these particular waves. Since they were being subsidised by the German government, it was not difficult to deduce their other purpose. In time of war, the ships could be taken over by the *Kriegsmarine* and used as raiders. This, clearly, could not remain unchallenged. In 1903, the British Admiralty handed over a considerable sum of money to the Cunard Line as a contribution towards the building of two great ships. The official reason was 'to win back for the United Kingdom the honour of having the two fastest vessels on the Atlantic.'

It may have seemed to be a nice gesture, but the Admiralty is seldom subject to such generosity. Anyone who studied the specifications would have observed that there had to be a mounting for a pair of guns on each forecastle, and that parts of the promenade decks had to be strengthened to take four guns on each side. A minimum speed of between 24 and 25 knots was stipulated and it was made clear that, in the event of hostilities, the ships would be handed over to the Royal Navy. Thus Schwieger's assessment was not unreasonable. The *Lusitania* had been built with a wartime role in mind.

The *Lusitania* and her sister, the *Mauretania*, came into service in 1907. In terms of speed, they matched up to everything that was asked of them. But there was a price: coal. Their consumption was prodigious. Had they been protected by adequate armour, the furnaces would have become even more rapacious.

Neither ship was ever used as an armed merchant cruiser. Until her demise in 1915, the *Lusitania* handled the Atlantic run. The *Mauretania* spent most of World War I at Liverpool. Her only contribution was to serve as a troopship during the Dardanelles campaign.

The rules for the treatment of merchant shipping in wartime had been laid down by the Hague Convention of 1907. The gist of them was that a hostile warship had the right to stop and search. If the vessel was unarmed, and if she was not carrying any cargo classified as contraband, she should be allowed on her way. Whatever the case, suitable provision had to be made for the safety of her crew and passengers.

That was in 1907. The submarine had yet to be recognized for the killer it turned out to be (Germany had only recently constructed her first U-boat). There were, indeed, doubts as to whether it would ever be used against merchantmen. As late as 1 January 1914, Winston Churchill said, 'I do not believe this would ever be done by a civilized power.' But it was done.

The Kaiser and Hitler had two things in common: impatience and a disregard for treaties. On 4 February 1915, the German government declared the sea around Britain as a war zone. 'From 18 February onwards,' the announcement ran, 'every enemy vessel found within this war zone will be destroyed without its always being possible to avoid danger to the crews and passengers.' And: '. . . owing to unforeseen incidents to which naval warfare is liable, it is impossible to avoid attacks being made on neutral ships in mistake for those of the enemy.' At least it was frank.

In theory, the *Lusitania* seemed to be safe against U-boat attack by reason of her considerable speed. She was far faster than any submarine yet produced. Indeed, in early 1915, she had escaped one possibly deadly encounter by making a run for it and getting out of range. But it does not seem to have occurred to anyone to wonder what might happen if, for one reason or

211

another, the liner had to slow down.

During the first week of May 1915, *Lusitania* was berthed in New York waiting to make a return passage to Liverpool. By a coincidence, two advertisements appeared in the city's newspapers. One was placed by the Cunard Line, giving notice of the sailing and proudly proclaiming the great liner as 'the fastest and largest steamer now in Atlantic service'. The other was the work of the German Embassy in Washington. Headed, simply NOTICE!, it had this to say:

Travellers intending to embark on the Atlantic voyage are reminded that a state of war exists between Germany and her allies and Great Britain and her allies; that the zone of war includes the waters adjacent to the British Isles; that, in accordance with formal notice given by the Imperial German Government, vessels flying the flag of Great Britain, or any of her allies, are liable to destruction in those waters and that travellers sailing in the war zone on ships of Great Britain or her allies do so at their own risk.

Perhaps the Cunard advertisement was more persuasive. The stern words of the German copywriter were certainly not heeded by the 1,600 travellers who had booked their passages in the *Lusitania* and who intended to make them, war zone or no war zone. What was more remarkable was that, on the eve of departure, the millionaire Alfred Vanderbilt, Carl Frohman the theatrical producer, and nine others received telegrams warning them not to sail. They were traced back to the office of the *Providence Journal* and dismissed as a newspaper stunt in rather bad taste. It may have been, but, as it happened, the newspaper's editor was receiving payments from British Naval Intelligence. Inevitably one must ask whether the messages were sent at the behest of that organization; and, if they were, why? Was there any reason to suppose that the liner might indeed run into trouble on this particular trip? There is no answer.

As the cargo manifest suggested, she was carrying war materials, although this document was less than honest. It listed 5,000 cases of cartridges (whether for rifles or sporting guns it was not made clear), and some fulminate of mercury fuses. In fact, there

212

were 4,527 boxes of .303 small-arms ammunition for the Royal Arsenal at Woolwich and 1,250 cases of 3.3-inch shrapnel shells (it was later indignantly denied that they contained explosive fillings). And then there was the matter of the cheese and the furs. There were 313 boxes of what purported to be cheese addressed to a dairy in Liverpool. The furs, or so the list suggested, came in 325 bales. But was this true? There is now reason to believe that these were, in fact, aliases for ill-prepared packages of gun cotton – and that these, and not a second torpedo from the U-20, caused the fatal explosion.

The first five days of the voyage were without incident until, approaching the southwest coast of Ireland, the *Lusitania* ran into fog. The master, Captain William Turner, reduced speed to 18 knots and then to 15 knots (the U-20 could accomplish 15.5 knots on the surface, 9.5 submerged). At some point, Turner received a radio message transmitted to all shipping in the vicinity. Its essence was that there were U-boats about, but it gave no details. No signal was addressed to the *Lusitania* specifically.

Captain Turner had his instructions and he tried to abide by them. He was to steer clear of all headlands by a margin of at least 5 miles. He was to follow a zigzag course, to give all ports a wide berth, to be sure that all the portholes were closed, and to keep to the centre of St George's Channel as he steamed towards the Irish Sea. Possibly he did not zigzag sufficiently, and one passenger noticed that several portholes had been left open on D Deck. He recalled thinking that this was rather strange.

On the other hand, Turner very properly doubled the watch, ordered the lifeboats to be swung out, and intended to put 12 miles between his ship and the Old Head of Kinsale on the southwest corner of Ireland.

U-boat commanders understandably favoured this patch of ocean. It covered the approaches to the Irish Sea and, indeed, to the English Channel. Consequently there were plenty of targets – either on their way to or from Southampton and London, or else Liverpool. On 6 May, the U-20 torpedoed the Harrison freighter *Candidate*. Schwieger was (for him) unusually meticulous about observing the niceties of war. The ship, assumed to be innocent, was stopped and searched. A six-pounder and two machine-guns were discovered. When, later that day, her sister, the *Centurion* came into view, she was sunk on sight.

Just before 1 p.m. on the 7th, the submarine lay submerged 12 miles off the Old Head of Kinsale. The crew was taking its lunch when in, Schwieger's words, 'a craft with very powerful engines is running above the boat'. He brought the U-20 up to periscope level and identified her, wrongly, as a small cruiser of the *Pelorus* class. In fact, she was HMS *Juno* of the *Eclipse* class hurrying back to her base at Queenstown (Cobh). The mistake was excusable: the two were very much alike.

The fog seemed to be persisting and Schwieger intended to leave the area: to move towards the Irish Sea in the hope of faring better. But then, at about 2 o'clock, the mist cleared – and there, steaming towards him, was this four-funnelled giant, immaculate in Cunard livery, but which he may have assumed to be an armed merchant cruiser. As she came closer, the captain altered course, presenting him with her flank. The target was too good to ignore; too easy to miss. He fired a torpedo, waited for a few minutes to watch the consequences, and then departed.

Although the sea was tolerably calm and land was only 12 miles away, the business of evacuating the *Lusitania* was a shambles. She sank 18 minutes after the second explosion. The din of escaping steam drowned Captain Turner's commands. The list the liner developed made it impossible to launch many of the boats. Those on one side swung out too far. Those on the other were smashed against the hull. HMS *Juno*, who might have given assistance, was well on her way back to Queenstown – ironically fleeing from the U-boat scare. There was no other vessel in sight. In the end, the only attempts to save life were made by Irish fishermen. The Royal Navy stayed at home.

The loss of the *Lusitania* so enraged Britain against Germany that it seems to have deprived the nation of logical thought. It is popularly thought to have been the reason why, on account of the 128 Americans that died (they included Vanderbilt and Frohman), the United States joined the war against Germany. But this is untrue. Nearly two years were to pass before President

Wilson sufficiently stiffened his sinews to take such a step.

Viewed with hindsight, the disaster poses a number of disturbing questions that ought to have been asked, but which seem to have escaped attention. Why, for example, was Captain Turner not given more specific warnings? A team at the Admiralty, housed in Room 40, not only intercepted German radio signals; its members had also succeeded in cracking the codes. They knew the position of just about every enemy submarine that was out on business. In some cases, they even knew the names of the commanding officers.

The naval force at Queenstown was, admittedly, small. The admiral in charge of it had been given the appointment following criticisms of the way in which he had conducted the Dover Patrol. Four aged cruisers (1897 vintage) were at his disposal and four armed yachts. On the other hand, a division of destroyers was available at Milford Haven on the far side of St George's Channel. The *Lusitania* could have been given an escort, but no escort was given. Alternatively, Captain Turner could have been instructed to proceed up the west coast of Ireland and so to Liverpool by way of the North Channel. Had he done so, he would have avoided the submarine-infested area. He received no such instructions. Then again, he might have worked up the liner to full speed after clearing the fog, and thus have made Schwieger's task more difficult.

Lord Mersey, who had headed the Board of Trade inquiry into the *Titanic*'s sinking, was charged with investigating the loss of the *Lusitania*. Turner, who survived, was exonerated of all blame. It was, Mersey remarked enigmatically, 'a damned dirty business'. To whom or what was he referring? The German U-boat arm? The fact that he knew the *Lusitania* was carrying war materials greatly in excess of those listed in the manifest? To the incompetence of the Admiralty in its handling of the situation (lack of handling might be a better way of putting it)? Or what?

The First Lord of the Admiralty, Winston Churchill, and the First Sea Lord, Admiral Sir John Fisher, were less kind to the unfortunate Turner. Fisher, in a note to Churchill, described him as 'a scoundrel' and hinted that he had 'been bribed'.

Churchill agreed. 'We shall pursue the captain without check,' he replied.

Mersey was right: there was much dirt in the business. Documents have gone missing from the Public Records Office. Records of signals that should be in the Post Office archives are not. The mystery of what happened behind the scenes in the *Lusitania* tragedy will never be completely cleared up – although Colin Simpson has gone as far as anyone can in his admirable book *Lusitania* (1972). The final grisly thought is whether the *Lusitania* was deliberately lured into the U-20's trap by Churchill: a sacrificial lamb that, once sacrified, might bring America into the war on the Allied side. After all, he did say, 'At the summit, true politics and strategy are one. The manoeuvre which brings an ally into the field is as serviceable as that which wins a great battle.' Was he thinking of the lost Cunarder? Were one liner and 1,198 lives a reasonable price to pay for the possibility of making the Triple Alliance a Quadripartite Alliance? The evidence is missing: the mystery remains.

THE HAUNTED U-BOAT

The captain of the American submarine L-2, on patrol off Cape Clear on the west coast of Ireland, could hardly believe his luck. There on the surface, well within range, a German U-boat drifted aimlessly. Through the periscope, he could read the number on her conning-tower: U-65. Quickly, he gave the order to attack.

The L-2 manoeuvred into position, opened her outer torpedo-tube doors — and then something happened that saved her the trouble of firing. With a tremendous detonation, U-65 blew up. The American captain stared in bewilderment. Who or what had intervened at the last moment to rob him of his prize? And had his eyes deceived him, or had he really seen a man standing motionless on the vessel's deck in the seconds before her destruction? If he had, no man aboard the doomed boat would have been in the least surprised. For the strange fate of U-65 was only what every crew member had been expecting: the culmination of a chain of events which had earned her the name of the 'the death-boat'.

The jinx on her could be traced back to the time of her birth, a little over two years earlier. She was built at Bruges early in 1916, one of 24 U-boats of a new design then under construction. Unlike those already in action, whose task was to patrol Belgian waters, harassing fishing fleets and disrupting Britain's supply lines, the new craft were to range farther afield, in search of rich pickings around the coasts of Britain and Ireland. They had a surface speed of 13 knots, twice as fast as their predecessors, and each of them would accommodate a crew of 34, including three officers. Conditions aboard were cramped in the extreme: the men who served on U-boats needed great courage and unusual powers of tolerance to endure being cooped up for days on end in a narrow steel tube at sea, literally breathing down one another's necks. Any outbreak of fear in that claustrophobic environment was sure to have dire consequences.

Fear, however, was far from the minds of the shipyard workers of Bruges. They would never go to sea in the U-boats they were building. But one day, as two of them stood talking, a steel girder being lowered into place for the hull of U-65 suddenly jerked and slid sideways out of its sling. With a fearful crash it fell directly on the two men, who had no time to react to the warning shouts around them. One was killed outright; the other, pinned by the legs, screamed in agony while his colleagues struggled to release him. The girder's tackle was broken, and the wretched man was trapped for an hour before they could lift the massive weight off him. He was rushed to hospital, only to die there soon afterwards.

Horrible though it had been, the fall of the girder was quickly passed off as an accident, and work resumed. A few weeks later U-65 was almost finished, and the day of her launching was at hand, when three workmen went into the engine-room to make a few final adjustments to the diesels. Minutes later, they were heard coughing and crying for help. The men who ran to see what was wrong found the sliding door in the bulkhead unaccountably jammed. Even as they tried to force it open, the anguished voices on the other side fell silent; and, when the rescuers at last broke through to the engine room, they found the men dead on the floor, asphyxiated by poisonous fumes.

Remarkably, an inquiry was unable to establish what had happened. No one could explain how the fumes had escaped, or even what kind of fumes they were. In peacetime, a more thorough investigation might have been held, and U-65 withdrawn from service; but with World War I at its height every vessel was needed, and she was hastily declared seaworthy. With any luck, the bottle broken over her bows when she was launched would fulfil its original purpose of appeasing the wrathful gods of the sea.

On a calm, clear day, with no problems on the horizon, U-65 sailed out with her sister ships for diving trials off the Scheldt estuary. Her captain was determined to start off on a successful note. Before giving the signal for her first dive, he took the precaution of sending a rating up to inspect the hatches and check that the breech of the deck-gun was closed.

What happened next was a matter of some debate. According to the bridge watch, the young man simply walked across the deck and stepped overboard, surrendering himself to the sea like a lemming calmly willing to be drowned. A boat was lowered to search for him, but no trace of his body could be found. U-65 had claimed her sixth life, and she had not yet been once under water.

A successful dive was essential now to keep the crew's spirits up. The watchmen came down from the conning-tower, the hatches were closed, and the tanks opened to let in the water which would remove the boat's positive buoyancy. Smoothly and gradually she sank, until the captain gave the command to level off at 5 fathoms. But U-65 failed to respond. She went on sinking, down and down, stopping only when she came to rest on the sea-bed. And there she stuck.

Apparently, there was a leak in one of the tanks. Compressed air was blown in to clear the water out, but still she refused to move. Minutes dragged into hours as the crew strove desperately to repair whatever had gone wrong. Fumes, perhaps due to water in the batteries, began to poison the air. For 12 hours the horror lasted, and then, almost beyond hope and for no obvious reason, she rose to the surface. The crew staggered out like drunkards, choking, sick, and gasping for oxygen — but the wonder was that they had all survived. Twelve hours was reckoned the absolute maxiumum that it was safe for a U-boat to stay submerged. If they had been trapped in that coffin-like tube minutes longer, the men would have started dropping like flies.

Surely, they thought, the worst was behind them now. They could not have been more wrong. The troubles of U-65 had scarcely begun.

After a complete overhaul at the shipyard, she was pronounced fit for service and sent off on her maiden patrol. The crew took her out to sea with trepidation in their hearts, but the trip was uneventful and she returned safely to Bruges. There she reloaded, taking on fresh supplies of food, ammunition and torpedoes. As the last of these was being lowered through the forward hatch, its warhead exploded.

When the panic and confusion had subsided, five men were found to have been killed, some inside the U-boat and some on

219

deck. Many others had suffered grievous injuries. One of the dead men was the second officer, known to the crew as *der Schwarze* because of his dark complexion. He was by all accounts an imposing figure.

The five dead were buried in a cemetery at Wilhelmshaven, the chief German naval station. U-65 meanwhile, herself badly damaged in the blast, was towed into dry-dock to be repaired. But what had caused the torpedo to explode? The crew muttered darkly of a jinx on their vessel, while the authorities took the view that it was just another unfortunate accident. No one was prepared to consider the idea that a saboteur might be at work.

All too soon, U-65 was ready for action again. The crew, who had been enjoying an extended period of shore-leave, was summoned to assemble a few days before she was due to sail. Evening was drawing on as they trooped up the gang-plank, being counted on board by a petty officer. He was glad to see that they had all turned up — all 31 of them, including the men drafted in to replace those killed with the second officer. But wait! There was a 32nd figure, silently following the others — and it was someone he recognized, someone with a dark face . . .

The captain and his new second officer were discussing plans in the wardroom when the door was suddenly flung open. There, ashen-faced and out of breath, stood the petty officer. The captain rose, frowning angrily. What was the meaning of this interruption? Stammering, the petty officer tried to explain. He knew it sounded impossible, but he had just seen the second officer — the last second officer, he meant — the one buried at Whilhelmshaven: yes, *der Schwarze!*

The captain was a level-headed man, not easily to be convinced by such a wild story. Then again, the petty officer was not the kind of man who usually told wild stories. His cool behaviour during the near-calamitous diving trials had been an example to the rest of the crew. He was clearly not drunk; but perhaps, in the failing light, he had seen someone who looked like the dead man? No, he was adamant, it was *der Schwarze*. Besides, he was not the only witness. A rating called Petersen had seen the figure as well. Keeping cool, the captain asked for Petersen to be brought to the wardroom to give his version of events. But the petty officer explained that Petersen was up on deck, crouching behind the conning-tower and too terrified to move.

The captain, accompanied by his bewildered second officer, went up at once to speak to Petersen. In answer to the captain's questions he confirmed that he had seen *der Schwarze* walk up the gang-plank, move along deck to the bows and stand there, arms folded, gazing out to sea. He had not known that the petty officer had also seen the figure; all he knew was that he was scared out of his wits and had run to hide. When he dared to peep out again, the ghost — for what else could it be — had vanished.

One sighting could have been passed off as a hallucination, the product of one man's overwrought mind. But two? The captain was uneasy. He was no believer in ghosts, but he could believe that someone might have impersonated *der Schwarze*, playing a tasteless joke on the crew which could seriously damage their morale. Over the next two days he questioned everyone connected with U-65, but found no proof that the ghost had been a fake. Nearly all the men believed in it and were afraid – none more so that Petersen, who vanished like a ghost himself just before the vessel was due to sail. He chose to risk a deserter's punishment rather than go to sea in the vessel which he had told everyone was a 'death-boat'.

Yet many months were to pass before the jinx claimed its next victim. Against all expectations, U-65 performed well on her Channel patrols in 1917, sinking some enemy ships and evading pursuit. For the men on board, however, the Allied forces were not the only enemy. Far more powerful and insidious, wearing down their resistance day by day, ever-present among them, was the enemy within — fear.

One of the crew, a petty officer who served on the ill-fated vessel right up to the end of her penultimate patrol, later described the general standard of morale:

U-65 was never a happy ship though we were always fortunate in our officers. There was something in the atmosphere on board which made one uneasy. Perhaps, knowing her evil history, we imagined things, but I am convinced myself that she was haunted. One night at sea I saw an

221

officer standing on deck. He was not one of us. I caught only a glimpse of him, but a shipmate who was nearer swore that he recognized our former second officer. Several of the bluejackets saw the ghost quite often, but others were unable to see it, even when it was pointed out to them standing only a few feet away.

Our last captain but one would never admit the existence of anything supernatural, but once or twice, when coming on deck, I observed him to be very agitated, and was told by the men that the ghost had been walking on the foredeck. When the captain's attention was drawn to it he pretended to see nothing and scolded the watch for being a pack of nervous fools. But afterwards I heard from a mess steward at the officers' casino that our captain openly declared his ship to be haunted by devils.

On New Year's Day 1918, U-65 cruised from Heligoland to Zeebrugge. During their stay in the Belgian port for the next ten days, the crewmen saw nothing of the ghost. They began to hope that the change of year would herald a change in their boat's fortunes. And so it did — but the change was from bad to worse.

Her next mission was to patrol the Channel off Portland, hunting down enemy merchantmen and fishing fleets. All went well until the evening of 21 January. Then, as darkness fell and gale-force winds drove clouds across the moon, U-65 had to surface to recharge her batteries. She was close to a British naval base so three watchmen were on the bridge — two ratings, one facing to port and the other to starboard, and the second officer, looking forward. Peering into the dusk, he saw showers of spray rise and fall around the bows — and in the middle a figure, standing right out on the prow. What did the fool think he was doing? The second officer cupped his hands to his mouth and shouted, warning the man to get below before he was washed overboard. Slowly the figure turned and stared back at him. It was *der Schwarze*.

By now, the other two look-outs had also seen the figure. They called frantically for the captain, and he came into the conning-tower before the ghost had faded. His blood ran cold as the dark face fixed its implacable gaze upon him. What did it

222

mean? Was it an accusation of him for keeping the death-boat at sea, or a warning that the jinx had singled him out as its next victim? The captain saw it, and was afraid. Then he blinked, and when he looked again the apparition had gone.

Immediately, he swore the three look-outs to secrecy. On no account must the crew know what had happened. Try as he might, however, he could not keep a secret of his own altered attitude. A few days later, U-65 torpedoed a supply ship on its way to Plymouth and disabled another with gunfire. The captain had only to give the word to sink it; instead, he ordered evasive action to be taken. Was he afraid of provoking the wrath of forces beyond his ken? If so, he had started to make his peace with them too late.

His doom came like a bolt from the blue, at a time when he must have thought himself safe. Several weeks had passed and U-65 was back at Bruges, moored in a bomb-proof pen in a canal dock. The captain went cheerfully ashore to spend the evening at the officers' casino. As he walked through the streets, the air-raid siren sounded, soon followed by the crack of ack-ack fire and falling bombs. Deciding that his duty lay with U-65 — he turned round to go back. No sooner had he done so than a shell fragment flew at him like a discus, cleanly severing his head from his body.

This bizarre incident prompted the authorities to take the jinx seriously at last. A new captain was appointed — a tough, experienced submariner who was appalled to find his crew on the brink of mass hysteria. On his initiative, an official inquiry into the U-65 affair was held. High-ranking officers conducted the investigation, but all they could find out was the plain fact that most of the crew was in a state of terror. A wholesale transfer of the crew to another vessel, which was what the men wanted, was out of the question; but one by one those most demoralized were drafted to less demanding positions within the German navy.

With fresh crewmen uninhibited by old fears, it was hoped that the submarine would be free of her jinx once and for all. To be on the safe side, however, one of the investigating officers suggested calling in a priest to conduct a service of exorcism on board.

Nothing could have been more calculated to inspire terror in the new men. They had been assured there was nothing to worry about — yet here was a clergyman, commanding the evil spirits of the boat to be gone, in the name of God. So she was haunted, after all! The most hardened of them now believed all the rumours they had heard, and their morale sank lower than ever. With each patrol, their sense of impending doom deepened. The captain furiously forbade any mention of ghosts: but he was powerless to forbid the fear that possessed his men's souls.

The omens were gathering like sharks in May, when U-65 endured a harrowing voyage down the English Channel and across the Bay of Biscay. After two days at sea a torpedo-gunner named Eberhard went mad and screamed till he was bound hand and foot and given morphia to calm him. It seemed to work, and when he had quietened down he was sent on deck with a colleague for some fresh air. The moment he came up through the hatch he went berserk, took a running jump over the deck rail and was swallowed by the sea, never to be seen again.

A little later, as U-65 pitched and tossed in raging seas off Ushant, the chief engineer slipped and broke his leg. Then, while firing on a British tramp steamer with the deck-gun, one of the gun's crew was swept overboard by a huge wave and drowned.

The new captain was beginning to believe in the jinx. Like his predecessor, he adopted a policy of avoiding the enemy ships which ought to have been his prey, convinced that the malign force which seemed to hold the U-boat in its grip would use any combat encounter as an instrument of doom. 'The men were so depressed,' wrote the petty officer who survived, 'that they went about like sleep-walkers, performing their duties automatically and starting at every unusual sound.'

Their last ordeal on that trip came as they made their way home, running the gauntlet of the Straits of Dover. Three U-boats had recently been destroyed in those waters: what price U-65?

But a more mysterious fate was reserved for her. On this occasion, though detected by enemy hydrophones while submerged, and depth-charged on and off for half an hour, she came through unscathed. Then, when the captain decided it was safe to surface, Coxswain Lohmann led the look-outs up to their posts on the bridge. Before they got there, a shell splinter hurtled through the conning-tower and into Lohmann's neck, severing the jugular vein. Bloodied and very bowed, the submarine finally reached Zeebrugge. There, to his great relief, the petty officer was sent to hospital suffering from acute rheumatism. The day before the vessel was to sail again, he was visited by another officer, Wernicke by name, who brought most of his personal belongings to leave in the invalid's care. These were to be passed on to Wernicke's wife, in case . . . Neither man needed to put it into words. Both shared the feeling that the thread by which the keen-edged Damoclean sword of doom hung over U-65 was at last about to snap.

Two months passed before the petty officer heard the news he had known would come. On 31 July 1918, German naval headquarters posted U-65 missing, presumed lost. For a while it seemed that she had disappeared without a trace; then came the report of the American submarine captain who had witnessed her end on 10 July off the Irish coast. It was an end as baffling as any of the disasters that had blighted her two-year life — and could it be true that a lone figure was standing on deck, gazing out to sea, at the moment when she spontaneously blew up? Had *der Schwarze* stayed with her to the bitter end?

The cause of the explosion which destroyed U-65 was never known. One of her own torpedoes may have detonated while still in its tube; or another U-boat may have attacked her by mistake, then slunk away undetected. Perhaps it was an act of sabotage, carried out by an agent willing to lose his own life in the process; or perhaps one of the crewmen, unable to stand the strain any longer, was the agent of annihilation. All these, of course, are natural possibilities. Behind them, formless and inescapable, lurks the spectre of the supernatural.

The mystery of U-65 was thoroughly investigated after World War I by a German psychologist, Professor Hecht, who published a pamphlet on the subject. He was followed in 1932 by Hector C. Bywater, the English naval historian, who conducted his own exhaustive research into the case. Neither could offer a clear-cut solution. Though extremely sceptical Hecht was unable to prove that the ghost was a fake.

On that question the whole mystery hinges. For if the ghost was not genuine — if it was a trick, or else a hallucination arising from the crewmen's fear — then all the other disasters can be explained away as accidents, coincidences, the misfortunes of war. But if the ghost was real — what then? The terrors suffered by the men of U-65 assume a far darker complexion — dark and inscrutable as the face of *der Schwarze* himself.

WHO MINED THE *MAINE*?

Warships have for centuries represented floating 'gunpowder barrels', repositories of large amounts of explosives of many kinds, among which men work and live and sleep without fear of their environment. With proper handling, storage and vigilance, explosives are safe. At sea and in port, strict precautionary measures are enforced against carelessness and sabotage — and yet there have been not a few instances of large warships being blown to pieces without a known enemy in sight. Since the disasters have been so shatteringly complete, it cannot be certainly established whether they were accidental, or deliberately caused.

Such mysteries attend the blowing-up of no less than five Royal Naval ships during World War I: the battleship *Bulwark*, in 1914, at Sheerness, Kent, and two years later and only 5 miles from the same spot, the auxiliary minelayer *Princess Irene*; the cruiser *Natal*, in 1915 at Cromarty Firth, near Scapa Flow; two years after that, the dreadnought *Vanguard*, in Scapa Flow itself; and the monitor *Glatton* in Dover harbour, in 1918.

Each represented a dramatic and tragic loss of a warship and many lives; but none had consequences so far-reaching as the destruction in Havana harbour, Cuba, of the American cruiser *Maine*, on 15 February 1898. Whether it happened by accident or was intended, no one knows, but it was enough to start a war.

Cuba, which in recent decades has had fresh political prominence, was discovered by Christopher Columbus in that mnemonically familiar year, 1492, and was made a colony of Spain. The Monroe Doctrine, which in the nineteenth century pronounced the Americas inviolable by other nations, seemed to many people in the United States to justify their nation's taking under its wing those neighbouring territories already dominated by other powers. Since the Cuban people were in any case in revolt against the oppressive rule of their Spanish masters, this largest of the Caribbean islands seemed ripe for the purpose.

The supplying of Cuban rebels with arms did not prove

enough; it only provoked Spain to send out an even harsher overlord, Captain-General Valeriano Weyler, with a band of young thugs to put the protestors down. They held on, though, encouraged most vociferously by the sustained campaigning of one of the most powerfully irresponsible magnates in the history of the press, William Randolph Hearst, owner of influential newspapers across the United States. His *New York Journal,* in particular, stirred up animosity against Spain and trumpeted the down-trodden Cubans' cause, demanding direct American intervention.

The Spanish Prime Minister, Antonio Cánovas, recognizing the growing likelihood of such a move, promoted a bill advocating Cuban home rule. It caused much resentment in Spain, that once-mighty colonial power — and Cánovas was assassinated. This brought the prospect of America stepping up her aid to the Cuban rebels; and with the Hearst newspapers egging on their government to take Cuba over, the new Spanish premier, Sagasta, ordered the tyrant Weyler home and replaced him with a milder commander, Marshal Blanco, who had orders to smooth the way towards Cuban autonomy.

This was not enough for William Randolph Hearst and the firebrands of the Republican Party. They wanted a dramatic demonstration of America's power to make other nations toe the line, certain to prove a re-election winner for the McKinley administration, next time round.

Not all Cubans wanted home rule, either. Many had prospered under the Spaniards, while others preferred the devil they knew to the unknown one who might spring from their own midst. Spain took advantage of the divisions among Cuban sympathies, and of the helplessness of a poor, disease-stricken island people. Spanish soldiers provoked an outbreak of rioting in Havana on 15 June 1898, which they were easily able to put down, in what they believed would be seen as a show of strength. In fact, they had given the U.S.A. the excuse to take action. In classic terminology, the best interests of the Cuban people and the wish to promote friendship between nations was given as the excuse for sending out to Havana the USS *Maine.*

The cruiser's arrival on 25 January 1898 by no means heralded an attack or invasion. She exchanged the customary courtesies with the shore establishment and was conducted by a local pilot to a mooring place which met with the approval of her commanding officer, Captain Charles D. Sigsbee. Her crew was not allowed ashore.

The threat she posed was a silent one, an insult, in the eyes of the throng who watched her from the waterfront. Never mind that she lay under the harbour batteries at Morro Castle, which could have blown her out of the water at any time. Never mind that the only comings and goings between ship and shore were strictly formal, with the crew remaining pent up on board in the uncomfortable heat. Never mind that, in herself, she was unprepossessing, a second-rate warship of obsolete design, though only a few years old. If anything, this made the insult more acute; had she been the pride of the U.S. navy, the Spanish, with their own great naval history, might have felt a little complimented.

Sightseers on a ferry boat jeered her. Leaflets began circulating throughout the Spanish in Havana. One of them bore the bold heading, LONG LIVE SPAIN WITH HONOUR:

Why do you allow yourselves to be insulted in this way? If your brave and beloved Weyler had not been recalled he would have finished off the rebellious rabble who are trampling our flag and our honour. And now these Yankee pigs, who meddle in our affairs, humiliate us to the last degree with their man-of-war. Spaniards, the moment for action is come. Do not fall asleep. Let us show these vile traitors that we have not lost all our pride, and that we know how to protest with the vigour worthy of a nation such as our Spain has always been and always will be!

Death to the Americans!
Death to Autonomy!
Long Live Spain!
Long Live Weyler!

Less provocatively, Spain reciprocated America's 'friendly' gesture of sending the *Maine* to Havana by dispatching a cruiser

229

of the Spanish navy to New York. It was a polite by pointed tit-for-tat. Her captain and officers were courteously greeted by U.S. officials, as Captain Sigsbee and his officers had been by the Havana Spanish.

For three hot, humid weeks the *Maine* rested at her mooring. Distantly, in New York and elsewhere in the United States, the trumpetings of the Hearst newspapers sounded ever louder and wilder, denouncing Spain's promise of Cuban home rule as a sham, and insisting on action without more delay. Captain Sigsbee, in his fifties, distinguished as a hydrographer but not noted for sharp discipline or running a 'tight' ship, felt that the point had been made. If one U.S. warship could lie complacently in Havana harbour without the Spanish daring to act against it, Cuba could be taken over at any chosen time.

Only the *Maine*'s crew grumbled, in their cramped, stuffy quarters, while the watchers on the shore sipped their evening drinks in the sultry heat of the evening of 15 February. One detail was different this evening, though. The warship had swung to a new posture at her mooring. As she now lay, her main armament was trained on the city and the shore fortifications.

If those who imagined any significance in this could have seen aboard, they would have found Captain Sigsbee no more urgently occupied than writing in his cabin. The crew had turned in for another restless night in the heat. The bugler had sounded 'taps' for lights-out. Suddenly the *Maine* blew up.

She went with a thunderous roar and a flash like blue lightning, vivid enough to melt the darkness for some seconds. Debris flew high into the air, to clatter and splash all around, until at last there was nothing to be heard but the cries of men in pain and fear.

There were some cheers from those ashore whose instinctive elation overrode any natural compassion. But many others cried out with concern, and there were even tears for what must undoubtedly prove to be a heavy casualty toll. Spanish and Cubans hastened to launch rescue craft, to converge on the now blazing hulk, already listing to port and going down by the head.

The water was crowded with sailors, some splashing in a

dazed attempt to swim, others floating, dead or unconscious. Captain Sigsbee had ordered the magazines flooded, but it was happening already, by natural process. Only three out of 15 ship's boats could be used. One thing Sigsbee did not neglect to do was post watchmen. For all he knew, his ship had been the target for the first strike in an outbreak of war. He had heard the gruesome cheers of those fanatics who had seen the disaster as a cause for rejoicing, and there was no knowing whether attacks on the survivors might follow.

In fact, every effort was made to save them, the rescue boats risking the danger that the main magazines, menaced by the spread of flames, might go up at any time. Sigsbee saw that danger as he and the others aboard climbed further up the steepening poop, the only part clear of the water. He gave the order to abandon ship.

There was no further explosion. With a great hissing of steam and extinguishing flame, the *Maine* was settling on the harbour-bed. Sigsbee, the last to leave her, was able to step over the side straight into a boat without getting his feet wet.

It was not until morning that an approximate count of the casualties could be made. Many men were missing, drowned or entombed in the wreck, but it was obvious that of the *Maine*'s complement of some 350 officers and men, two-thirds had died. Bodies floated ashore for days afterwards, and several survivors died of injuries.

Spanish expressions of sympathy were immediately forthcoming. Sigsbee, in his dispatch to Washington, counselled calm judgement of what had happened, though, after a day or two's consideration and exchange of opinions with his officers, he cabled to the Secretary of the Navy that he surmised that his ship's destruction had been caused by a mine, 'perhaps by accident'.

William Randolph Hearst was having no talk of accident in his newspapers. War was their demand. Every one of them carried front-page, headline accusations of Spanish treachery and murder. There were even diagrams, explaining how the deed had been done by deliberately causing the cruiser to be moored over mines able to be detonated from the Spanish shore fortress.

231

While responsible Americans deplored Hearst's gutter journalism, it did not necessarily lessen suspicions that the *Maine* had been mined, or even torpedoed, or perhaps sabotaged by an explosive device smuggled aboard, although Captain Sigsbee had received few visitors and had kept them under careful scrutiny. The questions were: had the detonation been accidental or deliberate? And, if deliberate, had it been a tactical blow by the Spanish, or a ruthless trick by the Cuban rebels to discredit their oppressors and provoke the United States against them?

The implications were immediately obvious to the Spanish. Genuinely, or merely going through the motions of doing the correct thing, they sought to allay American hostility by ordering a court of inquiry and sending divers down to investigate the wreck, already subsiding into the harbour mud. In their anxiety, or guilt, they spoiled the gesture by rushing out a preliminary verdict, far too quickly to have been a fully investigated and considered one, that the *Maine* could not possibly have sunk from any external cause. One reason offered was that no dead fish had been found: the harbour abounded with fish, and an explosion outside the ship would be bound to have killed hundreds. This was subsequently refuted at the Americans' own hearing, with the suggestion that the fish had probably left the harbour for the night, or had been temporarily stunned, recovered, and gone on swimming.

With hindsight, Spanish anxiety to play down the incident as quickly as possible is understandable. Spain did not want war with the United States, having nothing to gain and a great deal to lose. Equally unlikely was the possibility that planting a big enough mine or firing a torpedo could have been done by rebels without detection.

Rational-minded Americans must have recognized all of this. The hysterical exhortations of the Hearst press were not directed towards the rationally minded; besides which, there were outwardly responsible Americans who would quite welcome a war with Spain. Their powerful nation was in a mood to cut an international dash, while, as one senator was ingenuous enough to declare, a war would bring welcome stimulus to manufacturing and transport industries throughout the United States.

232

Nor were the Hearst newspapers the only ones clamouring for war. It was amid an atmosphere of sincere desire for revenge, and with the preconviction that the disaster must have been caused by some hostile means, that the Americans conducted their own inquiry: the practice of independent international inquiries into disputes was not much established in those days.

Witnesses from the *Maine* herself were united in one thing — there had been two explosions. The first had been minor, like a small gun going off; the one immediately following it had been cataclysmic. No one could deduce a known instance of a mine touching off a warship's magazine, but there was a first time for everything. It was equally unheard of for contact mines to be sown in a harbour, where any ship of any nationality would be equally vulnerable. There was, however, the remote-control type of mine, as depicted in the *New York Journal*'s diagram of the *Maine* sitting unsuspectingly above devices which could only be exploded by a wire contact with the shore.

Captain Sigsbee's opinion was that his ship had been led to a prepared mooring place, above mines which could be used if the cruiser should do something offensive. Had the fortuitous swing to bring the biggest guns seemingly to bear on the town caused some nervous Spaniard to press the button? Had some fanatical rebel gained access to the control and fired the mine? The possibilities were myriad, rejected or embraced according to national and individual suspicions and prejudices. The Spanish case was not helped, after their denial of the presence of any mines at all in Havana harbour, by one of their newspapers printing a boast by their Navy Secretary that there need be no fears about American warships penetrating Cuban harbours, because they were all mined in readiness, Havana in particular.

The chief alternatives to the theory that the *Maine* had been mined was that she had blown up of her own accord — that some small internal explosion had set off the fatal one. If a saboteur's explosive plant were ruled out, and there had been no obvious accident, the most likely cause remaining was spontaneous combustion of her fuel.

Six bunkers adjoined the main magazines. They had alarms and safety devices to keep a check on any build-up of heat within them. Sigsbee, the easygoing captain, left their supervision to others whose vigilance he had no reason to mistrust. There were no hot steam pipes, dangerous electric wires or exposed light fittings in the magazines. At the time of the disaster, four of the six fuel bunkers were empty, and, because the ship was moored, the power systems were working at minimal capacity.

Explosion caused from within was rejected by the American tribunal on 21 March 1898. A month later, the U.S. Minister in Spain handed in an ultimatum that Spanish occupation of Cuba must cease. Queen Cristina herself presided over the cabinet meeting at which proud old Spain determined to fight rather than give in tamely.

'How Do You Like The *Journal*'s War?' gloated Hearst's headlines when the fighting began, bringing a consequent rise in his circulation figures. It was a squalid little war, over by August, with not many casualties, not much honour, but with the Spanish fleet annihilated and the territories of the Philippines, Guam, Puerto Rica, and, of course, Cuba, Spanish possessions no longer.

In 1909 the wreck of the *Maine* was declared a hazard to shipping in Havana harbour. At great financial cost to the U.S.A. the hulk was raised, the job taking the better part of two years. One expert who examined the damaged hull declared conclusively that a small mine had gone off against it, chancing to explode a small magazine where black powder used for firing salutes was stored, which in turn had set off the great explosion. Another expert stated equally categorically that the initial explosion could not possibly have occurred outside.

Many years later, in the atomic age, a further expert, raking over old reports and unpublished details, found what to him was incontrovertible proof that the *Maine* had exploded as a result of overheating of bituminous coal which she was carrying in too close proximity to an insufficiently insulated magazine. Many other instances of such disasters have been known.

ROBERT MAXWELL: WAS HE MURDERED?

The world was stunned when, on the afternoon of 5 November 1991, media bulletins carried the news that Robert Maxwell was missing from his yacht off the Canary Islands. Some hours later follow-up bulletins announced that a body believed to be that of the publisher had been picked up from the sea by helicopter. It was difficult to comprehend that this most vital of men, who had travelled from a poverty-stricken childhood in a remote part of Europe to a pre-eminent position among the super-rich and internationally mighty, had ceased to exist. But so it proved to be.

The body was taken to the mortuary at Gran Canaria and there identified by Maxwell's widow Betty and eldest son Philip. Three Spanish doctors began a post-mortem on the following day, and organs from the body were sent to Madrid for further forensic tests. Early conclusions, later to be confirmed in the final Spanish submissions, pointed to death from natural causes – there being insufficient water in the lungs to suggest drowning. The mystery of how he had come to fall overboard remained unexplained: was it an accident, his own premeditated act, or was he pushed?

His family was anxious that his body should be buried by the Sabbath as required by Orthodox Jewish law, and hasty preparations were made for it to be flown to Israel. The 200-kilo oak casket was too large to fit into Maxwell's Gulfstream jet, and a Challenger jet had to be urgently chartered in Geneva. In Israel a second autopsy was carried out just hours prior to his interment on the Mount of Olives.

On 9 January 1992 came sensational news which strengthened speculation that Maxwell might have been murdered. The French magazine *Paris Match* revealed that three Israeli doctors who assisted at the second autopsy had become convinced that he had been brutally beaten before disappearing from the *Lady Ghislaine*.

But before we can fully appreciate the manner in which he may have died, we must go back to the beginning of the story.

Robert Maxwell was born on 10 January 1923 at Slatinske Doly, a small Ruthenian village on the Czech side of the Czechoslovak–Rumanian border – a remote area of shadowy forest between the brooding mass of the Carpathian mountains and the frontier-marking River Tisza. His father, Mechel Hock, named him Abraham Lajbi, but when the birth came to be registered the authorities insisted that he should have the Czech names of Ludvik Jan.

Great changes were taking place in this hitherto neglected part of Europe. Carpo-Ruthenia, which had belonged to Hungary up to 1919, was awarded to the new state of Czechoslovakia in 1919 by the Versailles Treaty. Traditional attitudes altered abruptly; instead of looking towards Budapest Ruthenians now shifted their gaze to Bratislava and Prague. Jan Masaryk, founding father of the new state and a liberal democrat, lifted the age-old anti-Jewish laws and granted the Jews full Czech citizenship.

The new more liberal regime made the region one of the staging-posts of eastern Europe. There had always been the natural flow of transients – Slovaks, Hungarians, Germans, Rumanians, Ukrainians, gypsies and Jews in this crossroads, but now Slatinske Doly became a transit camp for Zionists from Poland and Russia on their way to Palestine.

The new frontier also greatly encouraged smuggling. Rumania with its different and higher taxes on the slaughter of animals provided a strong incentive for the illicit shipment of horses and cattle from Ruthenia across the Tisza. Smuggling became an endemic industry and the enterprising smuggler was able to thrive.

It was into this ferment of changing attitudes and opportunities that Maxwell was born, and it was to affect his outlook for life: anything, it seemed, was possible. His childhood nevertheless was one of poverty.

Mechel was a poor Jewish peasant scratching a meagre living from the soil; now and again he was able to add a little to his income by acting as a middleman between farmer and butcher. The normal diet of the young Maxwell and his six brothers and sisters was potatoes and coarse bread, relieved at weekends and holidays by a little meat and gefilte fish. He was later to remark that he did not have a pair of shoes of his own until he was seven.

His mother Hannah came from a better family than Mechel and was fiercely ambitious for her children. She made sure that they attended regularly at the Jewish primary school and that Ludvik, her favourite, went to the synagogue daily, there to study the scriptures and learn Hebrew. His education however hardly progressed beyond the elementary stage.

But he was learning much more out of school. He was drawn to his maternal grandfather, Yaacov, who in many ways substituted for his own father. Yaacov was a much more successful dealer than Mechel, and in addition was a shrewd trader. Most of his deals were done by barter, and he could carry many transactions in his head simultaneously: there is little doubt that the future wheeler-dealer learned the tricks of the trade on the Rumanian side of the River Tisza at dead of night smuggling horses and cattle with his grandfather and watching the clever old master haggling in the moonlight. Also by the time he was in his early teens his skilful ear had picked up most of the languages of central and eastern Europe from the polyglot stream of life around him.

By the late thirties the skies were darkening over Europe. In September 1938 the Western Allies ceded the Czech Sudetenland to Germany by the Munich Agreement; in March 1939 Hitler broke the Agreement by marching into Prague and taking over the country; in the same month the German dictator transferred Ruthenia from Czech to Hungarian control, and almost immediately a company of

Hungarian troops marched into Slatinske Doly. Jews of military age were impressed into labour battalions: the shape of the future was becoming ominously clear. Maxwell's parents bought him a railway ticket to Budapest where they hoped he would be able to lose himself in the anonymity of a large city. He was just sixteen.

Maxwell has given various accounts of the ensuing months, but the most likely story is the one he later told his cousin Alex Pearl who had travelled with him to Budapest. It seems that he fell in with a group of young Czechs determined to fight for the honour of their ravished country; they left the Hungarian capital, made their way by devious and stealthy means to Zagreb in Yugoslavia, and there took ship to Palestine where they enlisted in the Czech Legion. The Legion took part in the battle of France in 1940, and disintegrated in the general Allied defeat of that disastrous summer; Maxwell was evacuated in an Egyptian ship, the *Mers-el-Kebir*, bound for Liverpool, and arrived, he said, 'with a rifle in my hand and a desire to fight the Germans': he would no doubt have felt even more strongly had he the prescience to know that except for one sister his whole family would perish in the Holocaust.

Bored with the inactivity of life in the reformed Czech Legion, he volunteered to join the Pioneer Corps and was accepted. For the next two years he strove to transform himself; he shed his boorish appearance and behaviour and donned the manners and deportment of a well-bred Englishman; he cultivated a well-rehearsed charm; and with his brilliance at languages learned to speak English with an 'upper-crust' accent. He also changed his name to Du Maurier after a brand of cigarettes popular at the time. But he had not neglected to become an excellent soldier and crack marksman so that when he applied to join a fighting unit he was accepted into the Sixth Battalion of the North Staffs Regiment. He made a particularly favourable impression on Brigadier Carthew-Yourston, who felt that his command of languages would be very usefully employed in the Intelligence (I) section of the battalion.

The brigade sailed for France on D-Day +16, landed near Arromanches, and took part in the fierce fighting around the Caen hinge and in the Falaise Gap. Paris was liberated on 25 August and Maxwell, now under the name of Jones, arrived with his unit shortly afterwards. The charming city in the first flush of liberation cast its spell over everybody: Maxwell met Elizabeth (Betty) Meynard, an attractive French girl and his future wife, and they immediately fell in love. The paternal Carthew-Yourston suggested he adopt the name of Robert Maxwell as being more suitable than the others: the erstwhile Sergeant Jones concurred. And so was born the name and the legend.

The Paris idyll lasted only a few days before Maxwell, newly commissioned, returned to the fighting. He achieved the summit of his military career by winning the Military Cross at Paarlo on the Belgian–Dutch frontier; the citation was particularly glowing and the award was made personally by Montgomery. The end of the hostilities saw him in Hamburg: Maxwell had had a 'good war'.

But although he had survived the poverty of Slatinske Doly, the Holocaust and the dangers of the battlefield the future posed a huge question-mark. Unlike the great majority of his fellow officers he had no home to return to: what was he to do? It was obvious that in the short term he would have to remain in the Army where his languages made him a much-prized possession: few British officers spoke German, and to these he could add Russian, Czech, Hungarian, Ruthenian, Polish and Rumanian. After a short period of battlefield interrogation he was posted in the rank of captain to the Control Commission – in effect the replacement of the German civilian ministries by the Army – and to that particular section known as PRISC (Public Relations and Information Services Control). Any German wishing to publish books or newspapers, put on plays or show films had to obtain permission from this important body. Maxwell was appointed Berlin's press chief: he now had a position of power and authority and one that was to afford him the opportunity of making the contacts which were to prove vital for his future.

The first friendship he formed was with Arno Scholtz, to whom he recommended the granting of a licence to publish *Der Telegraf*, which soon became the most influential newspaper in Berlin. Maxwell played an active part in this success, exhibiting an uncanny flair for locating and moving the vital spare parts in the war-torn city for keeping the presses running. The dashing young multi-lingual officer in the huge American cars soon became a well-known figure around the city. Scholtz, in gratitude for help given, introduced Maxwell to Ferdinand Springer, an introduction which was to determine the course of his subsequent career. Springer was the head of the German publishing firm of Springer Verlag, of high repute for its distinguished scientific list. Scholtz told Maxwell: 'If you help re-establish the trade, the trade will kiss your feet. . .'

In the meantime however, in March 1947, Maxwell resigned from the Control Commission and moved his headquarters to London. He had acquired the controlling interest in an import-export company formed with a fellow Czech and called Low-Bell; he bought German newspapers for sale to prisoners-of-war in Britain, collecting them at Heathrow in a huge grey Dodge, and trafficked in any commodity in short supply.

In October of that year, remembering Scholtz's advice, he returned to Germany to renew his acquaintanceship with Ferdinand Springer. Springer had built up the family publishing business to be of its class the best in Germany: his list had specialized in science and engineering, and with Germany leading the world in many fields Springer's publications were eagerly sought internationally. Among those whose first works he had published were authors of the stature of Max Born, Paul Erlich, Max Planck and Albert Einstein. Springer and his partner Tönges Lange had cleverly dispersed their stocks so that the bulk of their publications survived the bombing: they were however suffering agonies of frustration in trying to get their books and journals out of Germany to meet the demand for them abroad. The Allied customs regulations relating to exports were of nightmarish complexity, and they desperately needed someone on the outside who could distribute their publications for them.

Maxwell came to the rescue and at the same time did himself a huge favour. He had already established a firm earlier in the year for the importation of German publications (EPPAC), and it was agreed that through this agency he should own the exclusive worldwide distribution rights of Springer's journals and books. Over the next nine years their joint business was to be worth 20 million Deutschmarks. Maxwell had achieved his ambition of becoming a millionaire.

But there were to be bumps along the way. An unsuccessful attempt to revive the ailing book wholesaler Simpkin Marshall called down the wrath of the official receivers when the firm was finally wound up. All the hallmarks of the later Maxwell management style were apparent: intercompany trading, sums owed to Maxwell which were difficult to reconcile, accounting of a wildly incoherent kind.

Maxwell bounced back from this débâcle by turning with fiendish energy to Pergamon Press, a small scientific publishing firm which he had bought as Butterworth-Springer in 1951. By the end of 1957 Pergamon was publishing over one hundred journals and books per year: editorial advisers included people of the eminence of Sir John Cockroft, Sir Robert Robinson and Sir Edward Appleton. Many prominent authors accepted minimal fees for the advantage of academic prestige; yet subscriptions, based on the huge Springer mailing list to which Maxwell had access, were paid in advance. The money rolled in.

In 1969 he began to negotiate the sale of Pergamon to Leasco. Relations between Maxwell and Saul Steinberg, Leasco's precocious financial wizard, became strained however when the latter suspected that the Pergamon lily

241

was rather too heavily gilded. A DTI investigation was ordered which condemned Maxwell's accounting and truthfulness, and concluded with the damning verdict that he was not fit to run a public company. It was the end of an extraordinary switchback of a decade during which Maxwell had also been MP for Buckingham for six years.

Again, it did not take him long to recover lost ground. Without his genius and drive the fortunes of Pergamon withered and declined, and in 1974 he was triumphantly able to buy it back at a bargain price: 'Even with your huge fees,' he gleefully told a lawyer, 'I've come out of it with a big profit.' Pergamon's health soon recovered and it boomed again: it was to remain Maxwell's flagship until he sold it to Elsevier in 1991 to meet the huge debts he was incurring elsewhere.

In 1981 he bought the ailing British Printing Corporation, and transformed terminal decline into a success story against all predictions. In 1984 he achieved one of the greatest of all his ambitions – newspaper proprietorship with its attendant aura of power and influence, by buying the Mirror Group from Reed International: the banking community, their confidence in him completely restored, lent him the money for the deal. The great Lord Northcliffe's former empire was his: grandfather Yaacov would indeed have applauded.

He took possession of the Chairman's desk at the Mirror Group building soon after midnight on 13 July, and at midday informed leaders of the print unions that if the threatened strike of the previous day had taken place he would instantly have shut all the papers down. He was determined to reverse the complex of ills that had brought the newspaper industry close to ruin, and started by a ruthless pruning of staff. The Spanish practices of the robber barons of the print unions were brought to a swift halt: and he brooked no delay in introducing the long-overdue new technology in typesetting and colour processing. More than anyone else Maxwell pioneered the transition of British national newspapers from antiquated to modern production techniques; this is something on the positive side which has been lost sight of through the dark shadows cast by his disgraceful financial dealings.

If Robert Maxwell had died in 1988 posterity's view of him might have been very different. He had created success-ful world-wide businesses and had saved others from destruction; he had helped to transform the newspaper industry; he had headed several notable charities and by common consent had been an excellent constituency MP; he was the owner of Oxford United and Derby County football clubs; and he was the embodiment of the sort of colourful and individualistic life-style which has always endeared itself to the British: the soubriquet 'Cap'n Bob' connoted affection as much as familiarity.

Such a scenario was not to be. Throughout his life Maxwell could not leave well alone and this trait was now to become intensified in a particularly virulent way at the worst possible time. The man who had always bought cheaply and sold expensively reversed this practice; he bought prodigiously at top prices on the edge of a slump. So dramatic was this change in his pattern of behaviour as to suggest a sudden decline in his powers.

He bought the US company Macmillan for 2.6 billion dollars, and *Official Airlines Guide* for 750 million. He further tilted the balance of his main company Maxwell Communi-cations towards the United States by buying the Berlitz language-teaching business. In the last year of his life he was increasingly beset by the double impact of the transat-lantic recession and high interest rates: this did not stop him from continuing his buying spree with the purchase of the New York *Daily News*, which he advertised in character-istically dramatic fashion by sailing up the East River in his yacht the *Lady Ghislaine*.

Since his death the contortions by which, Houdini-like, he sought to escape from his mountainous debts have been fully reported in the world's press. Huge misappropri-ations of funds, most disgracefully from the Mirror Group and MCC Pension Funds, had taken place; the Byzantine structure of his financial empire with its interlocking complex of private and public companies made it fiendishly difficult to track down the missing money now estimated at £2 billion. The anonymous Liechtenstein and Gibraltarian accounts are black holes whose secrets have yet to be revealed.

At the time that Maxwell departed for his fateful last voyage, financial nemesis was impending. The *Financial Times* was about to publish a report revealing that Maxwell's debts were double those publicly acknowledged; Goldman Sachs started to sell MCC shares when he failed to make a margin call; Seymour Hersh's book *The Samson Option*, suggesting that Maxwell was a Mossad agent, had a further effect on a jittery market. At 2.58 p.m. on 5 November, the day of the publisher's death, dealings in Maxwell company shares were suspended on the Stock Exchange.

At 6.30 a.m. on the morning of Thursday, 31 October 1991 Robert Maxwell climbed aboard a helicopter on the roof of the *Daily Mirror* building in Holborn. He had been suffering from a very heavy cold and had decided that a few days' cruising in the sun on board his yacht the *Lady Ghislaine* would restore him to fitness. The helicopter flew him to Luton where his Gulfstream jet was waiting: three and a half hours later he landed at Gibraltar, there to be greeted by Captain Angus Rankin, the yachtmaster. He was, it seems, in a good mood, and was to remain predominantly cheerful during the subsequent voyage.

The yacht set sail for Madeira at 4 p.m. and glided through the intervening 600 miles of sunlit sea to arrive at Funchal two days later. After looking round the town Maxwell, who enjoyed swimming in the nude, asked to be taken to the Desertas beach: that night the passionate and unsuccessful gambler visited the casino.

The next step was Tenerife, and the yacht made landfall at the little fishing port of Darcena Pesquera a few miles north of Santa Cruz at 10 a.m. on Monday, 4 November. Maxwell spent most of the day in relaxed and cheerful activity centred chiefly on jointly composing on the phone with his son Ian the speech he had been due to give to the Anglo-Israeli Association that night and which Ian was giving in his stead. Among his other telephone conversations was one with Samuel Pisar, an Auschwitz survivor and his French lawyer, in which jokes were exchanged about Maxwell's nomination for France's highest honour, the *Légion d'Honneur*. At almost lunch-time the yacht sailed south to Poris de Abona where Maxwell took a break for a swim.

But later calls may have served to darken his mood somewhat; these informed him of Sachs's decision to sell MCC shares, of the Swiss bank's threat to call in the Fraud Squad, and of the clamouring of two French banks for loan repayments.

By late afternoon the *Lady Ghislaine* had returned to Santa Cruz. Maxwell went ashore at 8 p.m. and was driven by a taxi-driver named Arturo Trujillo, to the Hotel Mencey, the tycoon finding the front seat of the Toyota Camry a tight fit. He ordered a green salad and hake with clams: the waiters would later say that he seemed quite calm though abstracted and apparently lost in his own thoughts. When he departed he left behind his jacket – a beige blazer – and a waiter had to run after him with it. Trujillo then drove him to El Olympo for coffee after which, there being no available entertainment within reasonable distance, Maxwell asked to be driven back to the yacht. Back on board, he instructed Rankin to put to sea for the night.

At approximately 10.15 p.m. Stewardess Lisa Kordalski went to see if Maxwell required anything further, and found him in bed wearing a night-gown – his customary attire for repose: as she was about to depart through the main stateroom door he asked her to lock that door and leave through his bathroom.

At 11 p.m. Rankin answered a satellite telephone call from the publisher's son Ian, which he connected; Ian was reporting on the Anglo-Israeli dinner of that night and,

245

his reporting concluded, asked if his father would be returning home the following day. 'You bet,' was the reply, and these were the last words to a member of his family. His Gulfstream jet awaited him at Los Christianos on Tenerife to fly him home.

At about 4.25 a.m. the second engineer reported seeing Maxwell on deck; and about twenty minutes later he called up the bridge to complain that the air-conditioning was too high. An unbroken silence then ensued. The yacht, having sailed southward during the night from Santa Cruz around Gran Canaria and then westward to Tenerife, dropped anchor at Los Christianos at 9.45 a.m.

At 11.10 a.m. the telephone rang: it was a call from New York; Rankin put the call through to the publisher's stateroom, and getting no reply went down to investigate. Finding the door locked, he opened it with his master key: the room was empty, and on the bed lay Maxwell's folded night-gown. The yachtmaster ordered an immediate search of the vessel, and when this failed to find the publisher two more searches were urgently made. Maxwell had indeed vanished.

The first call Gus Rankin made was to Maxwell's youngest son, Kevin: this was at 11.30 a.m. An inexplicable gap of time then ensued until 12.25 p.m. when the yachtmaster dispatched a satellite news signal that Robert Maxwell was missing: the world heard the news and gasped.

The Spanish Air-Sea Rescue Service went immediately into action. Ships and planes were alerted and three helicopters began a systematic search; it was a fishing-boat, however, which reported the first sighting of a body about a hundred miles east of Tenerife: within minutes of confirmation a Superpuma helicopter began winching aboard Maxwell's 22-stone corpse. 'It was naked, stiff and floating face up, not face down which is normal,' reported a rescuer.

The body was flown to the military airport at Gando on Gran Canaria, there to be officially identified by Maxwell's widow Betty and eldest son Philip. After the identification

246

Betty was briefly questioned by Dr Carlos Lopez de Lamela, the local forensic director, about her husband's general health status: she revealed that he had been taking drugs to counter pulmonary oedema – a condition known to put a strain upon the heart.

The following day three pathologists, Dr Carlos Lopez de Lamela, Dr Maria Ramos and Dr Louisa Garcia Cohen carried out an autopsy: they found a little water in the lungs, a graze on the forehead, a fissure behind the ear; samples from the lung, kidney, pancreas, stomach and other vital organs were taken for dispatch to Madrid and further forensic tests. After three and a half hours they reported to Judge Luis Gutierez: the verdict was that there was no suggestion of either murder or suicide, and that death had occurred from natural causes before Maxwell fell into the sea. There was talk of 'a cardiac or cardio-vascular attack'. The central mystery of how he had gone overboard after dying from natural causes on board was dismissed as an accident. 'The initial forensic reports suggest a natural death before Mr Maxwell fell into the sea,' Gutierez told Betty Maxwell. The imprecise and vague nature of these findings drew immediate criticism from British pathologists and a flood of further questions from the hosts of assembled journalists. These were met with a shrug and the bland and unilluminating answer that 'nothing is impossible'.

Thus the field was thrown open to speculation on how precisely the publisher had come to die, and into this maelstrom of conjecture and counter-argument exploded the bombshell of the *Paris Match* revelations of 9 January, 1992.

Let us consider each of these possibilities in turn.

Natural Causes Maxwell was a prime target for a heart attack: massively overweight, he was also suffering from a chest condition known to put a strain on the heart; moreover his life-style was of an exacting intensity that would have taxed the strength of an elephant and one that made no concession to a healthy regime; above all, he was under prodigious pressure occasioned by huge debt and the sure knowledge that the reckoning was imminent and would be dire.

He was hot and uncomfortable – the message to the bridge to turn down the air-conditioning and the discarded night-gown are evidence of that; and he had been seen moving about on the lower deck at dawn. Though the ship had a solid 5½-ft barrier around the deck, there was a place near the stern where the only barrier was a thin 3-ft chrome rail strung with wire beside which the publisher often stood. If he had been at this point trying to cool off and had had a heart attack he could easily have toppled into the sea: as the spot was invisible from the bridge noboby would have seen him.

Accident Maxwell could have been standing by the low rail, had a dizzy spell, lost his balance and fallen overboard: it has been reported that the planking was moist, and footing therefore unsure. The shock of finding himself in the sea with the yacht blindly ignorant of his fate sailing away from him would have been sufficient to precipitate a heart attack.

Suicide On 21 February 1992, the *Sun* newspaper published excerpts from the report of an insurance investigator, Roger Rich, which pointed towards suicide, although there was the reservation that: 'At this stage the pathological results do not exclude other possibilities.' His conclusion was based on findings that 'the tearing and bleeding into the muscles of the back of the left shoulder and into the muscles by the spine resulted from sudden physical stress to the muscles, causing them to stretch and tear.' The injury, it is maintained, showed that Maxwell was hanging on to something – like a yacht rail – with his left hand whilst his massive pendulous weight ruptured his shoulder muscles until he finally let go and fell into the sea.

Such assertions are furiously contested by those closest to Maxwell. They maintain that he was a man who never knew when he was beaten, and point out that he could never have overcome his primitive beginnings, won an award for valour in the field, and risen time and again from the ashes of defeat and disaster to renewed achievement unless he possessed the courage of a lion: such a man would never contemplate suicide.

Moreover, it has been estimated that he could not have gone overboard later than 5.30 a.m. If he had been contemplating suicide would he have been concerned about such a mundane matter as the state of the central heating just forty-five minutes earlier?

Finally, one has to bear in mind the objective fact that the finding of the Spanish autopsy, whatever its shortcomings, maintained that there was insufficient water in the lungs to justify a verdict of suicide by drowning.

Murder On 9 January 1992 the leading French magazine *Paris Match* published the sensational news that in the opinion of three Israeli doctors and two French pathologists Maxwell was brutally beaten and may have been murdered before going overboard: the Israelis had assisted at the second autopsy carried out in Israel a few hours before he was interred on the Mount of Olives. The report was based on an 80-minute video recorded in the laboratory of the Institute for Forensic Medicine in Tel Aviv and shows in gruesome detail the operation in progress; it was illustrated with many close-ups of the dead man.

During the examination pathologists are heard making comments about a broken nose and blows to the eyes, ear and forehead.

Paris Match showed the video to two French experts. Loic le Ribault, the founder of Carne, the respected forensic laboratory, concluded: 'It is highly probable that a violent blow was struck behind the head of the victim with the use of a weapon.' He added: 'Altogether our first impressions are that these lesions were caused as a result of injury which took place before death.'

Professor Louis Roche, a pathologist and former president of the International Academy of Forensic Medicine, highlighted three major areas of bruising: 'All these lesions were caused by injury. By themselves they are not serious but they prove that injury was suffered before death.'

Dr Bartholomew Levy, one of the Israeli pathologists who carried out the second autopsy, was quoted as saying: 'Listen to me who has actually seen the body itself. I can tell you that those bruises were not made by the Holy Spirit. If Maxwell had not been beaten up he would still be alive today.'

On the strength of these and other statements the magazine concluded that Maxwell 'received numerous heavy blows, which caused many bruises and even fractured his nose and tore the ear lobe.'

These murder theories were supported by people who believed Seymour Hersh's allegations that Maxwell had been an agent for Israeli intelligence and thus a likely assassin's target.

British pathologists however dispute these opinions. Dr Peter Vanezis, head of forensic medicine and toxicology at Charing Cross and Westminster Medical School, said: 'The idea that Robert Maxwell had been subjected to a violent assault or any way beaten up before his death is, in my view, totally inaccurate.' His view is shared by Austen Gresham, the Cambridge pathologist. Both incline to the view that the publisher died from natural causes.

Dr Iain West, a Home Office pathologist who led the Israeli team, had not delivered his judgement at the time of this book going to press: he was working for British insurance companies. Maxwell's life was insured for £20 million in the event of accident or murder, so much rides on the final outcome of these medical deliberations.

The way in which Robert Maxwell came to die will remain the subject of speculation for years to come. At his death he left scores of unanswered questions to perplex and harass his erstwhile associates and the world at large; but none is so stubbornly intractable as what happened during his last few minutes on board the *Lady Ghislaine* in the early hours of Tuesday, 5 November 1991.

SELECT BIBLIOGRAPHY

WHO WAS THE MURDERER?

Dr John Bodkin Adams
Bedford, Sybille. *The Best We Can Do*. Collins, 1958
Hallworth, Rodney, and Williams, Mark. *Where There's a Will*. The Capstan Press, Jersey, 1983
Hoskins, Percy. *Two Men Were Acquitted*. Secker & Warburg, 1984

The Lindbergh Baby Kidnapping
Waller, George. *Kidnap, The Story of the Lindbergh Case*. Hamish Hamilton, 1961
Whipple, Sidney B. *The Story of Richard Bruno Hauptmann*. Heinemann, 1938
Wright, Theon. *The Search for the Lindbergh Baby*. Tower Publications, 1981

William Herbert Wallace
Goodman, Jonathan. *The Killing of Julia Wallace*. Harrap, 1969
Hussey, Robert S. *Murderer Scot-Free*. David & Charles, 1972
Wilkes, Roger. *Wallace, The Final Verdict*. The Bodley Head, 1984
Wyndham-Brown, W.F. *The Trial of William Herbert Wallace*. Gollancz, 1933

Adelaide Bartlett
Hall, Sir John. *Adelaide Bartlett*. Notable British Trial Series
Morland, Nigel. *Background to Murder*. Werner Laurie, 1955

Lizzie Borden
Pearson, Edmund. *Masterpieces of Murder*. Hutchinson, 1964
Radin, Edward. *Lizzie Borden, the Untold Story*. Gollancz, 1961
Lincoln, Victoria. *A Private Disgrace*. Putnams, 1967
Pearson, Edmund. *The Trial of Lizzie Borden*. Heinemann, 1937

Tony Mancini
Lustgarten, Edgar. *The Murderer and the Trial*. Odhams, 1960

The Axeman of New Orleans
Tallant, Robert. *Murder in New Orleans*. William Kimber, 1953

John Cartland
Cartland, Jeremy. *The Cartland File*. Linkline, 1978

Jack the Ripper
Rumbelow, Donald. *The Complete Jack the Ripper*. W.H. Allen, 1975

Zodiac
Graysmith, Robert. *Zodiac*. St. Martins/Marek, 1985

WHAT HAPPENED TO THEM?

Grey, Anthony. *The Prime Minister Was a Spy*. Weidenfeld & Nicolson, 1983
Bryson, John. *Evil Angels*. Viking, 1985
Shears, Richard. *The Dingo Baby Case*. Sphere Books, 1982
Cooke, F.B. *Single-Handed Cruising*. 1931
Kastenbaum, R. and Aisenberg, R. *The Psychology of Death*. Springer Publishing, New York, 1972
Wilson, Colin, and Seaman, Donald. *Scandal!* Weidenfeld & Nicolson, 1986

IDENTITIES: TRUE OR FALSE?

Thomas, Hugh. *The Murder of Rudolf Hess*. Hodder & Stoughton, 1979
The Verdict of the Court. Edited by Michael Hardwick. Herbert Jenkins, 1960
Machlin, Milton, and Woodfield, William Read. *Ninth Life*. Putnams, 1961
Morland, Nigel. *Patterns of Murder*. Elek, 1966
Roughhead, William. *The Trial of Oscar Slater*. Notable British Trials Series

ACCIDENTS

Ennis, John. *The Great Bombay Explosion*. Duell, Sloane and Pearce, 1959
50 Strange Mysteries of the Sea. Edited by John Canning. Souvenir Press, 1979

ENIGMAS OF AIR AND SEA

Garrett, Richard. *Flight into Mystery*. Weidenfeld & Nicolson, 1986
Barker, Ralph. *Great Mysteries of the Air*. Chatto and Windus, 1966
Garrett, Richard. *Atlantic Disaster*. Buchan and Enright, 1986
Simpson, Colin. *Lusitania*. Longman, 1972
Hardwick, Michael and Mollie. *The World's Greatest Sea Mysteries*. Odhams, 1967
Bywaters, Hector C. *Their Secret Purposes*. 1932
Beaty, David. *Strange Encounters*. Methuen, 1982
Bower, Tom. *The Outsider*. Mandarin, 1991. (The most rounded portrait of Robert Maxwell to date.)
Thompson and Delano. *Maxwell, A Portrait of Power*. Corgi, 1991
Haines, Joe. *Maxwell*. Macdonald, 1987
Hersh, Seymour. *The Samson Option*, Faber, 1991

INDEX

Figures in *italics* refer to captions.